MODES
OF
RHETORIC

MODES OF RHETORIC

by LEO ROCKAS

STATE UNIVERSITY OF NEW YORK/GENESEO

 ST MARTIN'S PRESS / NEW YORK

ACKNOWLEDGMENTS

The chapter "Abstract and Concrete Sentences" is reprinted in
slightly different form from the May 1963 issue of *College
Composition and Communication* by permission of the National
Council of Teachers of English.

"Metaphors of a Magnifico," 1st stanza, from *Collected Poems*
by Wallace Stevens is reprinted by permission of Alfred A.
Knopf Publishers.

"Haiku" are reprinted from *Oku No Hosomichi or the Poetical
Journey in Old Japan* by Matsuo Bashō, transl. Yaichiro Isobe.
Kyobashi, Tokyo: San Kaku Sha, 1933.

"Maxims" from *La Rochefoucauld: Maxims*, transl. L. W. Tancock, is reprinted by permission of Penguin Books, Ltd.

"Inscapes" from *The Journals and Papers of Gerard Manley
Hopkins*, eds. Humphry House and Graham Storey, is reprinted
by permission of the Oxford University Press.

"Here, Dear Library, Are the Papers" by Stanley Walker is
reprinted by permission. Copr. © 1956, The New Yorker Magazine, Inc.

"In a Station of the Metro" from *Personae: Collected Poems* of
Ezra Pound. Copyright 1926, 1954 by Ezra Pound. Reprinted
by permission of New Directions.

"The Magi" is reprinted from *Collected Poems of W. B. Yeats.*
Copyright 1916 by The Macmillan Company. Renewed 1944 by
Georgia Bertha Yeats. Reprinted by permission of The Mac-
millan Company, New York, Mrs. W. B. Yeats, and The
Macmillan Company of Canada.

"Gargantua and Pantagruel," I, lv, from *The Portable Rabelais*, selected, translated and edited by Samuel Putnam. Copyright 1946 by Samuel Putnam. Reprinted by permission of The Viking Press, Inc.

Portion of Chapter II of *The Country of the Pointed Firs* by Sarah Orne Jewett is reprinted by permission of the Houghton Mifflin Co.

"Elegant Variation" from *A Dictionary of Modern English Usage* by H. W. Fowler is reprinted by permission of the Clarendon Press, Oxford.

The passage from *Lolita* by Vladimir Nabokov is reprinted by permission of G. P. Putnam's Sons, © Vladimir Nabokov, 1955.

"The Unicorn in the Garden" by James Thurber is reprinted by permission from *The New Yorker* of October 31, 1939. Copr. © 1939 The New Yorker Magazine, Inc.

The chapter "The Mode of Drama" is reprinted in slightly different form from the March 1963 issue of the *Bucknell Review*.

Selections from *The Cherry Orchard* and *The Sea Gull* by Anton Chekhov are reprinted by permission of The Estate of Stark Young. Copyright 1939, 1941, 1947, and 1950 by Stark Young. Copyright © 1956 by Stark Young.

Excerpt from "The Snows of Kilimanjaro" (Copyright 1936 Ernest Hemingway; renewal copyright © 1964 Mary Hemingway) is reprinted with the permission of Charles Scribners' Sons from *The Short Stories of Ernest Hemingway*, pp.52-54.

The passage from *Socratic Method and Critical Philosophy: Selected Essays* by Leonard Nelson, transl. Thomas K. Brown III, is reprinted by permission of Yale University Press. Copyright 1949 by Yale University Press.

The passage from the *Life of Johnson* by James Boswell is reprinted by permission of the Oxford University Press.

The passage from *The Apple Cart*, Act I, by George Bernard Shaw is reprinted by permission of the Public Trustee and the Society of Authors, London.

"Two Sides Not Enough" from *Simple Stakes a Claim* by Langston Hughes is reprinted by permission of Harold Ober Associates Inc. Copyright © 1957 by Langston Hughes.

The passage from *Boswell in Holland*, ed. Frederick A. Pottle, is quoted with permission of Yale University and McGraw-Hill Book Company, Inc. Copyright 1928, 1952 by Yale University.

The passage from *The Agamemnon of Aeschylus*, transl. Louis MacNeice, is reprinted from *Four Greek Plays*, ed. Dudley Fitts, by permission of Harcourt, Brace & World, Inc., and Faber and Faber Ltd.

The passage from *Ulysses* by James Joyce is reprinted by permission of Random House, Inc. and The Bodley Head Ltd. Copyright 1914, 1918 and renewed 1942, 1946 by Nora Joseph Joyce.

The passage from *Mrs. Dalloway* by Virginia Woolf is reprinted by permission of Harcourt, Brace & World, Inc. and the Hogarth Press Ltd.

The passage from "The Art of Fiction" by Henry James is reprinted by permission of The Macmillan Company.

The passage from "A Defense of Dramatic Unities" by G. K. Chesterton is reprinted from *Selected Essays of G. K. Chesterton* by permission of D. E. Collins and Methuen & Co. Ltd.

"The Future of Reading" from *The Second Tree from the Corner* by E. B. White is reprinted with the permission of Harper & Row, Publishers Inc. Copyright 1951, by E. B. White.

ΚΡΥΣΤΑΛΛΩ

Εἶτα, ὦ καταγέλαστε, οὐκ ἀκήκοας ὡς ἐγώ
εἰμι υἱός μαίας μάλα γενναίας τε καὶ βλοσυρᾶς;

Preface

Rhetoric has meant the art of persuasion, of decoration, and of composition. The first meaning is classical, the second medieval and Renaissance, the third modern. The modern rhetorician, if he exists, may rightfully take up any matters of language or discourse left over when the logician and the grammarian have finished—and the three together still form a dubious modern "trivium."

This book tries to answer one question of rhetoric: what are the basic modes of discourse? To this question there have been, as I see it, two different critical answers. Plato and Aristotle answered epic, drama, lyric. Nineteenth-century rhetoricians (especially Alexander Bain in *English Composition and Rhetoric*, 1879) answered description, narration, exposition, and argument (or persuasion). That these are answers to the same question has not previously been urged, so far as I know, anywhere, except in a couple of speculative sentences by my teacher Austin Warren, on p. 238 of *Theory of Literature*. My analysis has suggested that these poetical and rhetorical modes extend themselves naturally and elegantly to the concrete modes, description, narration, drama, and reverie; and to the abstract or plagal modes, definition, process, dialogue, and persuasion. These are also classified by means of procedure as the static modes, description and definition; the temporal modes, narration and process; the mimetic modes, drama and dialogue; and the mental modes, reverie and persuasion. Though the modes may be modulated and mixed, I consider them to be ex-

ix

clusive of each other, and together inclusive of whatever can happen in discourse, at least at the simplest level of rhetorical analysis.

I have tried, with imperfect success, to avoid both logic and grammar. Like grammar, unlike logic, rhetoric is con-concerned more with sentences than with the ideas they embody; but the basic unit of rhetoric, at least for division into modes, is, I take it, two sentences rather than one. Like logic, unlike grammar, rhetoric is largely superior to the strengths or weaknesses of any given language; and so my statements, unless marked "in English," are supposed to apply to any language. In close quarters, however, the subjects of the three are indistinguishable. The closest quarters, I have found, are in what might be considered the two primary modes of rhetoric. Narration, heading toward "story" or "imaginative writing," which loosely includes all concrete discourse with the Horatian goal of delight, has brought me to grammar. Persuasion, heading toward "essay" or "expository writing," which loosely includes all abstract discourse with the Horatian goal of instruction, has brought me to logic.

The readings are by both professionals and students, and are all in my opinion worthy of general literary as well as merely rhetorical examination. All are in prose, though all might have been in verse, as the examples within chapters often are. And all the readings are brief, about the length of student papers. No literary "types" I expect will be found here, such as "comedy," "elegy," or "short story." Those are concerned chiefly, I think, with shape of the whole work, and these are two-page "passages," with no shape but the development to a climax somewhere past the middle—the customary progression of any temporal passage of art. The readings have been chosen to demonstrate the greatest possible variety within the mode, between serious-light, formal-informal, realistic-romantic, old-new. Translations, where not otherwise noted, are mine.

I have been using this book in increasingly greater amounts over the past five or six years. In a one-semester course I spend two weeks on a Journal exercise of sentences or short entries (See "The Freshman Journal," *College English*, October 1958), accompanied by the first chapter here. For the next eight weeks I take up the eight central chapters, and each student does a paper a week, approximately in each of the eight modes. For the remaining five weeks of the course I take up the prose of a mature stylist who mixes modes freely (say E. B. White), and each student writes one or two longer papers in mixed modes. The book, especially the last chapter, is intended to provide a basic rhetorical literacy, leaving other more complicated stylistic effects largely unexamined. Though the progression of the book may seem rigidly systematic I try to apply it liberally, understanding that restriction to a single mode is perfectly arbitrary and artificial. The readings themselves, which are mainly in single modes, show many switches to other modes or hints of them, which I have recorded in the commentary. The implication of the course is that, having tried his hand briefly at every mode and at mixing the modes, the student has attained a basic rhetorical proficiency.

"Abstract and Concrete Sentences" appeared in slightly different form in *College Composition and Communication*, May 1963, and "The Mode of Drama" appeared in *Bucknell Review*, March 1963; I thank the editors for running them and for permitting me to reprint them here. I have recorded my indebtedness to printed works whenever I was aware it arose, but I have also profited from criticism of separate chapters by friends whose names I here gratefully record: Norman Burns, John Collinson, Leonard Deen, Joseph Grassi, Donald Hope, Eleanor Hope, the late Leo Kirschbaum, Edgar Mayer, Peter McNally, Emanuel Mussman, Bruce Olsen, Thornton Parsons, James Philbin, Bernard Schilling, Rudolf Schmerl, Gerald Smith. I am additionally and even more numerously indebted to students of Wayne State University, Rochester Institute of Technology, St. John Fisher College, and the State University College of Geneseo, who have cheerfully treated my unfinished work as finished.

Geneseo, New York
September 1963

Contents

THE TEMPORAL MODES

THE MIMETIC MODES

THE MENTAL MODES

Reverie   197

Persuasion   219

Rhetorical Dominance   245

Abstract and Concrete

Sentences

All discourse is really philosophy, a commentary on the world around you. Every sentence is a proposition. Rhetoric is simply the flesh of epistemology, the study of how men relate what they have come to know. The cause of composition is knowledge, and you cannot, except by the most posterior analysis, tell how to say something without telling first how to know something to say.

Take a baby, or an adult born hypothetically at age 25—making, that is, his first perceptions. He sees the window, the father, the dresser, the door, and other things. The window is light like the lamp, but rectangular like the door. The father is tall like the door, but moving like the mother. The dresser is brown like the door, but thick like the bed. He has begun arranging things and their qualities. Soon he will conceive of general classes of things—maybe the class of people, as distinct from dogs and other moving, responding things. Then he will isolate or abstract qualities from things—maybe the quality of motion, abstracted from both people and dogs. But besides classifying things he will declassify them too. His window will fall into the class of all other windows he has seen, but no other window will reflect

the sun exactly as his does. Other mothers will smile, but
his mother's will remain special. Every new thing presented
to his perception will suggest similarities and differences
from other things known before. You call a child perceptive
when he remembers all the things he has seen and keeps
track of their qualities, so that he can immediately assess
what is familiar and what new in anything you show him.

Of course the number of qualities in any one thing is not
fixed; what appears one quality to you will seem several to
someone else. It depends on how closely you have examined
things, and compared them with their nearest fellows. The
more things resembling one another you have seen, the more
qualities you can abstract, the better you can tell which
qualities are common to a class and which unique. A class is
general when the things in it share a majority of their qualities (people); a class is abstract when the things in it share
a minority—perhaps only one—of their qualities (all brown
things). But in hard cases this distinction is doubtful. Are
French doors windows or doors? That is, does the class of
windows or of doors more conveniently or generally accommodate French doors? It depends on whether you see their
basic quality as letting you, or the light, pass through them.

I consider perception to head in two directions recognized
by philosophers for centuries, abstraction and concretion.
Abstraction is the process of bundling things and qualities
in broader and higher classes, of discovering similarities between things. Concretion is the process of separating things
and qualities in exclusive niches, of discovering differences
between things. If you think of the unique qualities of things
as defects of the general class, then abstraction is also a kind
of perfection or idealization. In the other direction, toward
concretion, you cannot descend below the level of concrete
things given, but you can relish even their most sordid particularity. Not that either process can occur alone. You can't
abstract unless you can tell which qualities to dismiss because
of their novelty; you can't particularize unless you can tell

which qualities to dismiss because of their generality. Still, persons will have their preferences. The philosophic habit of mind runs to abstraction, the poetic to concretion. I am aware that a philosopher may, like Plato, be a poet too; and that a poet, when he has revealed his individuality, may have commented on the condition of all men. Such wonders remind you that experience is both single and diverse, both abstract and concrete.

> Twenty men crossing a bridge,
> Into a village,
> Are twenty men crossing twenty bridges
> Into twenty villages,
> Or one man
> Crossing a single bridge into a village.
>   (WALLACE STEVENS, "Metaphors of a Magnifico")

So far I have conceived of all things as coexisting in one moment of time. When you give a child a new toy he mentally compares it with the other toys he knows, as if they were all laid out on the same static network at once. But existence is temporal as well as static. I have mentioned the abstract quality of motion, and that presupposes a stretch of perceived time, however brief. Besides things, a child will begin to notice events. The mother awakens him, pulls up the shade, and changes him. Later, the father comes home, picks him up, and plays with him. He begins to expect the same process every day, but it never is exactly the same. One day is gray, not sunny; one day the mother drops the bottle; one night the father doesn't appear. Again he is classifying, now events instead of just things. Certain days will seem routine, others novel. And their novelty may be measured not merely by substance, as things are, but by sequence. A red-letter day will be marked not only by the unique substance of cake and toys and playmates, but by the unique train of circumstances at the party. Even so, children respond to their birthdays differently. The events of a given day may seem general or typical according to one selection, or quite singular according to another.

As the child begins to talk, and to understand talk, he enters a third order of existence, which may be called mimetic. His mother says certain things to him and expects certain responses. He is able to respond more and more elaborately and is rewarded for each new word or tone he learns. When his father comes home the three of them have a conversation. Sometimes they say about the same things as usual, and in the same order; sometimes they vary them. Sometimes they talk about things common to any family; sometimes they talk about things unique to themselves. The conversations verge toward abstraction or toward concretion in either substance or sequence. The child may take most pleasure in the typical, recurrent conversations, or in the novel, unpredictable ones.

The final order of existence is the contemplation of his own mind. All existence, all experience is progressively sifted through his mind, and if he is both analytic and introspective he sees that certain patterns begin tracing themselves out there, which may be stimulated by what he sees or hears, but which have a special substance and sequence of their own. Often he is aware of a familiar train of thoughts that any child might have: if you want milk, cry and mother will come. But sometimes he is aware of a secret thought or a novel train of thoughts: his mother's yellow beads and perfume remind him of a sunny day in the garden.

According to this pastiche of epistemology, then, abstraction and concretion may operate in four different orders of perception. The first order is static, a comparison and contrast of things only, without regard to how long they last or what they become. The second order is temporal, an extension of things (and especially people) to the events that grow out of them. The third order is mimetic, a direct concern with the conversational exchanges between people. The fourth order is mental, an intimate consideration of the

mind itself, how it operates, and what it thinks about. You
may take a concrete or an abstract view of things, events,
conversations, and thoughts.

If you turn from perception to composition, from epistemology to rhetoric, you must consider how words, phrases,
and sentences communicate these four orders of perception,
and how they differentiate between abstract and concrete
perception. First, words. I mean words with substantive or
lexical content, not mere "function words"—*the, may, not,
very, and, at, do, there, when, after, well* (See C. C. Fries,
The Structure of English, ch. VI)—whose only meaning is
structural. All other words are usually considered general,
in applying to a class of particular things, however small the
class. But some words are more general than others. *Existence* has a wider application than any other word. Even in
more specific areas you may observe that *dwelling* is more
general than *hut*. Nor are these distinctions applicable to
nouns only. Among verbs, observe that *move* is more general
than *amble*. Among adjectives, observe that *unhappy* is
more general than *morose*. Roget's *Thesaurus* is partly an
attempt to classify all substantive words according to higher
and higher abstractions. Though the actual word-lists mix
general and specific words, the headings and subheadings are
conceived on a scale of abstraction.

Words, then, are roughly divisible into general and specific,
or abstract and concrete. A concrete statement is first of all
an aggregate of words lowest on the scale of abstraction, or
referring to a minimum of things. An abstract statement is
an aggregate of words highest on the scale of abstraction,
whether you think of these as general classes of things (men)
or as qualities abstracted from things (virtue). But the
arrangement, as well as the selection, the sequence as well
as the substance, of words is relevant. A fully concrete statement is one in which the succession of concrete words is
novel or unpredictable. Consider this haiku by Bashō: "Turn
the horse across the moor. Hark! a cuckoo has cried over-

head." A fully abstract statement is one in which the succession of abstract words is typical or ideal. Consider this maxim by La Rochefoucauld: "Our promises are made in proportion to our hopes, but kept in proportion to our fears."[1]

I have now come to the basic unit of discourse, the sentence. Recent linguists have cleverly detected units smaller than the sentence, and including the sentence, but there is no basic unit larger than the sentence. The paragraph is an arbitrary and conventional unit, susceptible of extensive editorial tampering. Indeed, in recording conversations, the paragraph has not even a conventional status. There the unit is the "line"—not the poetic or typographical line, but "those chunks of talk that are marked off by a shift of speaker." (Fries, p. 23) The paragraph is really no more bounded than this "line" or "utterance unit," and includes, according to the whim of author or editor, one to any number of sentences. Some writers grow as rhapsodic over the "unity and development" of the paragraph (meaning the unit between indentations) as others do over the "integrity and innate necessity" of the sonnet. (See T. W. H. Crosland, *The English Sonnet*, p. 53) But the sonnet has at least precise metrical bounds, whereas the paragraph is simply a convenient grouping of sentences. In a progression of sentences a few places will be more suited to indentations than others, but you can justify an indentation before almost any sentence of sophisticated prose. The *paragraph* was originally, as the *period* now is, a mark of punctuation, a *beside-mark* or *marginal note*. The *sentence*, unlike the *period*, is never the dot at the end, but either the grammatical unit between dots, or the substance of that unit, a proposition or *sententia*.

The sentence, then is the first unit of composition. It is a real unit, and it is the smallest unit. You cannot talk without talking in sentences, but nobody talks in paragraphs. Of sentences, it is not only to be observed that they may be

---

1. The translations are by Yaichiro Isobe (*The Poetical Journey in Old Japan*, p. 2); and by L. W. Tancock (*Maxims*, no. 38).

either abstract or concrete, but that they are always both
at once. The Hegelian phrase "concrete universal," a popular
one with literary critics, is, I take it, a means of naming this
paradox. Obviously an abstract statement, or universal, includes or implies many concrete possibilities; a concrete statement may be read as an example of an abstract truth. Any
statement, you might say, specifies not only a single meaning, but a range of meaning, apprehensible at all levels of the
scale of abstraction. The agency of the statement, the actual
assemblage of words, will be either concrete or abstract, but
the significance of the statement will include all its legitimate
extensions up and down the scale of abstraction.

Do you read "A bird in the hand is worth two in the bush"
as advice to fowlers only? If the agency is concrete, the
significance may be as abstract as "A small certainty is better
than a larger possibility." But this is an easy case; the concrete statement seems almost to insist upon an abstract
significance. Take as purely concrete a statement as you
know.

> When yellow leaves, or none, or few, do hang
> Upon those boughs which shake against the cold,
> Bare ruin'd choirs, where late the sweet birds sang.
> (SHAKESPEARE, Sonnet 73, 2-5)

You do not need the rest of the poem to understand more
abstractly that there comes a sad time when things are,
while not quite ended, past their prime. Ransom is thinking
of this poem when he says: "By a *tour de force* which for
more reasons than one we are apt to call 'metaphysical,' the
Universal of a poem may be wholly translated into a natural
image, or a series of them, and never expressed in the abstract
language of the understanding at all." (*Kenyon Review*,
Summer '55, pp. 397-398)

Abstract statements, on the other hand, are numerously
realizable in concrete effects. The first line of the sonnets,
"From fairest creatures we desire increase," establishes the

abstract theme for the first seventeen sonnets, and is variously particularized in "Now is the time that face should form another," (3.2) "That's for thyself to breed another thee," (6.7) "Make thee another self, for love of me," (10.13) and "She carv'd thee for her seal, and meant thereby/ Thou shouldst print more, not let that copy die." (11.13-14) Often Shakespeare offers abstract and concrete conveniently together. Here are four "examples" followed by the "precept."

> Roses have thorns, and silver fountains mud;
> Clouds and eclipses stain both moon and sun,
> And loathsome canker lives in sweetest bud.
> All men make faults. . . .   (35.2-5)

The most useful knack to readers and writers is the ready apprehension of the concrete in the abstract and the abstract in the concrete. Beginning writers often follow the example of philosophers and poets, and record in a journal notable sentences by themselves and others, both abstract and concrete, and with frequent translations back and forth. Good writers should be skillful at either kind of translation, but most will find, since two different skills are involved, that they are better at one kind. Translation of an abstract statement (for instance the maxim of La Rochefoucauld above) is usually considered easier, the abstract statement somehow including some particulars out of any person's experience. Translation of a concrete statement (for instance the haiku from Bashō above) is harder, or less accurate. The writer must imagine other similar details alongside those given and see what abstraction seems to issue from them. Nor is absolute accuracy to be sought at once. If abstraction is the formulation of a general rule from particular cases it looks like induction; if concretion is the application of general rules to particular cases it looks like deduction. But abstraction and induction are not quite the same, nor are concretion and deduction. Deduction operates by orderly syllogisms, while concretion operates by enthymemes, by immediate transference of the idea to the illustration. And induction requires a majority of cases—indeed all cases for a "pure" induction—while abstraction may operate on just one case. A real thinker, whether poet or philosopher, grows suspicious over the first sign of something awry, and wonders whether it is the exception or the rule.

In passages of discourse longer than a sentence, the four orders of perception mentioned above begin to appear as four orders of rhetoric. This sonnet is clearly static, or non-temporal.

> *They that have power to hurt and will do none,*
> *That do not do the thing they most do show,*
> *Who, moving others, are themselves as stone,*
> *Unmoved, cold, and to temptation slow,*
> *They rightly do inherit heaven's graces*
> *And husband nature's riches from expense;*
> *They are the lords and owners of their faces,*
> *Others but stewards of their excellence.*
> *The summer's flower is to the summer sweet,*
> *Though to itself it only live and die,*
> *But if that flower with base infection meet,*
> *The basest weed outbraves his dignity;*
>   *For sweetest things turn sourest by their deeds;*
>   *Lilies that fester smell far worse than weeds.* (94)

The octave defines a general class of people in some detail, without engaging any temporal pattern. The sestet translates the abstraction concretely, and adds a new thought beginning, "But if that flower with base infection meet," which is equivalent to "They that have power to hurt and *perform it.*" Though the sestet is slightly temporal, its function in the poem is to define a new class of people, sweets turned sour. The last line is an eloquent conclusion to the poem, whose agency is as concrete as its significance is abstract.

Temporality is engaged in the next sonnet, which traces a recurrent natural process in the octave.

Full many a glorious morning have I seen
Flatter the mountain-tops with sovereign eye,
Kissing with golden face the meadows green,
Gilding pale streams with heavenly alchemy;
Anon permit the basest clouds to ride
With ugly rack on his celestial face,
And from the forlorn world his visage hide,
Stealing unseen to west with this disgrace.
Even so my sun one early morn did shine
With all-triumphant splendour on my brow,
But out, alack! he was but one hour mine;
The region cloud hath mask'd him from me now.
Yet him for this my love no whit disdaineth;
Suns of the world may stain when heaven's sun staineth.

(33)

However concretely descriptive the octave may be considered, the process is a typical, recurrent one, and the effect is general. The sestet applies the general process concretely to the poet's life with the sun-son pun in line 9. The third quatrain is no more concrete in agency than the first two, but its reference is particular as they are not. The couplet drops the temporal process and closes with a general justification of the friend's behavior.

The next sonnet has the direct address back and forth characteristic of the mimetic order of rhetoric. The second quatrain is "quoted" from the Muse; the rest is addressed by the poet to the Muse.

O truant Muse, what shall be thy amends
For thy neglect of truth in beauty dyed?
Both truth and beauty on my love depends;
So dost thou too, and therein dignified.
Make answer, Muse: wilt thou not haply say
"Truth needs no colour, with his colour fix'd
Beauty no pencil, beauty's truth to lay;
But best is best, if never intermix'd"?
Because he needs no praise, wilt thou be dumb?

> Excuse not silence so; for 't lies in thee
> To make him much outlive a gilded tomb,
> And to be prais'd of ages yet to be.
> > Then do thy office, Muse; I teach thee how
> > To make him seem long hence as he shows now.   (101)

The agency and significance of this poem are almost uniformly abstract, and the Muse's statement is so general as to lack any clearly direct address to the poet. But there are the three persons of mimetic exchange—I, you, he—and the abstraction of truth and beauty is concretely applied to the poet's friend.

The fourth order of rhetoric is mental or ruminative. This sonnet is wholly so.

> If there be nothing new, but that which is
> Hath been before, how are our brains beguil'd,
> Which, labouring for invention, bear amiss
> The second burthen of a former child!
> Oh, that record could with a backward look,
> Even of five hundred courses of the sun,
> Show me your image in some antique book,
> Since mind at first in character was done!
> That I might see what the old world could say
> To this composed wonder of your frame;
> Whether we are mended, or whether better they,
> Or whether revolution be the same.
> > Oh, sure I am, the wits of former days
> > To subjects worse have given admiring praise.   (59)

The first quatrain offers an abstract reflection. Its structure, with its hypothetical suspension (*if* . . . *then*), is not merely static, nor even temporal or mimetic, but mental. The second quatrain states an unrealizable wish and renders the general discussion concrete and personal in "Show me your image." The third quatrain, with its "could" and its "whether . . . whether," is speculative, and mental. The couplet insists upon a contrast unverifiable, or mental.

When you see how readily discourse (here heightened discourse) stays abstract or concrete, or switches back and forth according to the author's substance, you may recall the advice of the handbooks, Be concrete. Any legitimate writer would answer, If I feel like it. Or even, I can hardly avoid being both at once. If the agency of a statement is single, its significance is always multiple. A writer ranges over the four orders of rhetoric both abstractly and concretely, and settles wherever he is most comfortable. All the resting points are good—which is not to say he may not be a sloppy writer in need of revision. But being abstract or concrete—or static, temporal, mimetic, or mental—are never faults in themselves. The unphilosophic mind shuns abstraction, as the Statue complains to Don Juan in Shaw's play: "This is extremly abstract and metaphysical, Juan. If you would stick to the concrete, and put your discoveries in the form of entertaining anecdotes about your adventures with women, your conversation would be easier to follow." (*Man and Superman*, Act III) But the unpoetic mind just as insistently shuns concretion as obvious and wasteful, and so every *Critique* requires its *Prolegomena*. Socrates has to apologize for switching the conversation from abstract to concrete: "Like a feeble speaker, therefore, I will not take the whole of the subject, but will break off a piece of it to show you what I mean." (*Republic* 392D)

W. K. Wimsatt suggests that "the right degree of specification . . . is to be determined by the decorum of the level at which the writing proceeds," (*Verbal Icon*, p. 136) but he ends up nevertheless chasing a will o' the wisp known as the "the substantive level"—or calling a spade a spade instead of an implement, which is too general, or a rusty garden spade, which is too specific. He quotes Aristotle in support of his view: "When we say *what* it is, we do not say 'white' or 'hot' or 'three cubits long,' but 'a man' or 'a god.' " (p. 136) "I incline indeed," Wimsatt says, "to the view that both the inflation of the abstract style and the solid minutiae of imagism are best when they cut fairly close to the substantive level of discourse." (p. 145) But the substantive level varies with languages and speakers. What are you to say of languages that lack a word for *tree* but have dozens of words for different varieties of trees? Is the whole language to be recalled to the substantive level? What appears substantively to me as white wine, or even as wine, will appear to the connoisseur Bordeaux, Moselle, Chablis. One excellent reason for writing in the first place is the author's certainty that the right substantive level of his subject has been formerly misnamed; and if such a thing as a substantive level for all subjects can ever be derived, it may turn out to be the trite level of things well agreed upon, which need no confirmation.

What is to be avoided in writing, then, is not the abstract or the concrete, but the trite, at whatever level of abstraction. Triteness is of course forever relative: a Chinese commonplace may strike me as incisive; a student's novelty will seem stale to the teacher. Education is largely a matter of relating the student's personal life to the culture at large, anyway. If the student finds that his abstract sentences are platitudes, and his concrete ones clichés, he will be better able to detect his good ideas when they come along. It might well be argued that no one's experience is so limited as to preclude originality. Both children and experts know that life is a vast tangle of unsolved mysteries. And anyone who takes the trouble to probe his experience closely enough will come up with news to the human race. But if you seek ways to seize upon that originality, that precious distinctiveness, it is hard to improve on Sherlock Holmes's "Sharpen your powers of observation, Watson!" or Henry James's "Try to be one of the people on whom nothing is lost!" Probably most of the brilliance and the fun was not in the result, which the world sees and applauds, but in arriving at it, which the writer keeps secret even when he can tell how it happened himself.

Distichs

Whoever, hearing evil of himself, does not grow angry, gives proof of utter baseness. (614K)

Folly is a misfortune self-chosen by mortals: why blame fortune, when you are wronging yourself? (618K)

The incredible sometimes has greater power and is more credible to the mob than the truth. (622K)

Three-times unlucky, whoever by his thrift has earned hatred double his substance. (626K)

For it's not the number of drinks, if you notice, that makes for carousing, but the nature of the drinker. (627K)

Never mind whether I who speak am a younger man, but whether a wiser. (638K)

A marriageable daughter, even if she never babbles at all, through her silence says much about herself. (658K)

There is never a word of truth in the threats of a father to his son, or a lover to his beloved. (661K)

I hate a pauper giving presents to the rich; it's a sign of his sniveling lot. (690K)

For he who seeks to wrong another himself foretastes the outcome of the wrong. (696K)

If in giving help you chide the receiver you've sprinkled absinthe on Attic honey. (708K)

I never try to straighten a twisted branch; there's no changing what nature has forced. (711K)

MENANDER

14

Haiku

Even wood-peckers dare not touch the cottage standing in a clump of the summer trees. (p. 12)

Turn the horse across the moor. Hark! a cuckoo has cried overhead. (p. 13)

Over the hermit's cottage, the chestnut-tree is now in full bloom, unnoticed by people. (p. 17)

In honour of the festival, let me adorn the thongs of my sandals with the iris. (p. 24)

A wilderness of the summer grass,—ah, the reminder of the warriors' dreams. (p. 33)

Has it survived the rainy seasons of ages?—the Glittering Hall still glowing in gold. (p. 34)

Creep out, o croaking frog, and bear me company, in ennui, from under the veranda of the silk worm-house. (p. 37)

The sight of the safflower now in full bloom reminds me of the eyebrow brush used by the fair. (p. 37)

How grateful the influences of the sacred mountain! The perfumed wind melts the last winter's snow in the Southern Valley. (p. 41)

It has washed the burning sun down into the sea—the Mogami river. (p. 46)

Sitting on the sliding doors brought out, the families of the fishermen cool themselves in the evening breeze. (p. 49)

Cool is the autumn breeze. Let us peel melons and egg-plants, the delicacies of the season. (p. 54)

I would sweep the court of the temple before my departure; there are leaves of the willow fallen here and there by the wind. (p. 59)

Like the opened shell of a clam, I part with my friends to go to Futami in the departing autumn. (p. 65)

> MATSUO BASHŌ, Oku No Hosomichi or the Poetical Journey in Old Japan, transl. Yaichiro Isobe

Maxims

We have no more say in the duration of our passions than in that of our lives. (5)

Our self-esteem is more inclined to resent criticism of our tastes than of our opinions. (13)

We all have strength enough to endure the troubles of others. (19)

Greater virtues are needed to bear good fortune than bad. (25)

The evil we do brings less persecution and hatred upon us than our good qualities. (29)

All men have an equal share of pride; the only difference is in their ways and means of showing it. (35)

Our promises are made in proportion to our hopes, but kept in proportion to our fears. (38)

In order to succeed in the world people do their utmost to appear successful. (56)

Truth does not do as much good in the world as the semblance of truth does evil. (64)

There is only one kind of love, but there are a thousand copies, all different. (74)

In most men love of justice is only fear of suffering injustice. (78)

It is more shameful to distrust one's friends than to be deceived by them. (84)

Everybody complains of his memory, but nobody of his judgment. (89)

Old people are fond of giving good advice: it consoles them for no longer being capable of setting a bad example. (93)

The tastes of youth change because it is hot-blooded; those of age remain unaltered through force of habit. (109)

The surest way to be taken in is to think oneself craftier than other people. (127)

We would rather run ourselves down than not talk about ourselves at all. (138)

FRANÇOIS, DUC DE LA ROCHEFOUCAULD, *Maxims*,

transl. L. W. Tancock

Sentences

About a year ago, having set aside a bowl which had contained some rhubarb grated in water, without wiping it, I was astonished to find, a few days afterward, that the rhubarb had crystallized, covering the bottom of the bowl with perfect cubes, of the color and consistency of glue, and a tenth of an inch in diameter.   (Dec. 22, 1837)

The utmost nearness to which men approach each other amounts barely to a mechanical contact. As when you rub two stones together, though they emit an audible sound, yet do they not actually touch each other.   (March 14, 1838)

The halloo is the creature of walls and masonwork; the whisper is fittest in the depths of the wood, or by the shore of the lake; but silence is best adapted to the acoustics of space.   (Dec. 15, 1838)

Cheap persons will stand upon ceremony, because there is no other ground; but to the great of the earth we need no introduction, nor do they need any to us. (April 24, 1839)

The words of some men are thrown forcibly against you and adhere like burs.   (June 4, 1839)

The poem is drawn out from under the feet of the poet, his whole weight has rested on this ground.   (Jan. 26, 1840)

The ring-leader of the mob will soonest be admitted into the councils of state.   (Feb. 12, 1840)

I cannot turn on my heel in a carpeted room. What a gap in the morning is a breakfast! A supper supersedes the sunset.   (April 22, 1840)

Of what consequence whether I stand on London bridge

for the next century, or look into the depths of this bubbling spring which I have laid open with my hoe?

(June 18, 1840)

When we are shocked at vice we express a lingering sympathy with it. Dry rot, rust, and mildew shock no man, for none is subject to them. (June 22, 1840)

Go where he will, the wise man is proprietor of all things. Everything bears a similar inscription, if we could but read it, to that on the vase found in the stomach of a fish in old times,—"To the most wise." (July 12, 1840)

As I picked blackberries this morning, by starlight, the distant yelping of a dog fell on my inward ear, as the cool breeze on my cheek. (July 16, 1840)

The squeaking of the pump sounds as necessary as the music of the spheres. (Jan. 23, 1841)

For our aspirations there is no expression as yet, but if we obey steadily, by another year we shall have learned the language of last year's aspirations. (Feb. 2, 1841)

"Lu ral lu ral lu" may be more impressively sung than very respectable wisdom talked. It is well-timed, as wisdom is not always. (Feb. 6, 1841)

A greater baldness my life seeks, as the crest of some bare hill, which towns and cities do not afford. I want a directer relation with the sun. (April 11, 1841)

There are certain current expressions and blasphemous moods of viewing things, as when we say "he is doing a good business," more prophane than cursing and swearing. There is death and sin in such words. Let not the children hear them. (April 20, 1841)

I am struck with the pleasing friendships and unanimities of nature in the woods, as when the moss on the trees takes the form of their leaves. (April 25, 1841)

Better a monosyllabic life than a ragged and muttered one; let its report be short and round like a rifle, so that it may hear its own echo in the surrounding silence.

(April 29, 1841)

It is not a true apology for any coarseness to say that it is natural. The grim woods can afford to be very delicate and perfect in the details.   (Dec. 25, 1841)

As difficult to preserve is the tenderness of your nature as the bloom upon a peach.   (Aug., 1845)

The rays which streamed through the crevices will be no more remembered when the shadow is wholly removed.

(1845)

He is not the great writer, who is afraid to let the world know that he ever committed an impropriety. Does it not know that all men are mortal?   (1845-47)

The song sparrow, whose voice is one of the first heard in the spring, sings occasionally throughout the season,— from a greater depth in the summer, as it were behind the notes of other birds.   (1837-47)

Am I not as far from those scenes, though I have wandered a different route, as my companion who has finished the voyage of life? Am I not most dead who have not life to die, and cast off my sere leaves?   (1837-47)

HENRY DAVID THOREAU, *The Journal I*,
ed. Bradford Torrey and Francis H. Allen

Inscapes

Two swans flew high up over the river on which I was, their necks stretched out and wings billowing. (Jan. 27, 1864)

The sun coming with pennons of cloud, cloud-bannerets, an oriflamme, a "plump" or something of the sort, of spear-like rays.   (1864)

Moonlight hanging or dropping on treetops like blue cobweb.   (1864)

Also the upper sides of little grotted waves turned to the sky have soft pale-coloured cobwebs on them, the under sides green.   (1864)

Note that the beaded oar, dripping, powders or sows the smooth with dry silver drops.   (1864)

Grey clouds in knops. A curious fan of this kind of cloud radiating from a crown, and covering half the sky.

(Sept. 14, 1864)

Changeable; some flying scarf-ends; showers; later graceful oyster-shell mouldings.   (July 16, 1864)

In walking back saw a Scotch fir with pale and very thin foliage all except one tuft high up, which was as dark and thick as velvet and freshly edged with bright green.

(Sept. 8, 1867)

In some chestnuts the leafing is as if drawn with a pair of compasses.   (May 13, 1867)

Alpine cows dun-coloured and very well made. Melodious lines of a cow's dewlap.   (July 9, 1868)

The snow on the hills, it must be owned, looks like rags of cambric drying.   (July 17, 1868)

In the valley a girl with spindle and distaff tending cows.

(July 20, 1868)

We drove to St. Remy. As we approached it the hills "fledged" with larches which hung in them shaft after shaft like green-feathered arrows.   (July 28, 1868)

An owl has come even to Oak Hill and I saw it sheeling through the moonlight in front and presently there were scuffling sounds in the bushes.   (Aug. 7, 1868)

The sunset June 20 was wine-coloured, with pencillings of purple, and next day there was rain.   (1869)

The cuckoo has changed his tune: the two notes can scarcely be told apart that is their pitch is almost the same.

(June 28, 1869)

The slate slabs of the urinals even are frosted in graceful sprays. [Dec. 31, 1870. I have noticed it here also at the seminary: it comes when they have been washed.]

(Feb. 12, 1870)

The banks are "versed" with primroses, partly scattered, partly in plots and squats, and at a little distance shewing

milkwhite or silver—little spilt till-fulls of silver. I have seen them reflected in green standing farmyard water
(May 6, 1871)

A parhelion seen after dinner, the mock sun being almost as bright as the true. I was not there: they did not take the trouble to tell anyone   (Nov. 29, 1871)

Holy Saturday—warm, with thunder, odd tufts of thin-textured very plump round clouds something like the eggs in an opened ant-hill   (March 30, 1872)

This day (and often afterwards) we have had one or two bats flying at midday and circling so near that I could see the ears and claws and the purplish web of the wings with the ribs and veins through it   (May 13, 1872)

I had the bud of a purple flagflower in water and happening to touch it it broke open   (June 14, 1872)

It is pretty to see the dance and swagging of the light green tongues or ripples of waves in a place locked between rocks   (Aug. 10, 1872)

The ashtree growing in the corner of the garden was felled. It was lopped first: I heard the sound and looking out and seeing it maimed there came at that moment a great pang and I wished to die and not to see the inscapes of the world destroyed any more   (April 8, 1873)
GERARD MANLEY HOPKINS, The Journals and Papers,
ed. Humphry House and Graham Storey

Here, Dear Library, Are the Papers

(Author's Note to the Librarian of Congress: The following collection of documents was made in response to your letter suggesting that unless some other disposition has already been agreed upon, I bequeath my "papers" to the Library of Congress.)

Gladly, sir, in memory of the great patron, Thomas Jefferson,
Do I give, devise, and bequeath these historic documents.

Use them as you please, for no strings are tied to this bequest.
Collate them, annotate them, and let the scholars paw them.

They shed a curious light upon the dark crannies of our time,
And thinkers now unborn will gasp, "Could such things be?"

They are the fruits of a long lifetime, and they repose
In an old shoe box, bound with a frayed hangman's noose.

When I die (maybe soon, maybe not), they all go to you,
To have and to hold in perpetuity. And this is what they are:

A note from Henry L. Mencken written in the spring of
1946: "What's this I hear? So you have gone home to Texas,
leaving New York desolate. One report is that you are schem-
ing to restore the old Republic of Texas and make yourself
President, or Dictator. Another is that you are engaged in
breeding freak animals for zoos and circuses. All this is very
disturbing. Please enlighten me."

An appeal, in pencil, written on ruled paper, from an old
cowhand serving a life term in Arizona State Prison: "I do
not like it around here. They treat me fine, but it is all very
boring. Don't you think it's about time you got me out?"

Memorandum on an envelope dated August, 1935, at
Great Neck, Long Island: "Don Skene and John McNulty,
who are resting in my house, spent most of the afternoon
quarrelling. They do not like each other. They almost fought
when Skene advanced the idea that 'We can sleep all day
tomorrow' is the finest sentence in the English language.
McNulty held out for 'No date has been set for the
wedding.'"

Part of a letter from an old Denver editor, apparently referring to the failure of some miscreants to obtain clemency:
"After all, you can't really blame the Governor. Remember
these boys killed eight Mormons before breakfast."

A haunting sentence picked up in the lobby of the Paso
Del Norte Hotel, in El Paso, in 1937, and recorded on a
piece of hotel stationery: "There were these two brothers

and they were bachelors and they had onions on both sides of the river."

Sentiment, by an author unknown to me, found written on a menu at Arnaud's Restaurant, in New Orleans: "This funny old Cajun named Quimper came down with a case of distemper."

Memorandum of a snatch of literary criticism overheard during a discussion of a new popular novelist in the Lafayette Restaurant, in New York, in 1933: "There are only two things wrong with his writing. He makes an unfortunate choice of words and then the bum places them in infelicitous juxtaposition."

Message on a Western Union blank from an unidentified informer: "This fellow fancies himself a cosmopolite and a social success because he knows that the M.-P. in the name of Grayson M.-P. Murphy stands for Mallet-Prevost. That's all he knows."

Verbatim quote, taken down on the spot, from a broad-hatted nabob who was getting off the Santa Fe's Texas Chief at Houston: "It's been a hard day all around. First, my wife's pet kangaroo has to go and get poisoned, and then somebody stole my midget butler's stepladder."

Excerpt from a letter from Chicago dealing with an acquaintance who had just died: "Well, he's gone. Somehow I'll miss him. He sang a beautiful tenor, but he was crazy as a peach-orchard boar."

Anonymous missive from someone, apparently not an admirer, in Atlanta, Georgia: "You cad! May your hair turn green and your eyeteeth dissolve in sheep dip. You are so lowdown you would rob a widow's bee tree."

Taunting postcard from a detective friend, addressed to me at the *Herald Tribune* (when I was its city editor) and postmarked Fairbanks, Alaska: "So you can't find Judge Crater, eh? I didn't think you could. But don't feel bad about it. I can't find him either."

Transcribed remarks of an aged barber at the Astor, who

cut my hair while I was on a visit to New York, in March, 1956: "You remember Fritz Gutman? Used to have the first chair. Been here since the place opened, in 1904. Dead now. Guess you want to know what his last words were. Yes? Well, he was dying in the bedroom of his home, out in Queens. Cancer. Been in a coma for a day or two. You remember a big motion-picture man named Bernstein? Used to stay at the Astor when he was in town. He'd always have Fritz Gutman come up to his room to work on him. Tipped him big—maybe ten dollars a visit. Fritz thought a lot of him. Well, all of sudden, Fritz came out of his coma, and woke up and called to his wife, Emma—for that's her name. 'Emma,' he said, 'bring me my razor and my strop and the mug with my name on it and some witch hazel. I must go upstairs now to see Mr. Bernstein.' Then he died."

Letter from a Philadelphia dowager, written the morning after a lively party in the Warwick Hotel, in that city: "There is something about Philadelphia social life which I think you should understand. It seems that every time a Biddle gets drunk, he thinks he's a Cadwalader."

Note from William Muldoon, the aged Solid Man, written from his training camp in Westchester County shortly before his death: "The trouble with life, my young friend, is that when you get old enough to know what to do you are too old to do it."

Notation of a comment made by W. O. McGeehan, the sportswriter, concerning an editor for whom he had a low regard: "I think he has often really tried to fight the s.o.b. that's in him. It's no use. He's hopelessly overmatched."

And that, beloved Library of Congress, seems to be the crop: Use it, pray, for the enrichment of the American Way of Life.

STANLEY WALKER, New Yorker, Nov. 24, 1956

Commentary

I have included no student entries here for a reason I think worth noting: I have had too many good ones over the past few years to do justice to them in a short space. Instead I have chosen professional entries, mostly of single sentences which are pretty clearly either abstract or concrete. I consider the distichs and maxims mostly abstract, the haiku and inscapes mostly concrete. The Stanley Walker entries are also concrete, and dramatically comic. The sentences from Thoreau are some abstract and some concrete. I intend all of these entries as samples of what students can include in their Journals, and also as originals suitable for translation on the scale of abstraction.

Because the range of such translation may not be altogether clear, I include below several translations of the same sentences, all of which I consider valid. Of the maxim, "The surest way to be taken in is to think oneself craftier than other people": "I bought an old army sabre from a rummage sale and hurried home, delighted to have purchased it so cheaply. I had another at home I thought would make a perfect match. When I got home, I learned that my wife had given my army sabre to the rummage sale." (James Shappee) "I turned the speedometer back to 60,000 on the '48 Ford and fooled the dealer into giving me $500 on it toward the new Edsel." (Richard Knox) "He used another man's name when he entertained the widow. The other man was quite elated a year later when he inherited her estate." (Richard Dewey) Of the haiku, "In honour of the festival, let me adorn the thongs of my sandals with the iris": "Something special is always prepared for in some little way." (Barbara Hilton) "We think we need excuses to ornament ourselves." (Claudette Corwin) "People are quite ingenious when it comes to excusing their vanity." (James Shappee)

Students include in their Journals their five best translations of each kind. Translations from abstract to concrete can be quite easily judged for precision. Often students overlook a word or two and distort the thought considerably. Translations from concrete to abstract are less subject to precision, but should be as precise as possible. What is to be avoided is such vagueness as "Beauty is found everywhere," which is the abstract basis of every haiku and inscape. Sometimes I have been unable to see any connection at all between original and translation until I questioned the student, and then I made him revise it to show the connection. Some students include their translations unidentified and interspersed with their own entries, and I try to oblige them by guessing. I ask that entries be arranged in climactic succession according to effectiveness (best last, weakest first), which often turns up interesting differences of opinion between us.

THE
STATIC
MODES

For when I hear a man discussing virtue or any wisdom who is a true man and worthy of the words he speaks, I am overjoyed; I put the speaker and the speech together to see how they fit and harmonize. And such a man seems to me properly musical, tuned to the fairest harmony, not of the lyre or pleasant instruments, but actually tuned in his own life between words and deeds, not in the Ionian, nor yet in the Phrygian or Lydian, but in the Dorian, the only one of the harmonies truly Hellenic. Such a man makes me delight in his voice, and you would consider me a lover of talk, so eagerly do I take in what he says.

PLATO, Laches 188C

Description

Literature shares with music the mixed blessing of time. Painting is, except for the doubtful achievements of the motion picture, static: though you may ponder a painting or statue for an hour, that experience is not ordered by the artist in time, as is a poem or a sonata. Both literature and music require a time of performance, a real performance in the theater or concert-hall, or a mock performance, the reading of a manuscript in the study. The exploitation of this time by the poet or composer constitutes his mastery of form, whereas the painter's form is spatial. Music, except when based on a narrative program, refers to no time, though it consumes time. But literature, as distinct from music, is a progression of two times. Besides the time of performance there is the time of reference. The trip from Phaeacia to Ithaca takes Odysseus both 55 lines, and one night. (*Odyssey*, XIII, 70-124)

Description may be considered literature aspiring to become painting, and that is why Lessing's essay on the limits of painting and poetry almost excludes description from the province of literature. The business of each art, he says, is to discover and exploit its peculiar capabilities, what it cannot share with its fellows. Now bodies in space are the peculiar subjects of painting, as actions in time are those of literature (*Laocoön* XVI); and so the time of painting, and the space of literature will be minimal. Description is literature failing to mind its own business, as serious an encroachment as is, in painting, a cartoon progression of drawings that tell a story. (XVIII)

Though description takes time, as all literature does, the time referred to is or approaches zero. And its order is chiefly determined, not by time, but space. If I am describing a house I may well begin with the front door and vestibule, and proceed through the downstairs and then the upstairs rooms, but I will probably be more interested in what there is along the way, than in my tour: an alternate order might have begun with the roof and attic. Thus description as far as possible violates the sequentiality of literature. It aims to convey bodies existing in equal, or no, time, by means of the staggered words of discourse: "the coexistence of the bodies," says Lessing, "comes into collision with the sequence of the discourse." (XVII)

But even Lessing cannot deny that description exists, that literature, however feebly or inappropriately, can describe. Admonitions aside, description appears to be the simplest of the concrete modes of rhetoric.

> At the harbor's head is a thin-leaved olive tree,
> and near the tree is a lovely cave dim with clouds,
> sacred to the nymphs who are known as the Naiads.
> (*Odyssey*, XIII, 102-104)

You may mark here, in obedience to the dismissal of time, the virtual collapse of the verb. If you think of the normal sentence as composed of subject, verb, and complement, description as far as possible lacks the middle element, and unites the first and last by the simplest copulation, the verb *be*. Greek and Latin sentences (such as those from Homer above) more often lack any verb, and English-speaking students are taught this rule for translation: in the absence of a verb supply the simplest form of *be*. In description every verb is, or can usually be recast by, some form of *be*. The usual substitutes for *is* are simple verbs of rest: *rests, stands, sits, lies*; or static pictorial verbs: *extends, hides, slopes, hangs*; or verbs which, normally active, here lack their usual activity or significance: *has, goes, gives, looks, leads, rises, runs*; or passive constructions: *is filled with, is surrounded by, is built of, is covered by, is separated from, is adorned by*.

Nor is it to be expected that most sentences in description will avoid *be* or one of its dodges. The handbook rule of avoiding adjectives in description, in favor of vivid nouns and verbs, is almost a restatement of Lessing's rule of avoiding description altogether, for any attempt to vivify verbs will simply render a passage non-descriptive. And since the verb is thus exempted from life, both nouns and adjectives must be fully counted on. There is another verbal dodge, as strained as, in the narrative trappings of dialogue, the avoidance of *said* by *muttered, opined, interjected, cautioned, fluted*. Pope's descriptive verse, for example, sometimes shows a coy and elegant variation on the verb.

> Pale suns, unfelt, at distance roll away,
> And on th' impassive ice the lightnings play;
> Eternal snows the growing mass supply,
> Till the bright mountains prop th' incumbent sky.
>   ("The Temple of Fame," 55-58)

The verb *be* is a simple assertion of existence, and it is no more disturbing than a repeated mark of punctuation, an equal-sign. Sometimes it may be used for rhetorical repetition, and often, even in English, it may be omitted altogether. There may be a mere catalogue of descriptive details, preceded by the anticipatory "There is . . ."

The structure of a single descriptive sentence seems, then, the barest that language is capable of. The next place to look for rhetorical complexity is the connection between the two statements, or the means of proceeding from one statement to the next. Here there is the simplest connection possible, addition. Every two descriptive statements are connected, or might be most appropriately connected, by the word *and*, of all conjunctions the most noncommittal. The formula for a descriptive sequence you are thus reduced to is $a=b$ *and* $c=d$, where a and c are things to be described, $=$ is a form of *be*, and b and d are the means of describing: "The house is white, and the shutters are black."

This formula, you may now observe, is equally suited to another literary phenomenon, the analogy or comparison.

> Poor soul, the center of my sinful earth,
> Thrall to these rebel powers that thee array.
>
> (SHAKESPEARE, Sonnet 146)

The formula above may be readily discerned here: "My soul is the center . . . and my soul is a thrall . . ." In fact the formula may help to show that "My body is the earth . . . and my body is these rebel powers . . ." Or the formula may be elaborated to accommodate elaborations of the analogy: a as to $v, w, . . . = b$ as to $x, y, . . .$ The analogy is now better expressed: "My soul as to my body is (or is like) the center as to my sinful earth, and is the thrall as to these rebel powers." Another analogy shows the pattern more clearly:

> So are you to my thoughts as food to life,
> Or as sweet-season'd showers are to the ground.
>
> (Sonnet 75)

This similarity between typically descriptive statements and typical analogies may be considered merely incidental,

or it may be considered that all comparisons, and especially
those which mean to clarify an abstract or vague issue by a
concrete reference in the predicate, are, however deviously,
descriptive, so that every comparison may be rhetorically
seen as a momentary switch to the mode of description.
Cicero says: "Every metaphor . . . is directed to our senses,
but principally to the sense of sight, which is the keenest
of them all." (*Orator*, III, xl)[1] Certainly the comparison,
identical in structure to the descriptive statement, is a fitting
embellishment of description. Or, under its alternate name
of image, it may become dominant:

> The apparition of these faces in the crowd:
> Petals, on a wet, black bough.
> > (EZRA POUND, "In a Station of the Metro")

Though the Imagists insisted they were "not a school of
painters," it is clear that their chief interest was graphic.
Pound's oft-quoted definition of the image—"that which presents an intellectual and emotional complex in an instant
of time"—shows that in the course of a single image, no time
passes. Elsewhere Pound offers an analysis of the structure
of the image comparable to the formula of the analogy above:
"By the 'image' I mean . . . an equation; not an equation of
mathematics, not something about *a, b,* and *c,* having something to do with form, but about *sea, cliffs, night,* having
something to do with mood." (*Gaudier-Brzeska*, p. 106) And
at least some Imagist poems proceed by largely static images
and may be rhetorically considered exercises in description.

The major variant from this formula for the analogy is the
epic simile, which is rhetorically distinct from other analogies,
not chiefly in its use of "like or as," or in being "extended,"
but because it is narrative rather than descriptive. The verbs
are vivid rather than static, the equation is between actions,
not bodies.

---

1. The translation is by J. S. Watson, *Cicero On Oratory and Orators.*

> And as when the welcome earth appears to swimmers
> whose well-made ship Poseidon has struck in the sea,
> driven forward by the wind and the heavy waves,
> a few escape from the graying surf toward the land,
> their bodies crusted over with brine from swimming;
> they welcome earth, having escaped their misery.
> Just so was she, looking on her welcome husband—
> she could not release her white arms from round his neck.
>   (Odyssey, XXIII, 233-240)

The present tense in English is not used for present action. To do so is one of the first mistakes that learners of the language make. "I go to the market," they say, meaning at the present moment. This statement actually suggests habit or recurrence: *always, every Tuesday,* or *whenever we have guests.* The most skillful analysis of the modern English verb, that of Trager and Smith (*An Outline of English Structure*, p. 80), distinguishes only two tenses, the past from the *non-past*, well named since not present. The tense might be named aorist, since it involves no special commitment to time. It may be used for past actions: "In the Renaissance men rediscover the classics." Or it may be used for future actions: "Next week we go to New York." The normal recurrent force of the tense may be thought indeed to suggest both past and future more than present time. In order to represent an action as occurring at the present moment you must use the "present progressive": "I am going to the market."

The past tense, by comparison, involves a distinct commitment. "I went to the market" is a reference to an action that occurred once at some time in the past and is now over. In order to carry the special recurrent force of the present tense into the past you are reduced to a periphrasis: *I used to go, I would go,* or *I kept going.* The simple past tense may sometimes be used to express recurrence, but only with additional help: "I always went to the market." Or the simple past may be used when a series has already been established as recurrent: "I used to go to the market every Tuesday. The children came along." These observations apply only to verbs with some possibility of life. For verbs already dead or meaningless, such as *be* and the alternatives most appropriate to description, no form of the verb will be anything but aorist. "The book was (or lay) on the table" is just as noncommittal as its recurrent forms, "The book used to be (or lie) . . ."

Description may be conceived, and may occur, at any time—past, present, or future—though future effects will be whimsical and tangential. The past in description is a duration of time when things were always the same, not a unique or particular time in the past. The present is merely a general or universal assertion of existence. Once its time has been established, no time passes in the course of a description— or else it becomes narration. Static verbs are always aorist. If vivid verbs are introduced, they are usually in the present tense, one clear denial of unique action, or in a past recurrent tense, another. Description, of course, most purely prevails in an altogether timeless continuum, but special effects may require vivid verbs. Perhaps some action needs to be taken account of along the way, but without disturbing the aorist effect already established: "the dog chases his tail"; or "the dog would chase . . ." Whenever there is some reference that might be considered unique or narrative, recurrence may be specially stressed.

Description most appropriately deals with things rather than persons. An attention to persons, a literary as distinct from a graphic attention, will result in actions rather than bodies, to use Lessing's terms, or will result in narration rather than description. People, not things, move and act: things stay still, and invite description. There is a way of regarding persons as things, of course, as bodies or objects which may be pictorially represented as well as other largely stationary objects. The description of a person has no rhetorical difference from other descriptions. But persons, and authors' accounts of them, cannot be depended upon to remain lifeless very long: once the person moves, and the author records it, you are out of description. The "character sketch," like most literary types a mixture of rhetorical modes, may be partly or largely descriptive. But characterization may verge on narration, or on reflection. "She had small white hands" may become "She lit a cigarette" or "She was not used to hard work."

An author who presumes to describe, whether a person or a thing, implies that the subject he has chosen diverges far enough from its class or classes to deserve singling out. His subject will be concrete, specific, particular, and unique, and it will reflect, as critics have often said, what impression the subject makes on all his senses. "Let me tell you about this house," says the author, and if his description applies as well to every other house of the same class you can accuse him of failure to describe *this* house. The art of description therefore requires a large and pervasive view of every subject, a sifting of all its traits, to determine its membership in every possible class, and to see also where it differs from each class. Every trait shared with other members of the class can be dismissed, leaving only unique traits. In scientific description, for example of archaeological remains, it is especially important to differentiate common from unique traits. And literary descriptions may well require greate subtlety. The description of a car need not tell us it is a vehicle with four wheels. The description of a 1960 Cadillac can omit its tail-fins, unless they are dented or otherwise unique. Flaubert told his protégé de Maupassant: "by a single word, show me how one cab-horse differs from fifty others before or behind it." (See Preface to *Pierre and Jean*.)

Though apology is never a becoming stance in a writer, he might well offer a passing apology for general or typical traits appearing in his otherwise unique description. Perhaps there is some need to classify an object before describing it: "The house is one of those built in New England in the early eighteenth century." Or he may wish to introduce a general trait in the course of his description: "Like most cars of that year it was too long." When no such apology is offered, you can expect every trait to be unique. It is a paradox of description that, while the verb of every statement denies a unique occurrence, the complement positively insists upon a unique attribute.

The unique may be sought in either of the contrasting aims proposed to themselves by Coleridge and Wordsworth on the occasion of the *Lyrical Ballads*: Coleridge's, to render the supernatural and romantic credible, Wordsworth's, "to give the charm of novelty to things of every day." (*Biographia Literaria*, ch. XIV) These statements may be critically discovered to separate matter from manner, substance from style, or content from form. But the controversial divorce of form and content, whatever its validity for criticism, has certainly some validity in the biography of the writer, whose subject may occur to him before his treatment of it; and in either the subject or its treatment he may aim at the unique. According to the formula $a = b$ *and* $c = d$, he may aim at the unique in the things to be described, the a's and c's or in the descriptive attributes of the things, the b's and d's. The night club in Mozambique need only be plainly presented; the corner supermarket had better be invested with novelty. Such examples suggest that what is unique is relative to what is known at a given time and place: your novelty is my commonplace. The criterion of the unique then makes, like other literary criteria, a constant appeal to the judiciousness and taste of writer and reader.

However novel a writer can make his description, it may well seem that the endless parade of descriptive statements, of things equated with their attributes, results in a certain dullness. Lessing speaks of description as tiresome, dry, barren. (*Laocoön* XVI, XVIII) Description, though possible, he says, belongs to prose rather than poetry; "for such verbal

descriptions of bodies lack the special illusion of poetry."
(XVII) Beauty, whose elements must be seen at once, can
never be conveyed by description (XX); but ugliness may be
relegated to description, which, in its weakening of all pictorial effects, may render ugliness less repulsive. (XXIII)
Homer, he observes—and it is one of his most useful observations—never, or rarely, stops the progression of his narrative
to describe. I have already noted that similes, usually static
or descriptive, are in Homer moving or narrative. In the
places where description might be expected, says Lessing,
there is another embedded narrative: "Should Homer wish
to show us how Agamemnon was dressed, then the king must
put on all his clothing piece by piece before our eyes: the
soft tunic, the great mantle, the beautiful sandals, the
sword." (XVI) Lessing complains that perception of a scene
is momentary, but description is lengthy. Because all the
statements of a description must be slowly taken in an
equal suspension of time, you have forgotten the first detail
by the time you get to the last—whereas a painting can be
seen all at once. (XVIII) This perhaps explains why
Alexander Bain insists: "The chief rule in Description is to
include with the Enumeration of the parts a comprehensive
statement, or general Plan, of the whole." (*English Composition and Rhetoric*, II, i, 2) Such a plan may help the reader
to keep his place in the lineup of details.

Critics have sometimes boggled at Lessing's categorical rejection of the pictorial from poetry and of the narrative from
painting, but they have not questioned his basic assignment
of the powers appropriate to each art. He is careful to expect
different beauties from each, because, he says, if you force a
competition between picture and description, the picture
wins every time. But if you take this competition quite seriously—poet and painter standing together at a given scene
with pencils poised—you may find that the poet comes off
somewhat better than Lessing claims. It is true that painting
makes a more direct and vivid appeal to the eye than poetry,

whose appeal is indirect. But it might also be said that poetry, by appealing to no sense, appeals to all senses, or to the seat of the senses, the mind. Pictorial and descriptive poetry are not always identical. There are the smells, the tastes, the sounds, the touches of things—all within the province of description. If poetry makes only half the appeal to the eye that painting does, its indirect appeal remains five times broader.

It is also true that the painter's result can be perceived at once (even if the painter directs the eye in an almost temporal fashion), whereas you must spend time perusing the poet's result. But it might also be said that the painter must deliver up all his effects at once, whereas the poet can postpone his so that they strike your perception in the best order. A painting comes closer to real-life perception of a scene, if that perception is of one moment, but if, as is more likely, you pass through a real-life scene, receiving constantly shifting images of the scene, the poet comes closer to your perception, and may withhold his choicest secrets till the end. The restriction of one art is the glory of another.

Even in a short space the sequence of descriptive effects may be artful and significant. Yeats's "The Magi" has been cited by Pound as evidence of Yeats's Imagism:

> Now as at all times I can see in the mind's eye,
> In their stiff, painted clothes, the pale unsatisfied ones
> Appear and disappear in the blue depth of the sky
> With all their ancient faces like rain-beaten stones,
> And all their helms of silver hovering side by side,
> And all their eyes still fixed, . . .

This brief sequence reaches something like a climax in line 6, with a direct sight of the eyes. Lines 2 and 3 give a first, vivid but broad view; lines 4 and 5 show the faces and headpieces. By line 6 Yeats is ready to merge his descriptive climax with his comment on the scene:

> . . . hoping to find once more,
> Being by Calvary's turbulence unsatisfied,
> The uncontrollable mystery on the bestial floor.

Obviously such effects cannot be scattered or rearranged. And if they could be reduced to one word, or one painting, you would lose the special postponed sequence of the poem. From this point of view, a painting might be said to dump a careless jumble of effects in your lap all at once. Or perhaps the restriction of the visual arts is more apparent in sculpture, which cannot so readily as painting be seen all at once from one location. But the sculptor can prescribe no spatiotemporal sequence for the best perception of his work, a guided tour around his sculpture, as can a poet.

The ancient saying of Simonides, that painting is silent poetry and poetry talking painting, often cited to demonstrate the equivalence and interdependence of the arts, may also be found to reveal a preference, however trifling, for poetry. Beyond simply equating the two arts, this saying modifies both with an attribute of poetry, according to whether they talk. A painting that talks, a poem, gives you the best of both arts, but what good is a poem that doesn't talk, a painting? A critic anxious to exalt painting would have said that painting is visible or spectacular poetry and poetry invisible painting.

But far from being praised, descriptive passages have ordinarily been considered lapses from the writer's chief business. Horace, who with his phrase *ut pictura poesis* seems to urge a correspondence of painting and poetry, also provides the first warning against that correspondence. His other phrase, *purpureus pannus*, the "purple patch," is now often equivalent to any "fine writing"—and both terms are usually ironic. But for Horace a "purple patch" is simply a lapse into description.

> one widely gleaming purple patch after another is sewn on,
> when there are described the grove and altar of Diana and

> the winding stream that rushes through the goodly fields,
> or the River Rhine, or the rainbow. But here was not the
> place for these descriptions.
>
> (Ars Poetica 16-18)[2]

Pope adopted a view similar to Horace's, and repudiated his
earlier descriptive verse.

> Soft were my numbers; who could take offence,
> While pure description held the place of sense?
> (Epistle to Dr. Arbuthnot, 147-148)

A comment on this passage by Pope's friend and literary
executor William Warburton is quoted with relish by Lessing, who says the comment "may have the force of an explanation by the poet himself." (*Laocoön* XVII)

> He uses pure equivocally, to signify either chaste or empty;
> and has given in this line what he esteemed the true char-
> acter of descriptive poetry, as it is called—a composition,
> in his opinion, as absurd as a feast made up of sauces. The
> office of a picturesque imagination is to brighten and
> adorn good sense: so that to employ it only in description,
> is like children's delighting in a prism for the sake of its
> gaudy colors, which, when frugally managed and artfully
> disposed, might be made to unfold and illustrate the
> noblest objects in nature.

This comment suggests what has often been said, that
description is chiefly useful as a means of enriching and
coloring the other rhetorical modes, and is, or should be,
rarely found in a pure state. Even so recent a critic as Jean
Hagstrum affirms that "Pictorial imagery is most effective
when it is in some way or other metaphorical rather than
purely descriptive or purely imitative of visual reality." (*The
Sister Arts*, p. xx) As in poetry, so in prose-fiction. In the
history of the modern novel from Balzac to Flaubert you

---

2. The translation is by James Harry and Sara Catron Smith in *The
Great Critics*, ed. by James Harry Smith and Edd Winfield Parks.

may trace a growing insistence that description be function-
ally related to character. The Pension Vauquer tells much
about its inhabitants. Emma Bovary's view of a scene tells
much about her mood.

Of course no good writer will give a trvial version of reality;
if he is trivial in description perhaps he is elsewhere trivial.
Lessing warns poets that, if even Ariosto's attempts at
description must fail, so must theirs. (XX) But every modern
reader will recall memorable descriptions from Spenser,
Shakespeare, Milton, and Pope, which Lessing strangely
avoids. Description has not won a place in literature with the
other concrete modes, possibly because it does not necessarily deal with human beings and so provides no "criticism
of life." But I have tried to show that it has an unquestionable if elementary place in literature and may be considered
the mode of every metaphor and analogy. The condescen-
sion of critics toward description, however appropriate to a
particular task at hand, is therefore fruitless or absurd in
general. Certainly the poet, the story-teller, had better keep
his eye out for unique descriptive touches in a phrase or a
sentence. But he may also sometimes beg you to hold everything, overlook the usual nibbling away of represented time
in his story, while capitalizing as ever on recited time as it
passes—and tell you just how things strike him.

IN THE MIDDLE of the lower court was a magnificent fountain of beautiful alabaster, above which were the three Graces with cornucopias, casting out water through their breasts, mouths, ears, eyes, and the other openings of their bodies.

The interior of the portion of the dwelling that opened upon this court rested upon great pillars of chalcedony and of porphyry, fashioned with the finest of antique workmanship. Above were splendid galleries, long and wide, adorned with paintings, with the horns of deer, unicorns, rhinoceroses, and hippopotamuses, as well as with elephants' teeth and other objects interesting to look upon.

The ladies' quarters extended from the tower Arctic to the Mesembrine gate. The men occupied the rest of the house. In front of the ladies' quarters, in order that the occupants might have something to amuse them, there had been set up, between the first two outside towers, the lists, the hippodrome, the theatre, and the swimming-pools, with wonderful triple-stage baths, well provided with all necessary equipment and plentifully supplied with water of myrrh.

Next the river was a fine pleasure-garden, in the center of which was a handsome labyrinth. Between the towers were the tennis courts and the ball-grounds. On the side by the tower Cryere was the orchard, full of all sorts of fruit-trees, all of them set out in the form of quincunxes. Beyond was the large park, filled with every sort of savage beast. Between the third pair of towers were the targets for arquebus, archery, and crossbow practice. The servants' quarters were outside the tower Hesperia and consisted of one floor only, and beyond these quarters were the stables. In front of the latter stood the falcon-house, looked after by falconers most expert in their art. [14]It was furnished annually by the Candians, the Venetians, and the Sarmatians, with all kinds of out-of-the-ordinary birds: eagles, gerfalcons, goshawks, sakers, lanners, falcons, sparrow-hawks, merlins, and others, all so well trained and domesticated that, when these birds set out from the castle for a little sport in the fields, they would take everything that came in their way. The hunting-kennels were a little farther off, down toward the park.

All the halls, rooms and closets were tapestried in various manners, according to the season of the year. The whole floor was covered with green cloth. The bedding was of embroidered work. [19]In each dressing-room was a crystal mirror, with chasings of fine gold, the edges being trimmed with pearls; and this mirror was of such a size that—it is the truth I am telling you—it was possible to see the whole figure in it at once. [20]As one came out of the halls into the ladies' quarters, he at once encountered the perfumers and the hair-dressers, through whose hands the gentlemen passed when they came to visit the ladies. [21] These functionaries each morning supplied the women's chambers with rose, orange, and "angel" water; and in each room a precious incense-dish was vaporous with all sorts of aromatic drugs.

FRANÇOIS RABELAIS, *Gargantua and Pantagruel*, I, lv,
transl. Samuel Putnam

LONDON. Michaelmas Term lately over, and the Lord Chancellor sitting in Lincoln's Inn Hall. Implacable November weather. [4]As much mud in the streets, as if the waters had but newly retired from the face of the earth, and it would not be wonderful to meet a Megalosaurus, forty feet long or so, waddling like an elephantine lizard up Holborn Hill. Smoke lowering down from chimney-pots, making a soft black drizzle, with flakes of soot in it as big as full-grown snow-flakes—gone into mourning, one might imagine, for the death of the sun. Dogs, undistinguishable in mire. Horses, scarcely better; splashed to their very blinkers. [8]Foot passengers, jostling one another's umbrellas, in a general infection of ill-temper, and losing their foot-hold at street-corners, where tens of thousands of other foot passengers have been slipping and sliding since the day broke (if this day ever broke), adding new deposits to the crust upon crust of mud, sticking at those points tenaciously to the pavement, and accumulating at compound interest.

Fog everywhere. Fog up the river, where it flows among green aits and meadows; fog down the river, where it rolls defiled among the tiers of shipping, and the waterside pollutions of a great (and dirty) city. Fog on the Essex marshes, fog on the Kentish heights. Fog creeping into the cabooses of collier-brigs; fog lying out on the yards, and hovering in the rigging of great ships; fog drooping on the gunwales of barges and small boats. Fog in the eyes and throats of ancient Greenwich pensioners, wheezing by the firesides of their wards; fog in the stem and bowl of the afternoon pipe of the wrathful skipper, down in his close cabin; fog cruelly pinching the toes and fingers of his shivering little 'prentice boy on deck. Chance people on the bridges peeping over the parapets into a nether sky of fog, with fog all round them, as if they were up in a balloon, and hanging in the misty clouds.

Gas looming through the fog in divers places in the streets, much as the sun may, from the spongy fields, be seen to loom by husbandman and ploughboy. Most of the shops lighted two hours before their time—as the gas seems to know, for it has a haggard and unwilling look.

[17]The raw afternoon is rawest, and dense fog is densest, and the muddy streets are muddiest, near that leaden-headed old obstruction, appropriate ornament for the threshold of a leaden-headed old corporation: Temple Bar.

[18]And hard by Temple Bar, in Lincoln's Inn Hall, at the

very heart of the fog, sits the Lord High Chancellor in his
High Court of Chancery.

CHARLES DICKENS, *Bleak House*, ch. 1

THE STORES AND HOUSES was most all old, shackly, dried-up
frame concerns that hadn't ever been painted; they was set
up three or four foot above ground on stilts, so as to be out
of reach of the water when the river was overflowed. The
houses had little gardens around them, but they didn't seem
to raise hardly anything in them but jimpson-weeds, and
sunflowers, and ash-piles, and old curled-up boots and shoes,
and pieces of bottles, and rags, and played-out tinware. The
fences was made of different kinds of boards, nailed on at
different times; and they leaned every which way, and had
gates that didn't generly have but one hinge—a leather one.
Some of the fences had been whitewashed some time or another, but the duke said it was in Columbus's time, like
enough. There was generly hogs in the garden, and people
driving them out.

All the stores was along one street. They had white domestic awnings in front, and the country-people hitched their
horses to the awning-posts. There was empty dry-goods boxes
under the awnings, and loafers roosting on them all day
long, whittling them with their Barlow knives; and chawing
tobacco, and gaping and yawning and stretching—a mighty
ornery lot. They generly had on yellow straw hats most as
wide as an umbrella, but didn't wear no coats nor waist-
coats; they called one another Bill, and Buck, and Hank, and
Joe, and Andy, and talked lazy and drawly, and used considerable many cuss-words. There was as many as one loafer
leaning up against every awning-post, and he most always
had his hands in his britches pockets, except when he fetched
them out to lend a chaw of tobacco or scratch. [11]What a
body was hearing amongst them all the time was:

"Gimme a chaw 'v tobacker, Hank."

"Cain't; I hain't got but one chaw left. Ask Bill."

Maybe Bill he gives him a chaw; maybe he lies and says he ain't got none. Some of them kinds of loafers never has a cent in the world, nor a chaw of tobacco of their own. They get all their chawing by borrowing; they say to a fellow, "I wisht you'd len' me a chaw, Jack, I jist this minute give Ben Thompson the last chaw I had"—which is a lie pretty much every time; it don't fool nobody but a stranger; but Jack ain't no stranger, so he says:

"*You* give him a chaw, did you? So did your sister's cat's grandmother. You pay me back the chaws you've awready borry'd off'n me, Lafe Buckner, then I'll loan you one or two ton of it, and won't charge you no back intrust, nuther."

"Well, I *did* pay you back some of it wunst."

"Yes, you did—'bout six chaws. You borry'd store tobacker and paid back nigger-head."

Store tobacco is flat black plug, but these fellows mostly chaws the natural leaf twisted. When they borrow a chaw they don't generly cut it off with a knife, but set the plug in between their teeth, and gnaw with their teeth and tug at the plug with their hands till they get it in two; then sometimes the one that owns the tobacco looks mournful at it when it's handed back, and says, sarcastic:

[26]"Here, gimme the *chaw*, and you take the *plug*."

All the streets and lanes was just mud; they warn't nothing else *but* mud—mud as black as tar and nigh about a foot deep in some places, and two or three inches deep in *all* the places. The hogs loafed and grunted around everywheres. [29]You'd see a muddy sow and a litter of pigs come lazying along the street and whollop herself right down in the way, where folks had to walk around her, and she'd stretch out and shut her eyes and wave her ears whilst the pigs was milking her, and look as happy as if she was on salary. [30] And pretty soon you'd hear a loafer sing out, "Hi! *so* boy! sick him, Tige!" and away the sow would go, squealing most horrible, with a dog or two swinging to each ear, and three

or four dozen more a-coming; and then you would see all
the loafers get up and watch the thing out of sight, and
laugh at the fun and look grateful for the noise. Then they'd
settle back again till there was a dog-fight. [32]There couldn't
anything wake them up all over, and make them happy all
over, like a dog-fight—unless it might be putting turpentine
on a stray dog and setting fire to him, or tying a tin pan to
his tail and see him run himself to death. [30] On the river-
front some of the houses was sticking out over the bank, and
they was bowed and bent, and about ready to tumble in. The
people had moved out of them. The bank was caved away
under one corner of some others, and that corner was hanging over. People lived in them yet, but it was dangersome,
because sometimes a strip of land as wide as a house caves in
at a time. [37]Sometimes a belt of land a quarter of a mile
deep will start in and cave along and cave along till it all caves
into the river in one summer. [38]Such a town as that has to
be always moving back, and back, and back, because the
river's always gnawing at it.

MARK TWAIN, *The Adventures of Huckleberry Finn*,
ch. 21

[1]AT FIRST THE TINY HOUSE of Mrs. Almira Todd, which stood
with its end to the street, appeared to be retired and sheltered
enough from the busy world, behind its bushy bit of a green
garden, in which all the blooming things, two or three gay
hollyhocks and some London-pride, were pushed back against
the gray-shingled wall. [2]It was a queer little garden and
puzzling to a stranger, the few flowers being put at a dis-
advantage by so much greenery; but the discovery was soon
made that Mrs. Todd was an ardent lover of herbs, both wild
and tame, and the sea-breezes blew into the low end-window
of the house laden with not only sweet-brier and sweet-mary,
but balm and sage and borage and mint, wormwood and
southern-wood. If Mrs. Todd had occasion to step into the

far corner of her herb plot, she trod heavily upon thyme, and made its fragrant presence known with all the rest. [4]Being a very large person, her full skirts brushed and bent almost every slender stalk that her feet missed. [5]You could always tell when she was stepping about there, even when you were half awake in the morning, and learned to know, in the course of a few weeks' experience, in exactly which corner of the garden she might be.

At one side of this herb plot were other growths of a rustic pharmacopoeia, great treasures and rarities among the commoner herbs. [7]There were some strange and pungent odors that roused a dim sense and remembrance of something in the forgotten past. Some of these might once have belonged to sacred and mystic rites, and have had some occult knowledge handed with them down the centuries; but now they pertained only to humble compounds brewed at intervals with molasses or vinegar or spirits in a small caldron on Mrs. Todd's kitchen stove. [9]They were dispensed to suffering neighbors, who usually came at night as if by stealth, bringing their own ancient-looking vials to be filled. One nostrum was called the Indian remedy, and its price was but fifteen cents; the whispered directions could be heard as customers passed the windows. [11]With most remedies the purchaser was allowed to depart unadmonished from the kitchen, Mrs. Todd being a wise saver of steps; but with certain vials she gave cautions, standing in the doorway, and there were other doses which had to be accompanied on their healing way as far as the gate, while she muttered long chapters of directions, and kept up an air of secrecy and importance to the last. [12]It may not have been only the common ails of humanity with which she tried to cope; it seemed sometimes as if love and hate and jealousy and adverse winds at sea might also find their proper remedies among the curious wild-looking plants in Mrs. Todd's garden.

SARAH ORNE JEWETT, *The Country of the Pointed Firs*,

ch. 2

I SIT ON THE BEACH in front of the "Lakeside" summer resort looking out over the waters of Lake Huron. In back of me a sandy hill rises to the flat plot of ground where the twelve small cabins of the "Lakeside" are huddled together. There is a sign advertising cheap rates, and one look at the sad, dusty cabins and surrounding grounds shows why. The dry brownish-green grass is always thin and patchy, and the flowers next to the cracked cement doorsteps look droopy and sick. From the outside the buildings look like shacks, from the inside like one-half car garages. A stuffy bedroom and a crowded kitchen with a tiny window are the only two rooms in the cabins. And, here there is no cheery yellow paint on the kitchen walls, or "eye-rest green" in the bedrooms; instead, the four walls are made of raw, unpainted boards and two-by-fours. There is no ceiling either and plump, black spiders spin intricate webs from one rafter to another. The walls, too, have been decorated with the carvings of many a young boy's jackknife.

[10]At night the vacationists of the "Lakeside" enter into their usual evening diversions. Every night from cabin number six you can hear the continuous slap-slap of the cards against the kitchen table, the rattle of the beer bottle caps as they fall to the floor, the bursts of blatant laughter, the frequent swearing. These sounds rush out of the hot cabin through the screen door and into the night air. There they mingle with the noise coming from the television set in cabin number one; this cabin is dark except for the bright, luminous glow of the television. [14]From another cabin the only sound that drifts into the night is the faint rustle of human fingers turning the pages of a magazine.

[15]The other cottages are completely dark, and a passer-by would be inclined to think that the occupants have taken an evening walk along the beach. [16]But this is not so; each night as soon as supper has been finished these families will hurry over to a nearby town, so they may roller-skate to the tunes of a wailing organ, or sit in their automobiles and

watch a movie at the drive-in theater. [17]Sometimes, too,
it is the whirling lights and fantastic thrills of a carnival
which lure the cabiners into town.

[18]The beach in front of the sad, ugly, little cabins bears
no similarity to the rest of the grounds at the "Lakeside";
it is clean and beautiful. After the hot searing sun has dis-
appeared the sand feels wonderfully cool to walk or sit on.
More enjoyable to the ear than the desperate clamor in the
cabins are the softer sounds of the night. One can hear the
waves of Lake Huron slap gently against the hard packed
sand on the shore. [22]The night breeze swashes through
the trees and with its breath makes their branches twitch
and toss. Then, the breeze, swooping down to the golden
beach will pick up a few tiny grains of sand, toss them into
the air, watch them sparkle for an instant in the moonlight,
and blow up the hill to cool off the pitiful occupants of the
sad, hot cottages. [24]Out on the lake a few tiny white-caps
have a moment of glory as they rise to a peak and gleam
under the silvery pool of the moon; then they fade again
into the vastness of the deep, blue lake.

[25]It is strange that this beach is always deserted at
night. There are no vacationists sitting on the sandy hill,
no one hearing and seeing the beauty of the night, no one
walking along the beach and feeling the cool sand on the
bottoms of his hot feet. [27]Instead the summer vacationists
scurry into their automobiles when darkness approaches
and ride to the nearest town, or remain in their cabins
watching television, staring at the black and red spots on the
faces of their cards, turning the pages of a magazine.

CAROL SCHULTZ

MY PARTNER AND I called it the North Tract. There were 400
acres in this stand of timber which lay just north of a power-
line that crossed the Adirondack Mountains in an east-west
direction. The terrain of this region was considered inac-

cessible for logging, and as a result, its timber was virgin. It was the value of this timber that had tempted us to look there to fill a contract for hard maple and black cherry.

[5]When I first surveyed it, I could not help but notice the icy, north-east wind that whirred in the towering hardwoods. [6]Its ominous sound seemed a warning, begrudging my intrusion, and I felt as though it was cutting through my several layers of clothing to freeze my life's fire. Its chill made me shiver and ache throughout my body, something like the numbing pain of rheumatism.

[8]Turning my back to the wind, I could see a dark, razorback ridge running off to the south. The trees that crested the ridge were ragged fringes of black lace against the stormy, lead-belly clouds. Farther down the steep slope, dark protruding boulders scowled from the shadows. [11]From my bird-like view on a high promontory, I followed with my eye down this slope to what appeared to be the level floor of a valley, but was really a broad expanse of tree tops, a false bottom.

The opposite ridge ran parallel to the razor-back and was heavily wooded with black-trunked cherry and occasional spears of hemlock. Here and there ghostly fingers of white birches became more and more prominent in the impending gloom.

[14]With the coming of dusk, the wind increased its force and snow began to spit against my face and frost-encrusted beard. The advancing night brought a sharp drop in temperature, causing the sap in the maples and other hardwoods to crack and pop like pistol shots. The wind continued to blow, but rising and falling in an uneven cadence. [17]The snow flocked, paused and then whisked away as the wind ebbed and surged.

[18]As I thought about starting the long trek back to the cabin, I saw a large owl swoop down from a tall tree and out over the ravine. The wind caught his gliding body and hurled him far off the course he was headed for. [20]Just as the

owl was tossed out of sight by this sudden gust, the wind seemed to be nudging me from behind in an effort to rid his domain of the transient.

[21]The howl of the wind and cold were only too good persuaders to make me wish myself at home by a warm, wood fire. I kept telling myself the terrain was too rugged for cutting timber, but whether it was or not I could not help but feel the wind was *pushing* me out. [23]Maybe someday they'll get it out, I thought, but the wind laughed at my back.

JAMES SHAPPEE

Commentary

(NOTE: The bracketed numbers within selections identify sentences discussed in the commentary.)

A mode often allied with description is process, possibly because both favor present tense. Here, process is found most extensively in the Twain, sentences 11-26, where the lines of conversation seem more dialogue than drama from the process that contains them; the concrete humor of them is heightened by the implication that the conversation is in fact recurrent. Another process is in 29-30, and others in 32 and 37. In the Dickens, 8 is distinctly process, and other sentences could be construed as brief processes, to show the movement of the fog. In the Jewett, 1 and 2 have a trace of process in "At first" and "the discovery was soon made"; and 4-5, 9, and 11 are clearly process. In the Schultz much of the description is contained by process, 10-14, 16-17, 22-24, and 27. Slight traces of process also occur in the Rabelais, 14, 20, and 21.

Narration is most extensive in the Shappee, where the description is contained by the story of his visit, especially 5, 8, 11, 14-17, 18-20. Reverie occurs in the Dickens, 4; in the Jewett, 7 and 12; in the Schultz, 15; and in the

Shappee, 6 and 21-23. Drama occurs in a characteristic intrusion, in the Rabelais, 19.

Hints of abstraction may be found in the Rabelais intrusion, 19, on the marvellous luxury; in the Dickens, 17-18, on the Chancellor deserving the fog; in the Twain, 38, on the town deserving to be gnawed away; in the Jewett, plainly in 12; in the Schultz, 18 and 25, on the people missing the beauty; in the Shappee, 20-23, on the place having a will.

Descriptions often fail from a wishy-washy typicality in the selection of details. All these examples seem authentic, that is, as if the writer was really there, and struck by the things he saw. The Rabelais has a gorgeous explicitness, like a Renaissance tapestry. The Dickens is a modern atmospheric study, a succession of hazy impressions whose sentences usually lack verbs altogether. The Twain is naturalistic in selection of details and in style ironically naïve. The Jewett is quiet, careful, Flaubertian. The Schultz and Shappee may stand, respectively, for the familiar invested with novelty, and for the exotic made credible. Not everyone has seen the woods in the Shappee, though perhaps everyone has seen something that remote; but everyone has seen the miserable cabins in the Schultz, though perhaps without observing them so carefully.

Definition

Definition is abstract description, just as description is concrete definition. If you have a thing before you, the first in a new universe, and you tell all you can about it, you will not know whether you have described or defined it. Only by comparisons and contrasts with like things in the universe everybody knows can you tell whether you have preferred the unique, distinctive qualities in your account, resulting in description, or the common, typical ones, resulting in definition.

Description is of a thing, definition of a class. In actual practice description may require a rarer, poetic perception of the unique qualities of a thing, but definition would seem theoretically the more difficult mode. For if the unique qualities of a thing can be isolated, its description is simply composed of their total. But definition requires a judicious sifting of things and qualities to find which of the thing's membership in various classes is the most real or useful. And once a class is decided upon, the job is not finished. For an elegant definition is not composed of all the qualities common to the class, but only of those common qualities distinctive of the class. The class of all sports cars has many qualities common to all other cars, but they should be excluded or else you are defining cars in general. The traditional analysis of definition as genus plus differentia suggests two halves of equal importance; but the genus is ordinarily a mere passing mention, an apologetic location of the given class in one of the larger classes it belongs to; the definition actually occurs in the sometimes lengthy total of common qualities distinctive of the class under examination, which are the differentiae. Properties, as Aristotle define them ("which belong only to that thing"—*Topics* I, 5) are rarer than he suggests. Qualities often belong to many things, and it is the exact combination of qualities which differentiates the class.

There are general classes of things, sharing a majority of their qualities, such as men, and abstract classes of things, sharing a minority of their qualities, such as the class of virtuous actions. Both are subject to definition. An abstract class may seem further removed from things, and so more abstract than a general class, but definitions of either are arrived at through abstraction, through sifting and arranging of things and qualities into the most equitable classes. Nor are general and abstract classes always clearly differentiable. If virtue is my subject for more than a few sentences, I must use classes of both men and actions. For that matter, neither are descriptions and definitions always clearly differentiable. All the most concrete words in the dictionary (toad, forsythia, butterscotch) can after all be defined; apparently their definitions must be less abstract than those of recognized abstractions, such as virtue and truth. Then there may be literary techniques and types which are founded on a mixture of description and definition, such as Theophrastan "characters" which seek to define a general class of men, using various concrete agencies ("Boorishness," "Newsmaking," "Late-learning," "Friendship with Rascals"). Such a definition including concrete particulars wittily suggests that, however novel these particulars seem, you will find them duly repeated in every case.

The two modes can be distinguished, but they have much in common. Both description and definition read as a static enumeration of qualities, a telling of beads on a string. You take up the beads one at a time, and possibly in the best order, but the important thing is that you have the string of beads in your hand all at once. If I am defining the ranks of English nobility I may begin with the lowest and proceed to the highest, but this sequence is not temporal, nor, except metaphorically, even spatial. I may also begin with the highest. Both static modes are, however, remotely spatial. Just as description may often be spatially rendered in a picture, so definition may often be schematized by lines and boxes, like a family tree. Both modes are relatively free of time, but a skillful writer, even though no sequence is demanded, will strive to find the most convenient or graceful sequence, as if he were under an obligation to time all along.

Logicians have contrived various intricate rules for definition, but rhetorically all abstract, static discourse is definition. Pascal quarrels with Plato's definition of man as a biped without feathers (since you can't make a man by plucking a chicken), but a rhetorician must accept not only Plato's definition but attempts even further afield: "a man is a two-face, a worrisome thing that leads you to sing the blues in the night." This already appears a violation of one of the rules, that a definition "should not be expressed in obscure or figurative language." But these traditional rules are probably too constricted, not only for rhetoric, but for logic as well. Definition is too often regarded merely as a tool of lexicography, or of persuasion. "Define your terms" is a rule anticipatory to debate. But however brief or extended, definition has an interest in its own right. An author may set forth his static perceptions of a class, and stop there; if he has taught you the secrets of heaven and earth in the attempt, you will not complain that he has been occasionally figurative, or even obscure.

Like description, definition is based on a pattern of static equations simply added to each other: $a=b$ *and* $c=d$. In this formula for definition, $=$ represents *to be* or any other static verb, usually in the present tense, a and c are classes or parts of classes, and b and d are the qualities which differentiate those classes. Any statement, or series of statements, filling this formula with abstract terms may be said to define the terms in positions a and c. The chief "rules" for definition (but they are not rules at all) is that no temporal sequence be engaged in the progression of verbs; and that no particular or concrete things sit for subjects. If these rules are disobeyed, the rules for some other mode of rhetoric will be obeyed. So long as discourse remains abstract, and static, it will define something.

Clearly this view of definition is broader than is usual, including most of what is called exposition. Whatever it is called, this mode is probably the commonest of the modes of rhetoric. Any answers to the questions "What is it like?" or simply "What is it?" will be definitions. The conveying of simple information, or the most sophisticated exchange of wisdom, will make large use of definition. If no material rhetorical differences can be found between the various types and styles of definition and exposition, there is no need to clutter the board with distinctions.

Some philosophers have distinguished between real and nominal definition. The statement *a is b* conceals an ambiguity, and may be taken to mean either "I assert a to be really b," or "I take a nominally to be b." The first defines a thing, the second a word. It is one of the achievements of Robinson's book (*Definition*, ch. VI) to have shown that only nominal definition is an activity clear and simple enough to pass under one name; and that what has been called real definition had better be known by other names, such as abstraction or analysis or naming. Perhaps an easier, if less accurate, means of distinguishing between the two so-called kinds of definition is to say that real definition is what passes in the writer's thoughts and researches before writing; nominal definition is what he writes. However neatly Robinson would like us to separate the two, clearly real definition must somehow precede nominal definition.

If you begin with one thing, and aim to derive from it one of its classes, you will regard the thing as illustrative of the class. Perhaps this is how most abstraction takes place. You perceive the thing not for its particularity but for its generality—still it is only one thing. Illustration also serves in the nominal result both of definition and of persuasion. One of the means of clarification recommended by the handbooks is by concrete example or illustration. But a concrete example is a contradiction in terms, or at least a paradox. As an example or illustration actually exemplifies or illustrates something, some general type or principle, it presents only the qualities common to the class, and lacks any concrete integrity of its own. Minneapolis as illustrative of American cities of its size is the total of its qualities shared with other cities, rather than any of those unique to itself. From this point of view an illustration is nothing other than a static, abstract equation, an enumeration of the qualities common to a class—or a definition.

Analysis and synthesis are means of illustration. It may be that the handiest means of understanding, or of presenting, the thing illustrative of the class will be to separate the thing into its parts, and see how they are related. If you begin with the whole and isolate the parts you analyze it; if you begin with the parts and form the whole you synthesize them. But sequence is a matter of time, and the mode of definition is static. Consequently the sequence of a definition, whether real or nominal, is of little importance; the finished result will show no difference between an analysis and a synthesis. A violin is a whole, and it has separate, organically related parts. If you know your subject you may begin either with the whole or the parts; any sequence will define the violin, or the class of all violins. Sequence will only prove crucial if you are tracing a temporal process— how to make a violin, or how to play one—but those will not be definitions at all, if you take definition to be a static enumeration of the qualities of a class.

If you begin with two things instead of one, and aim to derive one or several classes from them, both become illustrations. Perhaps you will be most interested in the qualities shared by the two things, and so derive a single class to be defined. Or perhaps you will be interested in both the similarities and differences between them, and so partly define the class of qualities shared by the two things, and partly the separate classes of which each is a member. This procedure is called comparison and contrast, and it is unavoidable in even the simplest act of abstraction. Even illustration must introduce other like things into the reckoning; otherwise there is no sign of what the thing illustrates. In more intricate abstractions the ranking of similarities between things, or comparison, and of differences between them, or contrast, may become a more necessary procedure. Think of how many ways city and country businessmen resemble each other, and differ from each other, and you see the use of comparison and contrast. But note that you have only ended up with three classes, one of qualities common to the two, and the two of qualities peculiar to each—or three definitions.

Analogy is a special form of comparison and contrast, a comparison between the relations of things or classes otherwise contrasting. As an accompaniment of description analogy will usually prove particular or concrete; as an accompaniment of definition ideal or abstract. Often the most elevated abstractions cannot be talked about handily in their own terms, and so you must come down a notch or two to a place more spatially perceptible, and then superimpose the

clearer pattern found there on the abstraction. Socrates'
fondness for analogy is well known. In order to define justice in the individual or in the state, it may help to understand what harmony in the lyre amounts to. (*Republic*
443D) And, as the temporal extension of analysis is process, so the temporal extension of analogy is allegory, a story
duplicating an abstract process on a lower level. Socrates'
fondness for allegory is even better known. In order to understand how the philosopher feels who has perceived reality
and tries to define it to the world, consider how a man must
feel who has escaped from a cave of shadows to the light of
day, and returns to tell his old companions what the light
is like. (*Republic* 514 ff.)

If you begin with many or all possible things, and aim to
derive numerous classes from them, you will carry comparison and contrast to even greater lengths. You may find that
two or three classes of things fit into one larger class and that
the new class bears interesting comparison and contrast with
another like class containing two or three classes of its own;
and that the two larger classes together form one even larger
class. Perhaps you will limit yourself to one area of experience and try to separate all its classes, and find their inter-
relationships. Perhaps you will try, as Aristotle did, to define
the classes of all human experience. However limited or
grand, this procedure is called classification, and it is unavoidable in some measure in even the simpler forms of
abstraction above. You cannot tell whether a thing is illustrative of a class unless you have somehow classified many
separate things or classes; you cannot compare and contrast
things and classes without knowing more of their possible
classification than you include in the nominal result. But
sometimes the nominal result may prove more intricate than
a scheme of three definitions. The laws of taxation according
to classification of taxpayers show how intricacies of classification may prove convenient or necessary. But each class
along the way must be separately presented for its own sake,

and so you have ended up with nothing other than an intricate scheme of separate classes, or of classes within classes—or of many definitions.

Division is an alternate form of classification. Sometimes you may begin, not with separate things and the classes they immediately form, but with a large class, and try to find what its divisions are. This procedure may also be carried into the nominal result, in which case the sequence of presentation would be from large to smaller classes, or from up down, instead of the other way around. But as between analysis and synthesis there is no static difference, only temporal; so here the finished result will show no difference between classification and division. Only one variety of division proves of special interest. Aristotle offers a means of complete division of a class, called a dichotomous division, by isolating one quality of a class to make a smaller class, and forming another, remaining class of the negative of the quality. When a painter puts black marks on white paper he gets two configurations, one black, one white, each formed by the exclusions of the other. If you try to divide all human discourse into English and French you will have a great deal left over; but if you divide it into English and non-English you will have a complete, dichotomous division. Often, as perhaps here, the result will be trivial; and this may explain another of the traditional rules, that a definition "must not be in negative when it can be in positive terms." Or you may come up with a negative which is well recognized, as M. Jourdain did when he found that all discourse not verse is prose, and that he'd been talking it all his life.

Doubtless, these, then, are the varieties of abstraction or of real definition which must precede nominal definition. They are also the so-called methods of exposition, which as shown above result simply in one or many, or more or less highly abstract, definitions. None of these varieties are so abstruse that they could be missed by someone full of his subject. Unfortunately no adherence to these varieties, in part or in whole, insures the discovery of truth, which may sometimes come about haphazardly and then be rationalized by one or several of these varieties. A thinker's or a writer's obligation is to his material, not to ideal procedures of abstraction, and he had better let the material dictate his technique, however lopsided the result.

The members of the Pickwick Club are definers not quite but almost as irresponsible as Humpty Dumpty. "When *I* use a word," Humpty Dumpty says, in rather a scornful tone, "it means just what I choose it to mean—neither more nor less." The word "glory" he defines as "a nice knock-down argument." Mr. Blotton calls Mr. Pickwick a humbug, and refuses to withdraw the expression, but when the chairman asks whether he has used the expression in a common sense, Mr. Blotton "had no hesitation in saying he had not—he had used the word in its Pickwickian sense." Whereupon Mr. Pickwick generously responds that "his own observations had been merely intended to bear a Pickwickian construction."

Dictionaries are made to prevent such irresponsibility, which is not always so entertaining as here. Robinson differentiates two varieties of nominal definition: lexical, a report of how men in a given time and place have used a word; and stipulative, an announcement of how a given writer is about to use a word (p. 19). The first variety is bound by usage, the second is perfectly free. But while you may permit a writer to use a word however he likes for purposes of his own discussion, the dictionary provides one convenient set of bounds for ordinary discussion. Modern dictionaries define, not reality, but usage. A dictionary is worth consulting, but never worth quoting, for ideally it tells no more about a word than you already know, if you know the word at all. If you seek to refine upon the meaning of a word, the dictionary provides only the vaguest assistance, as vague, that is, as the combined uses of all the users. Webster is at best a stenographer, no oracle.

According to the traditional rules, definitions should not be circular—should not, that is, repeat the term or terms to be defined in the remainder of the statement. But all human knowledge forms an invincible circularity of relatedness; if I define enough words I must begin repeating myself. And not only are all definitions finally circular, but also Pickwickian —if you read the scene above, that is, as an attempt to reinterpret the word or the thing so as to provide a more comfortable and convenient disposition of reality. No word or idea can ever be definitively defined, not even "liberty" when Milton and Mill have finished with it.

For verbal discourse is not mathematical discourse, as Pascal insists, nor is mathematical discourse perfect. You can imagine, he says, an ideal discourse in which all terms are defined and all propositions proved, but even in geometry there remain some basic terms which cannot themselves be defined by simpler terms. How far from ever being settled, then, must be discourse in the ordinary talk of men.

Still there must always be some uncertainty about which words or ideas stand at present in need of further definition. Anybody may consult his dictionary; if you have nothing more to say than the dictionary, you may let the word rest. But a dictionary is only a crude repository of information. If a subject really interests you, you had better see what the best authorities have to say on the subject; you may have been anticipated or contradicted. But if you have really thought about the subject yourself, you will usually find that no one has thought about it exactly as you have.

You may also feel that if a definition is composed of the qualities common to a class of things, those qualities must already be common, or well known, to anyone who has bothered to think about the subject. But may I insist on a progressive view of human knowledge. Fresh evidence occurs every day; and if there is nothing but the old evidence to con-

sider on certain subjects, it is forever subject to fresh inter-
pretations. Your sifting of things and qualities will come
up with classes different from mine. If knowledge may be
metaphorically regarded as existing along a scale of abstraction, there are always new strata of the scale to be examined,
which have different qualities from those already examined.

And when you make your discoveries, you may, like Adam,
name them. But if you give old names they may already
mean something different to most people. If you give new
names they may be ugly and properly called jargon. If you
give new names based on old names they may have the
familiarity of old ones, and the accuracy of new ones.
Robinson seems to prefer the third of these alternatives,
and suggests that the second might be chosen in the interests
of accuracy oftener than the first. (pp. 88-90)

Lexicographers, or nominal definers, try to find many or all
the contexts for a word before setting out to define it. The
contexts they find dictate the definitions they compose—for
a meaning can exist only in relation to other meanings.
Similarly, real definers must sift their experience to think of
all the contexts in which they have observed the thing
which interests them—for a thing can exist only in relation
to other things. Since nobody's contexts, and nobody's equipment for distinguishing them, are the same as yours, truth is
forever just on the verge of being stated. Even Aristotle and
Kant oversimplified, if you stop and think about it.

VIRTUE THEN IS A HABIT of choice, lying in a mean determined for ourselves by reason, or as a prudent man would determine. It is a mean between two vices, one by excess and one by defect. [3]And again, they either fall short of or exceed what is right in feelings and actions, while virtue both finds and grasps the mean. Hence by its essence and the definition of what it is virtue is a mean, but by the best and good an extreme.

But not every action or every feeling admits of a mean. For some of their names immediately suggest wickedness, such as malice, shamelessness, envy, and among actions adultery, theft, murder. All these and others like them are wicked, not just the excesses or defects of them. So it is never possible to do well as to these, but only to sin. Nor does doing well or not well as to these lie in when or how or with whom to commit adultery, but simply to do any of these is to sin. For that would be like supposing unjust or cowardly or dissolute action to have a mean and an excess and a defect; there would thus be a mean of an excess and a defect, and an excess of an excess and a defect of a defect. But just as of temperance and justice there is no excess or defect, because the mean is a kind of extreme; so there can be no mean or excess or defect of these; however they are done they are sinful. For there can never be a mean of an excess or defect, or an excess or defect of a mean.

But we must not only speak of the whole, but suit it to the parts. For in discussions of actions statements of the whole are more universal, but those of parts are truer, for actions have to do with particulars, and we must agree with

those. [15]Let us take them down from the list, then. As to
fear and confidence, then, courage is the mean. Of the excesses, the man with no fear is unnamed (many are unnamed), and the man excessive in confidence is rash, while
the man excessive in fear and deficient in confidence is
cowardly. As to pleasures and pains (not all of them and less
as to pains) the mean is temperance, the excess dissolute-
ness. Men deficient in pleasures scarcely occur, so that no
name has been assigned to them either, but let us call them
insensible. As to giving and taking money the mean is generosity, and the excess and defect are wastefulness and stingi-
ness, and these are excessive and deficient in opposite ways,
for the spendthrift is excessive in spending and deficient in
taking, and the miser is excessive in taking and deficient in
spending. [21]Now we speak in outline and by heading, which
is enough here, but later they will be more accurately differentiated. As to money there are other traits—the mean
of magnificence (for the magnificent man differs from the
generous, the one having to do with large sums and the other
with small), the excess tastelessness and vulgarity, and the
defect paltriness. [23]These differ from those of generosity,
but how they differ will be later told. As to honor and dis-
honor the mean is nobility, the excess may be called vanity,
and the defect baseness. And as we said generosity is to
magnificence, differing from it as to small sums, so there is
a trait that is to nobility as small honor is to great, for
aspiring to small honors can be either more or less than is
right. He who exceeds in these aspirations is called earnest,
and he who is deficient easygoing; the mean is unnamed
and the traits are also unnamed, except the one of the
earnest man, earnestness. So that the extremes claim the
middle position, and we ourselves sometimes call the mean
earnest and sometimes easygoing, and sometimes praise the
earnest man and sometimes the easygoing. The reason we do
so will be told in what follows. For now let us speak of those
remaining by the foregoing method. As to anger there are

also an excess and a defect and a mean, which are almost unnamed, but since we speak of him in the middle as gentle let us call the mean gentleness; of the extremes let the man excessive be called nasty and the vice nastiness, and the man defective spiritless and the defect spiritlessness. There are also three other means having some resemblance to one another but also differing from one another. They all have to do with words and actions in company, but they differ in that one has to do with truth in these things, and the others with pleasantness, one in amusement, the other in all the affairs of life. [33]Let us talk about these too, then, in order to see better that the mean should always be praised, while the extremes are neither right nor praiseworthy but blamable. Here too most are unnamed, but we must try, as with the others, to name them ourselves for the sake of being clear and easily followed. As to truth, then, he in the middle is truthful, and the mean may be called truthfulness, while pretending to more than the truth is boastfulness and he having it boaster, and to less, irony and he having it ironist. As to pleasantness in amusement he in the middle is witty and the trait wittiness, the excess is buffoonery and he having it buffoon, and the man deficient boorish and the habit boorishness. As to the other pleasantness of life as a whole, the man properly pleasant is friendly and the mean friendliness; the man excessive, if for no reason, fawning; if for his own benefit, a flatterer; and the man deficient and unpleasant in everything, quarrelsome and surly. There are also means in and as to the feelings. For in these too one is spoken of as in the middle; another is excessive, as the bashful man ashamed at everything; another deficient or ashamed at nothing is shameless; and he in the middle is modest. For though modesty is not a virtue it is praised, and so is the modest man.

ARISTOTLE, *Nicomachean Ethics*
II, vi 15-vii 14

IN THAT GREAT SOCIAL ORGAN which, collectively, we call literature, there may be distinguished two separate offices that
may blend and often *do* so, but capable, severally, of a severe
insulation, and naturally fitted for reciprocal repulsion. There
is, first, the Literature of *Knowledge*; and, secondly, the
Literature of *Power*. The function of the first is—to *teach*;
the function of the second is—to *move*: the first is a rudder;
the second, an oar or a sail. The first speaks to the *mere*
discursive understanding; the second speaks ultimately, it
may happen, to the higher understanding or reason, but always *through* affections of pleasure and sympathy. [5]Re-
motely, it may travel towards an object seated in what Lord
Bacon calls *dry* light; but, proximately, it does and must
operate—else it ceases to be a Literature of *Power*—on and
through that *humid* light which clothes itself in the mists
and glittering *iris* of human passions, desires, and genial
emotions. [6]Men have so little reflected on the higher
functions of literature as to find it a paradox if one should
describe it as a mean or subordinate purpose of books to
give information. But this is a paradox only in the sense
which makes it honourable to be paradoxical. Whenever we
talk in ordinary language of seeking information or gaining
knowledge, we understand the words as connected with
something of absolute novelty. But it is the grandeur of all
truth which *can* occupy a very high place in human interests
that it is never absolutely novel to the meanest of minds: it
exists eternally by way of germ or latent principle in the
lowest as in the highest, needing to be developed, but never
to be planted. To be capable of transplantation is the immediate criterion of a truth that ranges on a lower scale. Besides which, there is a rarer thing than truth—namely, *power*,
or deep sympathy with truth. What is the effect, for instance,
upon society, of children? [13]By the pity, by the tenderness,
and by the peculiar modes of admiration, which connect
themselves with the helplessness, with the innocence, and
with the simplicity of children, not only are the primal

affections strengthened and continually renewed, but the qualities which are dearest in the sight of heaven—the frailty, for instance, which appeals to forbearance, the innocence which symbolizes the heavenly, and the simplicity which is most alien from the worldly—are kept up in perpetual remembrance, and their ideals are continually refreshed. A purpose of the same nature is answered by the higher literature, viz. the Literature of Power. [15]What do you learn from *Paradise Lost*? Nothing at all. What do you learn from a cookery-book? Something new, something that you did not know before, in every paragraph. But would you therefore put the wretched cookery-book on a higher level of estimation than the divine poem? [20]What you owe to Milton is not any knowledge, of which a million separate items are still but a million of advancing steps on the same earthly level; what you owe is *power*—that is, exercise and expansion to your own latent capacity of sympathy with the infinite, where every pulse and each separate influx is a step upwards, a step ascending as upon a Jacob's ladder from earth to mysterious altitudes above the earth. [21]*All* the steps of knowledge, from first to last, carry you further on the same plane, but could never raise you one foot above your ancient level of earth: whereas the very *first* step in power is a flight—is an ascending movement into another element where earth is forgotten.

THOMAS DE QUINCEY, "The Literature of Knowledge
and the Literature of Power"

IT IS THE SECOND-RATE WRITERS, those intent rather on expressing themselves prettily than on conveying their meaning clearly, & still more those whose notions of style are based on a few misleading rules of thumb, that are chiefly open to the allurements of elegant variation. [2]Thackeray may be seduced into an occasional lapse (*careering during the season from one great dinner of twenty covers to another of eighteen*

guests—where however the variation in words may be de-
fended as setting off the sameness of circumstance); but the
real victims, first terrorized by a misunderstood taboo, next
fascinated by a newly discovered ingenuity, & finally addicted
to an incurable vice, are the minor novelists & the reporters.
[3]There are few literary faults so widely prevalent, & this
book will not have been written in vain if the present article
should heal any sufferer of his infirmity.

The fatal influence (see SUPERSTITIONS) is the advice
given to young writers never to use the same word twice in
a sentence—or within 20 lines or other limit. The advice has
its uses; it reminds any who may be in danger of forgetting
it that there are such things as pronouns, the substitution of
which relieves monotony; the reporter would have done well
to remember it who writes: *Unfortunately* Lord Dudley *has
never fully recovered from the malady which necessitated an
operation in Dublin some four years since, during* Lord
Dudley's *Lord-Lieutenancy.* It also gives a useful warning
that a noticeable word used once should not be used again
in the neighbourhood with a different application. This point
will be found fully illustrated in REPETITION; but it may be
shortly set out here, a kind providence having sent a neatly
contrasted pair of quotations:—(A) *Dr Labbé* seriously
maintains that in the near future opium-smoking will be as
serious *as the absinthe scourge in France;* (B) *The return of
the Nationalists to Parliament means that they are prepared
to treat* seriously *any* serious *attempt to get Home Rule into
working order.* Here A would be much improved by changing
serious to *fatal,* & B would be as much weakened by changing
serious to *real;* the reason is that the application of *seriously*
& *serious* is in A different, the two being out of all relation
to each other, & in B similar; *I am serious in calling it serious*
suggests only a vapid play on words; *we will be serious if you
are serious* is good sense; but the rule of thumb, as usual,
omits all qualifications, & would forbid B as well as A. Half
a dozen examples are added of the kind of repetition against

which warning is needed, to bring out the vast difference between the cases for which the rule is intended & those to which it is mistakenly applied:—*Meetings at which they* passed *their time* passing *resolutions pledging them to resist.*/ *A debate which took wider ground than that* actually *covered by the* actual *amendment itself.*/ *The observations made yesterday by the Recorder in* charging *the Grand Jury in the case of the men* charged *with inciting soldiers not to do their duty.* / *We much* regret *to say that there were very* regrettable *incidents at both the mills.* / *The figures I have* obtained *put a very different complexion on the subject than that generally* obtaining./ *Doyle drew the* original *of the outer sheet of Punch as we still know it; the* original *intention was that there should be a fresh illustrated cover every week.*

These, however, are mere pieces of gross carelessness, which would be disavowed by their authors. [11]Diametrically opposed to them are sentences in which the writer, far from carelessly repeating a word in a different application, has carefully not repeated it in a similar application; the effect is to set readers wondering what the significance of the change is, only to conclude disappointedly that it has none:—*The Bohemian Diet will be the second Parliament to elect* women *deputies, for Sweden already has several* lady *deputies.*/ *There are a not inconsiderable number of* employers *who appear to hold the same opinion, but certain* owners—*notably those of South Wales—hold a contrary view to this.*/ *Mr John Redmond has just now a* path *to* tread *even more thorny than that which Mr Asquith has to* walk. [12]What has Bohemia done that its females should be mere women? Are owners subject to influences that do not affect employers? of course they might be, & that is just the reason why, as no such suggestion is meant, the word should not be changed. And can Mr Asquith really have taught himself to walk without treading? [15]All this is not to say that *women* & *employers* & *tread* should necessarily be repeated—only that satisfactory variation is not to be so cheaply secured as by the mechanical replacing of a word by a synonym; the true corrections are here simple, (1) *several* alone instead of *several women* (or *lady*) *deputies,* (2) *some* alone instead of *certain employers* (or *owners*), (3) *Mr Asquith's* instead of *that which Mr Asquith has to tread* (or *walk*); but the writers are confirmed variationists —nail-biters, say, who no longer have the power to abstain from the unseemly trick.

H. W. FOWLER, "Elegant Variation,"
A Dictionary of Modern English Usage

BETWEEN THE AGE LIMITS of nine and fourteen there occur maidens who, to certain bewitched travelers, twice or many times older than they, reveal their true nature which is not human, but nymphic (that is, demoniac); and these chosen creatures I propose to designate as "nymphets."

It will be marked that I substitute time terms for spatial ones. [3]In fact, I would have the reader see "nine" and "fourteen" as the boundaries—the mirrory beaches and rosy rocks—of an enchanted island haunted by those nymphets of mine and surrounded by a vast, misty sea. [4]Between those age limits, are all girl-children nymphets? Of course not. [6]Otherwise, we who are in the know, we lone voyagers, we nympholepts, would have long gone insane. Neither are good looks any criterion; and vulgarity, or at least what a given community terms so, does not necessarily impair certain mysterious characteristics, the fey grace, the elusive, shifty, soul-shattering, insidious charm that separates the nymphet from such coevals of hers as are incomparably more dependent on the spatial world of synchronous phenomena than on that intangible island of entranced time where Lolita plays with her likes. [8]Within the same age limits the number of true nymphets is strikingly inferior to that of provisionally plain, or just nice, or "cute," or even "sweet" and "attractive," ordinary, plumpish, formless, cold-skinned, essentially human little girls, with tummies and pigtails, who may or may not turn into adults of great beauty (look at the ugly dumplings in black stockings and white hats that are metamorphosed into stunning stars of the screen). A normal man given a group photograph of school girls or Girl Scouts and asked to point out the comeliest one will not necessarily choose the nymphet among them. You have to be an artist and a madman, a creature of infinite melancholy, with a bubble of hot poison in your loins and a super-voluptuous flame permanently aglow in your subtle spine (oh, how you have to cringe and hide!), in order to discern at once, by ineffable signs—the slightly feline outline of a cheekbone, the slenderness of a downy limb, and other indices which despair and shame and tears of tenderness forbid me to tabulate—the little deadly demon among the wholesome children; *she* stands unrecognized by them and unconscious herself of her fantastic power.

Furthermore, since the idea of time plays such a magic part in the matter, the student should not be surprised to learn that there must be a gap of several years, never less than ten I should say, generally thirty or forty, and as many as ninety in a few known cases, between maiden and man to enable the latter to come under a nymphet's spell. It is a question of focal adjustment, of a certain distance that the inner eye thrills to surmount, and a certain contrast that the mind perceives with a gasp of perverse delight.

VLADIMIR NABOKOV, Lolita, ch. 5

ONE, WHEN IT OCCURS as the difference between zero (absence of quantity) and one (presence of quantity) or as the difference between one (single presence) and two (plural presence), is an infinite number. The difference between zero and one is infinite, as is the difference between one and two.

The difference between being a homeless wanderer and being the proprietor of one small dry cave in which to curl up during inclement weather is an infinite difference, because possession of the cave negates absolutely your homelessness. It also gives you responsibilities—suddenly there is something to care for and defend, and to return to.

The difference between having one cave and having two caves is also infinite, for two caves provide a choice to be made about where to stay and how to distribute your possessions. But two caves also bring a problem: how are you to care for and defend both places at the same time? Choice and decision are lacking in the first situation, but they are inevitable in the second. Thus the two situations are infinitely different.

The difference between having one broken arm and having no broken arms is infinite. With no broken arms you can carry things that are bigger than your hand; you can use a knife and fork; you can play the piano and type (assuming that you have these skills). But to have one broken arm is infinitely different because it limits you to carrying only things which can be held in one hand, using only one implement at a time, and typing hit-or-miss with one hand. Playing the piano properly with only one hand is impossible.

It is infinitely worse to have two broken arms, because then you are totally unable to carry things, use any implements, type or play the piano, whereas before you were only in difficulty about these things.

Human relationships are not exempt. The difference between having one friend and having no friends is an infinite difference. Having one friend provides an opportunity to communicate and to centralize your social instincts. This is infinitely different from having to keep all your ideas to yourself and finding no direction for your social instincts. One friend may also hurt you, physically or emotionally, by a slight or an insult. This is infinitely different from suffering only from your own clumsiness and recriminations of conscience.

It is infinitely different to have two friends, because there is always the chance that what one friend does not like or understand about you, the other will. There is also the opportunity to choose between two friends when you have something to confide. [22]One friend can hurt you, but two can ostracize, and to be rejected by what has become a majority is infinitely different from being the object of scorn or anger from someone with whom you are on equal terms.

These examples are basic; many more occur. Once you have got past two, the difference is no longer infinite; whether or not it decreases is another argument; but there is no longer the infinite difference between total absence and presence, or between single presence and plural presence.

BARBARA SHERMAN

ALL PUNS ARE BAD, but some are worse. Illogical as it may seem, the worse they are, the better they are. And they always come in bunches. It is not enough for the intellect to be assassinated merely once. [5]Surely it takes several loud groans before the punster is assured that the victim is thoroughly dead. And if he be a good punster, that is to say thoroughly bad, he will kick the victim once more for safety's sake. The audience (which is probably made up of fellow punsters, for the rascals hang together) is playing possum. [8]This is the only defense, which of course serves a dual purpose: it gives the audience time to contemplate sweet revenge against such an onslaught. [9]Resolved!

This self-regenerative power of puns assures its existence forever, a status before accorded only the common cold. Puns are always present in the intellect in a passive state. Like the passive cold germs, exposure activates the inherent punning qualities of the intellect. In the best spirit of potlatching, puns beget puns of a worse nature. Each pun includes all the bad qualities of the previous pun, plus whatever the author can add of his own invention.

[15]Thus assured of a grandiose future, it is safe to predict that the art of punning will take a turn for the worse, that is, get better. Of course this undoubtedly will cause quite a stir among the medical men of the punning world, the rhetoricians. For a pun is a hard opponent to grapple with. Having made its appearance, done its damage, it disappears. [19]The rhetorician will make a good show of it and perhaps carry on a chase lasting several centuries, but ultimately will go down to defeat, punning himself—probably the most notable of punning victories. In such fertile soil as the mind of the resigned rhetorician, punning undoubtedly will take on new dimensions; it might even become respectable. Of course when that happens, someone will write a book about it, decide who was *the* worst, establish criteria of bad taste, and categorize all puns so that the art of punning will become a science. [22]Such a modal approach will deal the death blow to this degenerate art.

[23]But let's not become sentimental too soon. [24]Let's give these pundits a pun for their money.

WILLIAM LINDSAY

Commentary

Process is suggested in the Aristotle, 3; in the DeQuincey, 5, 13, and 21; in the Fowler, 2 and 11; in the Sherman, 22; in the Lindsay, 5-8, 19-22. Dialogue is suggested in the Aristotle, 15, 21, 23; in the DeQuincey, 15-20; in the Fowler, 12-15; in the Nabokov, 4-6; in the Lindsay, 9, 23-24. Persuasion is suggested in the Aristotle, 33; in the DeQuincey, 6; in the Fowler, 3; in the Lindsay, 15.

Of the concrete modes, description occurs in the Nabokov, 3 and 8.

Definitions may achieve originality by making a serious,

or merely a whimsical, addition to knowledge. The Aristotle here is perhaps the most important and influential definition in western culture; its beauty, however, as always in Aristotle, lies in its substance rather than its style. By contrast the Nabokov is a whimsical "character," which nevertheless is based on a distinctive insight. The DeQuincey division of literature has become a standard one, though it is only one of many that might be made. The Fowler presents one of the many cares that reader of the London *Times* was harrassed by, probably the most original and useful of them. The Sherman and Lindsay also make their distinctive contributions: the Sherman a disarmingly basic treatment of the first two numbers, the Lindsay a purely amusing treatment especially of the relationship between puns in conversation. According to the traditional varieties of "exposition," the Aristotle might be considered a case of division or classification, the DeQuincey of comparison and contrast, the Fowler of analysis, the Sherman of illustration, and the Lindsay of analogy. But each example also shows some signs of most of the other varieties too.

THE
TEMPORAL
MODES

The comrades of Pelops were the first in Hellenic drinking parties to play on flutes the Phrygian song of the great mother; and these too struck on high-pitched harps a Lydian hymn.

HERACLIDES PONTICUS citing Telestes of Selinus

Narration

A rt is often considered a perfection of life. Life itself is unreliable, shifting, imperfect. The artist recasts life in a shape dearer to himself and his audience. At least for the time of composition, or perception, of a work of art, life seems controlled, articulated, noble. Or even if the artist's aim is to show life as mean, at least he can do so neatly and thoroughly: no arbitrary sunbeam or overheard joke will intrude to dispel the gloom. Schopenhauer sees life as an oscillation between pain, when your wishes are not satisfied, and boredom, when they are. The only temporary release from this bondage is in art, where you sometimes apprehend the perfection of Platonic forms. And the end of the work of art, the curtain, comes none too soon, says Schopenhauer: there is nothing more for the artist to show you now but the failure of his hero's every hope and happiness. (*The World as Will and Idea*, IV, 58) Instead he sends you off to your own fumbling life.

Of attempts to fix and improve life, none seems so bald as narration. Painting atones for the sloppy sights you might encounter; music for the sloppy sounds; but poetry deals with the actual dreary details of existence, and tries to make them seem worth it. Even the earliest narrative form, the annal or chronicle, may be seen as an attempt to reduce the whimsical mysteries of life to a single statement, comprehensible at a glance, like a picture. The earliest accounts are in fact both picture and writing, the letters themselves being pictorial. Of course the special excitement of narration is that it can't quite be comprehended at a glance, or in a moment—but that it almost can. A story catches you in the vise of time, but it releases you soon, and rewards you with what ought to happen instead of what does. And as soon as the story is over it can all be comprehended in a moment, reviewed at a glance. You hurry through a story in order to render your narrative experience as statically comprehensible as a picture. Epic or novel is only amplified annal, fact fictionalized or life perfected. But before perfecting life the artist must first "capture" it, for it is, like Proteus, in constant transformation.

Like life, narration flows through time. Whether oral or written, narration is a prolonged art. The metaphors applied to storytelling, of spinning, of weaving, of tying and untying, of thickening, refer to other prolonged arts. All literature, all discourse, takes time, but narration also refers to a passage of time: while the bard sings, Odysseus travels. Literature may be consequently regarded as essentially narrative, temporal in its reference as in its recitation. Lessing considers the province of literature distinctively narrative. And narration may well be considered the central mode of literature—"its most typical mood," says Stevenson, "the mood of narrative." ("A *Humble Remonstrance*") All concrete discourse is generally perceived as story. Description often falls into a temporal pattern; drama and reverie are often seen (especially in retrospect) as heightened plots or stories. Certainly there is in narration a nice dependence between the sentence itself and what it expresses, both enduring through time. But the duration of a sentence is usually

shorter than its narrative reference. Equality of time between
reference and recitation, or action and perception, occurs
only in drama.

The temporality, the sequentiality of narration is clearly
featured in its rhetorical structure.

> When early-born Dawn shone forth with rosy fingers,
> then Odysseus' dear son arose from out of bed.

Of these two statements the first may be considered descriptive, if Dawn is thought of as a natural agency, and narrative if Dawn is a person; but the second statement presents
the unmistakably narrative action of the human agent Tele-
machus. In the actions of these agents, the predicates of
these subjects, you find, not be or another static or passive
verb, but verbs as they are defined in old grammars, words
of action. The whole range of verbs, in all their variety and
color, is almost the exclusive property of the narrative mode.

The past tense is the tense of narration. The action of
Dawn, from Homer above, seems single or narrative because
of the past tense; only by additional tampering, for example,
"whenever" instead of "when," could you suggest recurrence,
and description. Unless so tampered with, every English
statement in the past tense is a reference to a finite action
that occurred once some time in the past and is now over
with. These implications amount to an assertion of historical
actuality, and are consequently ideal for all narration. From
the annal to the novel, narration minimizes the present and
unclouds the future by recounting the past: all story is history,
just as the two words are one in origin. The storyteller,
whether he purveys fact or fiction, adopts the stance of the
historian: you the reader may attain your aesthetic distance
whenever you like. "Caesar conquered Gaul" lends its authen-
ticity to "Jane conquered Rochester," and may help suspend
the reader's disbelief.

Present-tense narration, the so-called "historical present,"
is usually strained and improbable, not, as is often claimed,

vivid. There is some folk use of the present tense to recount past events, but its ordinary colloquial use is identical with its most distinguished literary use, that is for synopsis or retelling. "There's this guy, see?" begins the synopsis of a movie, and suggests, like all present-tense statements, recurrence: whenever you go to see the movie, this is how it will be. The special suitability of past tense for narration is artificially stressed when it is used even for telling future events (1984)—though such fantasies may be imaginatively presumed to be addressed by a writer to a reader after the fact. Narration actually in the future tense is rare, but sometimes occurs in the course of drama as prophecy or directions, especially in the second person: "You will enter the room, and there you will find . . ." What Circe foretells Odysseus of his trip to Hades in imperative and future tense he later retells in indicative and past tense.

A narrative statement is then basically composed of a person and his action. Rhetorical progression, or the means of proceeding from one statement to the next, is ordinarily accomplished in narration by the word *then*, signifying that between the reference of the two statements thus connected is to be assumed an indefinite lapse of time. If the exact lapse of time is important it can be specified; otherwise it is only important to know *what happened next*. Children are very early intoxicated by the stream of narration, and demand, at every pause in the story, "And then?" or "What then?" From such reflections may be derived the following formula for narrative progression: avb then $cv'd$, where a and c are persons, v and v' are vivid verbs in the past tense, and the remainders b and d may or may not also be persons, or may be absent: "I hit him, then she ran in."

The conduct of narration in English is assisted by various words and phrases, which regulate the time and rate of the story. The time of the story, the time of reference as distinct from the time in which the story is read, has also been called the "fictive present." (A. A. Mendilow, *Time and the Novel*, p. 96) A story is always being read in somebody's present, but it refers to another, earlier time than that—rarely, in fantasy, to a later time. Lamb distinguishes between the *my Now*, in which he writes, and the *your Now*, in which his correspondent reads it ("Distant Correspondents"); but there is also a narrative *his Now*, in which the hero of the story acts. Except in epistolary fiction the time of composition is not important; the two important times are those of the reader and of the hero. The disparity between these times is established, often at the beginning of stories, by various means, some vague and consequently useful in "romantic" narration—*once upon a time, in days of old, in earlier times*; some specific and consequently useful in "realistic" narration—*about ten years ago, in 1937, on the 12th of October, 1928*. Such tags indicate the earliest time to be referred to, unless the author makes a special point of regressing.

The rate of the story also needs to be carefully regulated, for the rate of reading is constant, each page taking about the same time, while the story proceeds at very different rates. Signals of rate are least frequent in passages where the rate of the story more or less consistently corresponds with the rate of the telling—simple past-tense statements connected by actual or implied *then's*. The rate of the story shifts the time of reference, usually forward, sometimes backward, according to the internal necessities of the action.

The aspect, and form, of narrative verbs is chiefly altered by two words, more "function words" than verbs, *had* and *was/were*, which govern the "past participle" and "present participle," respectively. *Had* accompanies an action already completed or perfected at the time of reference so far arrived at. ("He had written the letter the day before.") It may begin a passage in which the actions, though continuous in themselves, together constitute a regression from the general or previous time of reference. *Was* accompanies an action which may have continued or progressed for some time, but is now viewed instantaneously, often at the same instant that it crosses the path of another action. ("When I came in, he was writing.") This form of the verb is therefore, like the "present progressive" form, more instantaneous than "progressive"; the purely "progressive" aspect is not achieved without additional help, which itself signifies progression. ("He was always writing.")

These two aspects may be clarified by a pair of words, *now* and *then* (above a conjunction, here an adverb equivalent to *beforehand, earlier* or *previously*), whose meaning or function is clear enough in a present context, *now* signifying the present time, *then* any earlier time. In a past context, however, *now* is *then* to reader and writer—the past time of reference as it shifts—and *then* is even earlier. These terms are especially useful after a regression in time: *now* can stand for the time before and after the passage of regression, and *then* for the time of the regression. Though there is no necessity of accompaniment between these terms and the two oblique aspects of the narrative verb, they may be joined thus: "He had then written; she was now writing." The *now* may be omitted if the statements are reversed, giving the effect of a narrative afterthought: "She was writing; then he had written." Here, the "past perfect" is the only sign that *then* is an adverb, not a conjunction—or that it refers to an earlier, not a later, time than the first statement. If you have "then he wrote," *then* becomes a conjunction and refers to a later time than the first statement.

Numerous English words, besides *then*, are useful in joining two narrative actions. I adopt again the hypothetical actions *avb* and *cv'd*, the first preceding the second in time: "I hit him, then she ran in." In this formula, *then* may be replaced by *afterwards, later, next,* or *thereafter* with no change in temporal relation, and little change in effect: *afterwards* and *later* suggest a longer lapse of time between actions than *then; next* suggests a shorter lapse, especially between members of a numbered series; *thereafter* suggests that the second action will be prolonged rather than single. Any of these terms may occur at the middle or tail, as well as the head of the second action: "she then ran in," or "she ran in then."

The word *after*, like *then*, shows simple sequence, but heads the first action instead of the second: *after avb, cv'd*; the statements may also be reversed, providing *after* still heads the first action: *cv'd, after avb*. Either way, these statements may replace the original formula without change of effect; in fact, the first sequence may include *then: after avb, then cv'd*. The term *once* may replace *after* in any of these sequences—for example, *once avb, cv'd*. The antonym of *after*, *before*, heads the second action: *avb, before cv'd*; or reversed: *before cv'd, avb*. Here, though the temporal relation between the two actions remains the same, there is some difference of effect; either pair of statements including *before* suggests that a different sequence of actions might have been expected: "Before she ran in, I managed to hit him."

Expectation contrasted with reality provides, in fact, the basis for numerous temporal distinctions. A shorter lapse of time between actions than might be expected, for instance, is shown by *soon* at head, middle, or tail of the second statement, or by the phrases *soon after* or *not long after* at the head of the second statement; or by the constructions *as soon as avb, cv'd*, and *no sooner had* (or *did*) *avb, than cv'd*. (*Did*, unlike *had*, governs the "present" form of the verb.)

Narration must also take account of actions occurring, not one after the other, but together. Here I must take the hypothetical actions *avb* and *cv'd* as concurrent. The simplest and briefest concurrence is signaled by the word *as*, which, because the actions it joins are in fact concurrent, may head either action: *as avb, cv'd*, or *avb, as cv'd*. (The reservation of *as* as a headword for this temporal use is the only legitimate objection to *as* as a logical synonym for because.) The word *while* may replace *as*, but it usually suggests a concurrence between longer actions, though still contained in only two statements. Often *while* heads a review of past action (with *was*), and is followed by new action: "While I was hitting him, she ran in." These statements are reversible, so long as *while* always heads the action reviewed. Concurrence between longer actions than these, often between whole passages of narration, is signaled by *meantime, meanwhile* or *in the meantime*. These terms, like those above, may show concurrence between two statements, if the second statement is simply in the past tense; or they may signal a concurrence between two entire passages, if the second statement contains *was* or, especially, *had*. Thus two whole chapters of a novel may run concurrently. The terms of concurrence also often indicate, besides a shift in time, a shift in place: "meanwhile, back at the ranch . . ."

Several remaining words variously join narrative actions. The most versatile, and therefore the most complex, of these is *when*. This word usually heads the first action and is interchangeable with *after*: *when* (or *after*) *avb, cv'd*. But it may also, like *while*, show concurrence, if it heads a review of past action, with *was*: "when I was hitting him, she ran in." This use of *when* still heads the action nominally first, but if the first statement is "progressive" or "perfect," it may also head the second action. The second statement may then be exclamatory: "I was hitting him, when suddenly (*or* when of all things) she ran in." Or it may be accompanied by one of two adverbs, which are never themselves headwords: *a had* or *was already vb, when cv'd* suggests that the first action was unexpectedly early; *a had* or *was just vb, when cv'd* suggests a very short lapse of time (a moment) between actions. Here, *just* may be replaced by *barely, hardly*, or *scarcely* at head or middle, but only with *had*: *scarcely had avb, when cv'd*. In this sequence *when* may be replaced by *before*, rendering *when* equivalent at last both to *after* and *before*.

The word *since* is sometimes used as a logical synonym for

because. Temporally, it heads an action, usually single, completed or perfected before a second, prolonged action. Often both actions, in either a present or a past context, are "perfect": "since he has/had left, she has/had worked." In a present context, the simple past tense as well as the "present perfect" adequately represents an action as perfected: "since he left (*or* has left), she works (*or* has worked)." But in a past context (when *now* is really *then*), an action already perfected cannot be represented otherwise than by "past perfect." You may, however, have: "since he had left, she worked," the simple past tense here serving for prolongation, because the verb *work* itself suggests a prolonged action.

The word *till* (or *until*), like *since*, heads a single action juxtaposed with a prolonged action, but now the single action, not the prolonged one, comes second in time: "she worked, till he left." This word also suggests the end of the prolonged action at the single time of the second, sometimes as a result of the second. Any sequence of statements with *since* or *till* is reversible, providing the word always heads its accompanying action; the latter sequence, that is, may read: "till he left, she worked."

These are the more significant means of joining two narrative statements, but there exist numerous more obvious means of regulating narrative time. All the parts of speech provide temporal distinctions. The choice of verbs, for example, not only their aspect, is significant. Most verbs above considered narrative verbs are sometimes called "terminates"; they signify, that is, a whole, often short action. Other verbs, such as *worked* above, (and *stayed, remained, kept, continued*) are prolonged. Some verbs focus on the beginning of an action (*began, started, commenced*); others on the end of an action (*ended, quit, stopped, ceased*). The same focus on beginning, middle, or end of an action may be achieved by adverbs: *originally, initially, at first; gradually, little by little; finally, at last*.

Nouns provide words for various measurements of time,

from *second* to *century*, including the additional divisions for *day* (*morning, afternoon, evening, night*), *week* (from *Sunday* to *Saturday*) and *year* (from *January* to *December* and *spring, summer, fall, winter*). Most of these words may refer either to a stretch of time, or to one point of time, depending on context: *He worked all day long; next day he escaped.* A few words (*daybreak, noon, sunset, midnight*) refer only to a point of time. A few words count on their relation to a given point of time: *yesterday, today, tomorrow,* counting on *now; the day before, that day, the next day,* the equivalent terms counting on *then,* the past time of narrative reference.

A few adjectives and adverbs are of special temporal interest. The pair *early* and *late* designate a modification sooner or after the time expected; the pair *slow* and *fast* longer or shorter than the time expected. The pair *frequent* and *infrequent,* or *frequently* (*often*) and *infrequently* accompany a duration of time and indicate many or few occurrences within it. The pair *ever* and *never* indicate all or no times after a given time of reference. The word *ago* follows a duration of time, usually numbered ("three years ago . . .") separating the narrative time of reference from the actual present of the writer writing, or the reader reading.

Prepositions are indispensable in showing temporal relations. Almost all the prepositions make phrases of time when followed by one of the nominal units of time listed above. Several of the conjunctions above (*after, before, since, till*) also serve as prepositions, with the same functions already noted, except that now they are followed, not by a sentence, but by a nominal unit of time (for example, "after sundown . . ."). Certain prepositions designate a point of time: *on* followed by a day of the week, or a date; *at* followed by a time of day; *in* followed by a season or a year. Other prepositions designate a point of time more vaguely: *towards,* when the likelihood is on or before a given point; *about,* when the likelihood is either before or after a given point. The preposition *by* heads a particular point of time, usually of the day,

and accompanies a perfected action, with *had*. ("By noon
he had left.") The preposition *for* heads a duration of time,
usually numbered, and accompanies a prolonged action.
("For three hours he worked away.") The preposition *during*
heads a duration of time, and accompanies a single action.
("During the morning he came home.") A duration of time
may be specified by the prepositional phrases *from . . . to
. . .* or *between . . . and . . .* All single prepositions may serve
as narrative conjunctions when followed by "the time that
. . ." To the patterns of joined actions above may then be
added this one: *p the t that avb, cv'd.* Here, the *p* stands for
any of the prepositions listed here, and *t* stands for the word
"time" or for any of the nominal units of time. In this pattern each preposition retains its characteristic function.

I have occasionally distinguished here between single and
prolonged actions. These differ according to the passage of
time referred to within sentences of about the same recited
length. "I hit him" is obviously single or short compared
with "I raised three children." Similarly, the passage of time
between narrative statements may be short or long. Compare
"I hit him, then she ran in" with "I raised three children,
then they had grandchildren." When narratively extended,
these result in passages of single or of prolonged actions. A
series of single actions results in a minute view of action, and
a series of prolonged actions in a remote view. Though the
time necessary to read aloud each page of narration is about
the same, the time referred to may be very long or very short.
A shortening of the time of reference results in a lengthening of the time of recitation, and a lengthening of the time
of reference results in a shortening of the time of recitation.
Thus the most exciting passages, those told at greatest
length, are rhetorically the slowest, and the most leisurely
passages, those told most briefly, are rhetorically the fastest.
Skipping to the end of the story is a sign of impatience
with minute narration—the reader's, not the writer's, yoke
to remote narration.

Most stories are readily divisible into passages of remote or minute narration, even though the duration of time within and between actions is rarely specified. Such specification as occurs ("ten years later"—"the next second") will usually be in the most remote passages (that is, beginnings and endings), and in the most minute passages (that is, climaxes), where simple, brief succession of actions cannot as elsewhere be assumed. Whole stories may be predominantly composed of remote or minute narration. In fact, the tale and the short story may be distinguished by the lapse of time from beginning to end, the tale long, the story short—though both are only ten pages long. According to the Aristotelian elements of drama, the tale shows a predominance of plot, the short story of character. A more important rhetorical distinction between them is the heavier reliance of the short story on the modes of drama, and reverie, than on narration. The modern short story is almost all climax, or scene. If Boccaccio and Chekhov were assigned the same story to write, Boccaccio would begin "at the beginning"—with a remote build-up—and concentrate on the circumstances by which the story occurs: Chekhov would begin at an arbitrary middle, disregard all circumstances, and pose characters dramatically against each other. The charm of Isak Dinesen's stories, coming after a steeping in the Chekhovian-Joycean story, results partly from their return to the literary form of the tale, to the rhetorical mode of narration.

The time of reference in stories usually proceeds chronologically, but regressions or flashbacks may occur for a sentence or for a considerable passage. Even within a flashback the time of reference is continuous, but in the mystery story there is a different procession. The detective proceeds chronologically in his track, but running counter to his forward movement is a backward story, the gradual unravelling of the mystery itself. This is jigsaw-puzzle narration, an exception to many narrative practices. Even when largely chronological, however, the various temporal terms mark and signal the action to proceed by fits and starts, inspecting here more minutely, there more remotely, progressing and regressing from a given point—and thereby probing all the psychological eventualities that make stories stories. The course of true narration never runs smooth.

Narration most appropriately deals with persons rather than things. Only actors act, and stories deal with actions. And animate life, when non-human, also lacks that interesting unpredictability which may be the glory of the human race. Stories about dogs are intended for children, who have not yet learned that even new dogs can only be taught old tricks. A story about a man and a car, or even a windmill, is never as good as a story about a man and another man, because machines only run or break down, while men feel pleasure and pain. Narration is at best a differential calculus in which all elements are variable; things are dull constants. The traditional opening of stories, "Once upon a time," is conveniently ambiguous: *once*, at a certain time in the past; *once*, unique, and impossible to have happened twice. The rhetorical structure of narration—the opening, the use of human agents, the vivid verbs, the past tense—all amount to a pretense of novelty. The storyteller implies that you have never before heard such a train of circumstances; if then the story turns out to be a process already well known you rightly feel cheated.

Though the number of characters appearing in a story is theoretically limitless, certainly in a small space more than three characters are rarely manageable. Even *War and Peace* restricts itself chapter by chapter. Sometimes the three characters are easily transferable to the grammatical concepts of first, second, and third persons. But aside from the epistolary novel, the second person has no status in narration; the second person is the reader or listener. As for the third person, critics in the James-Lubbock line sometimes speak of third-person narration as if any other kind were possible, but all narration has at least one third person, and it might be better to distinguish between narration with and without the first person. E. S. Dallas finds the third person as basic to narration as is the past tense. (*Poetics: an Essay on Poetry*, p. 99) Obviously the dramatic protagonist may be represented in either the first or third person. The third person serves for the protagonist as well as the first when the degree of impersonation is slight. (Compare *The Ambassadors* with *David Copperfield*.) But when the impersonation, by means of irony or dialect (*Gulliver's Travels, Huck Finn*), becomes drastic, the first person has a more necessary status: the author is felt to be so clearly separate from the narrator that the whole work is silent drama, and might as well be in quotation marks.

The epistolary novel may also be considered near-drama. A letter is written immediately after the event, and may be addressed to someone dramatically implicated. Richardson pompously quotes one of his own characters in support of the epistolary novel. "*Much more* lively and affecting must be the Style of those who write in the heights of a *present* distress; the mind tortured by the pangs of uncertainty (the Events then hidden in the womb of Fate); *than* the dry, narrative, unanimated Style of a person relating difficulties and dangers surmounted, can be; the relater perfectly at ease; and if himself unmoved by his own Story, not likely greatly to affect the Reader." (Preface to *Clarissa*) But if this pronouncement condemns narration (or at least Henry Fielding) in favor of Richardson, it just as easily condemns Richardson in favor of drama. Narration and drama have each their separate interests and attractions, and if I must choose between Tom Jones and Clarissa Harlowe I have a right to consider their characters and actions as well as the rhetorical mode of their authors.

Narration and drama actually accommodate each other with unusual ease. In all drama offstage or previous events (removed in space or time from the presence of the stage) are related by a speaker who temporarily exchanges his role of dramatic interlocutor for mere storyteller. In all narration, a minute view of action results in an actual minute-by-minute account, or drama: if you come close enough to the characters you hear what they are saying. Between "indirect discourse" and "direct discourse" is the closest embrace of narration and drama. "She said that she loved him" is a statement respecting the third person and past tense of narration. "She said, I love you" involves the first and second persons and the present tense of drama.

Compared with drama, any narration is remote from the action—perhaps, if you consider the action morally suspicious, safely remote. For this reason the objections accumulated against narration are few. Like all pleasurable activities, storytelling has sustained a Puritanical charge of idleness and vice, but the major literary target of Puritanism was always drama. Gosson's attack on the poets, pipers, and players of his day only peripherally objects to stories. Sidney's answer to him, easy in its splendor, still never demonstrates any necessity for poetry to teach virtue instead of vice. In key passages Sidney is so frank as to comprehend both the wonder, and the danger, of narration. The poet, he says,

> dooth as if your journey should lye through a fayr Vineyard, at the first give you a cluster of Grapes: that full of that taste, you may long to passe further. He beginneth not with obscure definitions, which must blur the margent with interpretations, and load the memory with doubtfulnesse: but he commeth to you with words sent in delightful proportion, either accompanied with, or prepared for the well inchaunting skill of Musicke; and with a tale forsooth he commeth unto you: with a tale which holdeth children from play, and old men from the chimney corner.

[1]AS THEY ADVANCED there appeared the track of horses, and dung. [2]It seemed to be the trail of about two thousand horses. These in their advance had burned the grass and anything else useful. And Orontas, a Persian gentleman related to the family of the king and said to be in matters of war among the noblest of the Persians, now conspired against Cyrus; he had previously been at war with him, but was reconciled. [5]He now told Cyrus, that if he were given a thousand horsemen, he would either kill the horsemen burning ahead, or taking many of them alive, he would prevent them from burning in the future, and so arrange matters that they could never see Cyrus' army and report it to the king. This seemed a serviceable project to Cyrus when he heard it, and he urged him to take a division from each of the commanders.

[7]And Orontas, thinking the horsemen were ready for him, wrote a letter to the king saying that he would come with as many horsemen as possible, and so he urged that the king's cavalry receive him as a friend. There were also in the letter reminders of previous friendship and trust. This letter he gave to a trusty man, as he thought; but he took it and gave it to Cyrus. And when Cyrus read it he arrested Orontas, and called into his tent seven of the noblest Persians among his attendants, and urged the Greek generals to bring forth hoplites and stand at arms around his tent. And they did so, bringing forth about three thousand hoplites. Clearchus was summoned inside as well to act as advisor, for he seemed both to Cyrus and the others the worthiest of the Greeks. And when he came out, he reported to his

friends how the trial of Orontas had gone, for it was not secret. He said that Cyrus began his speech thus:

[15]"I have summoned you, gentlemen and friends, so that we may together determine what is just for me to do, before both gods and men, with this Orontas. For first my father offered him to be obedient to me. Then he fought against me, stationed, as himself says, by my brother to hold the acropolis of Sardis. So I fought back and made him realize it best to stop the war against me. And so we shook hands, and after that," he said, "Orontas, did I ever wrong you?" He answered, no. And again Cyrus asked, "Well then later, as you yourself grant, never wronged by me, did you revolt to the Mysians and cause damage to my territory as much as possible?" Orontas admitted it. "Well then," said Cyrus, "sensing once more the limits of your strength, did you come to the altar of Artemis and insist that you repented, and prevailing on me give your word and accept mine?" [24] Orontas granted this too.

[25]"Then how," said Cyrus, "have you been wronged by me, to conspire so a third time, as it becomes clear, against me?" When Orontas said he had never been wronged, Cyrus asked him, "You grant that you have acted wrongly toward me?" "It seems I must," said Orontas. At this Cyrus asked again, "Still you might once more become hostile to my brother, and a faithful friend to me?" The other answered, "Not even if I should, Cyrus, could you ever believe it." With this Cyrus told the company, "The man has done these things, and speaks thus. Now first among you, Clearchus, you state your opinion of what seems best."

[32]And Clearchus spoke thus: "I advise that this man be taken out of our way as soon as possible, so that there is no need to guard him, and we can give this attention to rewarding honest friends." He offered this opinion and the others agreed. After that, he said, at the bidding of Cyrus, the whole company, including his kinsmen, took Orontas by the belt, signifying death, and the attendants led him out.

And when those who formerly bowed down before him saw him, they bowed down again, even if they saw him led to his death. So he was led into the tent of Artapatus, the trustiest of Cyrus' marshals, and after that no one ever again saw Orontas either alive or dead. Nor could anyone say just how he died, though some guessed one thing, some another. And no one ever found his grave.

XENOPHON, *Anabasis*, I, vi

[1]IT IS NO LITTLE JOY to me, to find the force of smart and witty replies so well set forth in what has already passed among us. [2]And, as it is accounted a mark of good sense in men to aim at ladies of superior quality to themselves, so is it no less a token of the greatest discretion in women, to take care never to be surprised in love by men of higher degree. For which reason I shall now relate how a woman by her wit and address may ward off an attack of that kind, when there is a design upon her honour.

The Marquis of Montferrat was a person of great valour, and, being standard-bearer to the Church, was gone in a general crusade of the Christian princes against the Turks. [5]And one day as they were discoursing of his prowess at the court of Philip, surnamed the Short-sighted, who was preparing in France for the like expedition, a courtier said, in the presence of the king, that the whole world had not so accomplished a pair as the marquis and his lady; for as much as he excelled other cavaliers in valour, so much was she superior to the rest of her sex in worth and beauty. These words so affected the king that from that very moment, though he had never seen her, he began to be passionately in love. [7] And he resolved to go by land as far as Genoa, that he might have an honourable pretext for paying her a visit, thinking that, as the marquis was absent, he could not fail of accomplishing his desires. With this design, having sent the greatest part of his company before, he set forward with a small retinue, and, being come within a day's journey of the place, he sent her word that on the morrow she might expect his company at dinner. [9]The lady very cheerfully replied that she should esteem it a singular favour, and would make him heartily welcome.

[10]For a long while she could not conceive why so great a prince should come to see her, when her husband was from home; but supposing at last that the fame of her beauty must have drawn him thither, she resolved nevertheless, as she was of a noble spirit, to show him due respect: for which purpose she summoned the principal gentry who were left in the vicinity to consult them about what was necessary for his reception, reserving the entire management of the feast to herself. And, buying all the hens that were in the country, she ordered the cooks to get nothing else for his majesty's dinner, but to dress them all the different ways possible.

Next day the king came, and was received by the lady with great joy, and had all due honour paid him; and finding her even exceed what had been said before in her favour, he was greatly astonished; he then retired a while into the apartments which were provided for him, to repose himself; and when dinner was ready his majesty and the lady sat down at one table, and their attendants at other tables, all placed according to their respective qualities.

Here the king was served with dishes one after another, and with the most costly wines, feasting his eyes yet more with the sight of the lady, and was extremely pleased with his entertainment. [14]But observing at last that all the different courses, however variously cooked, were nothing but hens, he began to wonder; and though he knew that the country about was well stored with venison and wild-fowl, and he had signified his intention time enough for them to have provided both, yet, being unwilling, how great soever his surprise might be, to mention anything but concerning the hens, turning a merry countenance to the lady, he said,

"Madam, are only hens bred in this country, and no cocks?"

[15]The lady, who well understood the meaning of this question, now thinking that she had a fit opportunity of letting him know her sentiments, boldly answered: "Not so, my lord; but women, however they may differ in dress and titles, are the same here as in other places."

[16]The king hearing this, immediately found out the meaning of the entertainment; as also what virtue lay couched under her answer. [17]And being sensible that words would be spent in vain on such a lady, and force he could not use, he therefore judged it more becoming his honour to stifle his ill-conceived passion; and so without more words (as being afraid of the lady's replies), when dinner was over, that he might shadow his dishonourable coming by a hasty departure, he thanked her for the honour he had received, took his leave, and posted away to Genoa.

GIOVANNI BOCCACCIO, Decameron
I, v., transl. anonymous

ABOUT THIRTY YEARS AGO, Miss Maria Ward, of Huntingdon, with only seven thousand pounds, had the good luck to captivate Sir Thomas Bertram, of Mansfield Park, in the county of Northampton, and to be thereby raised to the rank of a baronet's lady, with all the comforts and consequences of an handsome house and large income. [2]All Huntingdon exclaimed on the greatness of the match, and her uncle, the lawyer, himself, allowed her to be at least three thousand pounds short of any equitable claim to it. She had two sisters to be benefited by her elevation; and such of their acquaintance as thought Miss Ward and Miss Frances quite as handsome as Miss Maria, did not scruple to predict their marrying with almost equal advantage. [4]But there certainly are not so many men of large fortune in the world as there are pretty women to deserve them. [5]Miss Ward, at the end of half-a-dozen years, found herself obliged to be attached to the Rev. Mr. Norris, a friend of her brother-in-law, with scarcely any private fortune, and Miss Frances fared yet worse. Miss Ward's match, indeed, when it came to the point, was not contemptible; Sir Thomas being happily able to give his friend an income in the living of Mansfield; and Mr. and Mrs. Norris began their career of conjugal felicity with very little less than a thousand a-year. But Miss Frances married, in the common phrase, to disoblige her family, and by fixing on a lieutenant of marines, without education, fortune, or connections, did it very thoroughly. She could hardly have made a more untoward choice. Sir Thomas Bertram had interest, which, from principle as well as pride—from a general wish of doing right, and a desire of seeing all that were connected with him in situations of respectability, he would have been glad to exert for the advantage of Lady Bertram's sister; but her husband's profession was such as no interest could reach; and before he had time to devise any other method of assisting them, an absolute breach between the sisters had taken place. [10]It was the natural result of the conduct of each party, and such as a very imprudent marriage almost always produces. To save herself from useless remonstrance, Mrs. Price never wrote to her family on the subject till actually married. Lady Bertram, who was a woman of very tranquil feelings, and a temper remarkably easy and indolent, would have contented herself with merely giving up her sister, and thinking no more of the matter; but Mrs. Norris had a spirit of activity, which could not be satisfied till she had written a long and angry letter to Fanny, to point out the folly of her conduct, and threaten her with all its possible ill consequences. [13]Mrs. Price, in her turn, was injured and angry; and an answer, which comprehended each sister in its bitterness, and bestowed such very disrespectful reflections on the pride of Sir Thomas, as Mrs. Norris could not possibly keep to herself, put an end to all intercourse between them for a considerable period.

Their homes were so distant, and the circles in which they

moved so distinct, as almost to preclude the means of ever hearing of each other's existence during the eleven following years, or, at least, to make it very wonderful to Sir Thomas, that Mrs. Norris should ever have it in her power to tell them, as she now and then did, in an angry voice, that Fanny had got another child. By the end of eleven years, however, Mrs. Price could no longer afford to cherish pride or resentment, or to lose one connection that might possibly assist her. [16]A large and still increasing family, an husband disabled for active service, but not the less equal to company and good liquor, and a very small income to supply their wants, made her eager to regain the friends she had so carelessly sacrificed; and she addressed Lady Bertram in a letter which spoke so much contrition and despondence, such a superfluity of children, and such a want of almost everything else, as could not but dispose them all to a reconciliation. She was preparing for her ninth lying-in; and after bewailing the circumstance, and imploring their countenance as sponsors to the expected child, she could not conceal how important she felt they might be to the future maintenance of the eight already in being. Her eldest was a boy of ten years old, a fine spirited fellow, who longed to be out in the world; but what could she do? Was there any chance of his being hereafter useful to Sir Thomas in the concerns of his West Indian property? [20]No situation would be beneath him; or what did Sir Thomas think of Woolwich? or how could a boy be sent out to the East?

The letter was not unproductive. It re-established peace and kindness. Sir Thomas sent friendly advice and professions, Lady Bertram dispatched money and baby-linen, and Mrs. Norris wrote the letters.

JANE AUSTEN, Mansfield Park, ch. 1

[1]ONCE UPON A SUNNY MORNING a man who sat in a breakfast nook looked up from his scrambled eggs to see a white uni-

corn with a gold horn quietly cropping the roses in the garden. The man went up to the bedroom where his wife was still asleep and woke her. [3]"There's a unicorn in the garden," he said. "Eating roses." She opened one unfriendly eye and looked at him. [6]"The unicorn is a mythical beast," she said, and turned her back on him. The man walked slowly downstairs and out into the garden. The unicorn was still there; he was now browsing among the tulips. [9]"Here, unicorn," said the man, and he pulled up a lily and gave it to him. The unicorn ate it gravely. With a high heart, because there was a unicorn in his garden, the man went upstairs and roused his wife again. [12]"The unicorn," he said, "ate a lily." His wife sat up in bed and looked at him, coldly. [14]"You are a booby," she said, "and I am going to have you put in a booby-hatch." [15]The man who had never liked the words "booby" and "booby-hatch," and who liked them even less on a shining morning when there was a unicorn in the garden, thought for a moment. "We'll see about that," he said. He walked over to the door. [18]"He has a golden horn in the middle of his forehead," he told her. Then he went back to the garden to watch the unicorn; but the unicorn had gone away. The man sat down among the roses and went to sleep.

As soon as the husband had gone out of the house, the wife got up and dressed as fast as she could. She was very excited and there was a gloat in her eye. She telephoned the police and she telephoned a psychiatrist; she told them to hurry to her house and bring a strait-jacket. When the police and the psychiatrist arrived they sat down in chairs and looked at her, with great interest. [25]"My husband," she said, "saw a unicorn this morning." The police looked at the psychiatrist and the psychiatrist looked at the police. [27]"He told me it ate a lily," she said. The psychiatrist looked at the police and the police looked at the psychiatrist. [29]"He told me it had a golden horn in the middle of its forehead," she said. At a solemn signal from the psychiatrist, the police leaped from their chairs and seized the wife. They had a hard time subduing her, for she put up a terrific struggle, but they finally subdued her. Just as they got her into the strait-jacket, the husband came back into the house.

[33]"Did you tell your wife you saw a unicorn?" asked the police. "Of course not," said the husband. "The unicorn is a mythical beast." "That's all I wanted to know," said the psychiatrist. "Take her away. [38]I'm sorry, sir, but your wife is as crazy as a jay bird." So they took her away, cursing and screaming, and shut her up in an institution. The husband lived happily ever after.

[41]*Moral: Don't count your boobies until they are hatched.*

JAMES THURBER, "The Unicorn in the Garden,"

JOHN WAS SITTING with his buddy Bert at the bar. You can always tell when someone has something on their mind even if you don't know them very well. I didn't know John at all but we were in the same Anthropology class. [4]He wore one of those plastic pencil holders in his pocket and looked like the kind of guy in Engineering, but I found out later that he had been kicked out of Engineering and was in Liberal Arts and not doing very well there either. I could always tell when he had something on his mind because I had watched him in class. He never asked many questions but he pinched his lips and squirmed around on his seat. He looked puzzled at everything except when he looked at Ellen, his girl. I met her at a party. She was young and unsettled but she certainly was pretty. I think she was in Education but I never found out for sure. [11]Her eyes were very dark brown. She and John were engaged but John's misfortune in Engineering and his many doubts about the future had disappointed Ellen and delayed their wedding date. It would be cruel to call Ellen promiscuous. Her age allowed her to be a little unsettled and she was very pretty. I knew

Bert, John's buddy, had been attracted to her, but he was attracted to most girls simply because they were girls. She was younger than John and impetuous. John's worrying about school interfered with his judgment. He didn't believe Ellen when she told him that she and Bert were just watching television with friends. He suspected much worse.

Bert was trying to talk to John. He was a smart guy. He had a 3.2 in Engineering and was planning to go to M.I.T. The most outstanding thing about Bert was his laugh. [24]He laughed quickly and loudly, but his parted lips and pink gums formed a grimace, a Cheshire grimace as if he didn't really think anything was funny. Most people liked him because of his sincerity, but it and his laugh were of a kind. He was bright and ambitious and had learned early how to assume sincerity and heartiness when it could prove profitable, but when he laughed his eyes were blank. [27]His Cheshire smile and austere eyes rendered him calculating, and when he laughed, even a tint of fear paled his features and bleached into panic. I always got the idea that Bert had to be careful not to look at himself too closely in a mirror because once, when John must have said something amusing, Bert looked up into the mirror behind the bar, saw his wide mouth and blank eyes and looked quickly away.

I watched them sitting at the bar and the music was loud. [30]It came out of a flashy colored jukebox and it usually came out too loud. The bar was a student hangout and I think one of them must have put ten dollars in dimes into the jukebox because it didn't stop playing all the time I was there. Tables were in the middle of the floor; many people sat at them and the booths were almost full too. Every one was enjoying themselves; they sat in the cheap patent-leather booths and smoked and talked. [34]There was a yellow neon light circling the place and it shone up on the papered walls and through the plumes of smoke rising from the booths. Every time someone came in the door everyone would turn and look to see who it was.

Bert drank three beers to each of John's and smoked profusely. [37]The yellow smoke swirled around them and they seemed strange sitting there on the high red stools. Probably it was because they were too tall for the stools and their legs bent up when they put their feet on the rungs and they had to bend over to put their elbows on the bar. [39]Their heads were always bent downwards as if they were unhappy at something.

Bert was still trying to start a conversation with John, but John had his pencil out and was vacantly drawing over the silky designs in the formica bar top. Bert was making gestures with his hands and kept looking over his shoulder at the booth behind them trying to get John to look too. But John wasn't concerned with whatever it was Bert was trying to show him. He kept drawing on the bar top. I could see Bert was perplexed. Finally he turned away from the booth and just sat facing the yellow whisky bottles. I saw John look in the mirror at Bert's reflection and then look away. Then Bert turned around and started to unbutton his coat. He saw two guys and nodded his head and smiled. He kept looking and must have smiled and waved to at least seven girls. He had a reputation among his friends. He was far from handsome; John was probably better looking, yet Bert had a reputation. He didn't spend much time with one girl. He moved quickly among them. Most of his buddies didn't really like him, but you heard a lot about him. He sat with his back to the bar, took out a cigarette and put it in his lips. [56]They were puffy lips; he had a round nose and his hands were huge and freckled. He kept smiling at the booth which he wanted John to look at before. There were three girls sitting there. One girl looked at him, smiled quickly and looked away, but Bert kept smiling. [60]He had his elbows on the bar behind him and his shirt was stretched across his chest and stomach. [61]He was fat and his shirt pulled at the buttons as if they were going to pop. He looked at the three girls for a while then turned around to look in the mirror and saw John's eyes turn jerkily down to the glass in front of him. They both just sat there for a while. Finally Bert asked John if he wanted a cigarette. John laid down his pencil, took a drink from his glass and took the cigarette from Bert at the same time. Bert lit it with a shiny lighter. John sucked hard on the cigarette and the end glowed red. John asked Bert a question and Bert faced him. John kept looking at his glass and shifted on his stool. Bert was moving his hands around trying to explain something to John. Once in a while John would raise up nervously and change his feet but he kept looking at his glass. Bert's eyes opened wide; his face was like an innocent little boy's.

Then the door opened and four girls came in bright faced and laughing. They were the sorority girls. I recognized Pat and Ellen. I had seen these four girls having coffee together. They always sat around and talked about guys and troubles. You'd think no one had troubles except these four girls the way they got so excited about them.

Bert and John looked around and saw them; they smiled and Bert really smiled. All the girls smiled, but Ellen's pretty smile was only momentary. The girls pointed to an empty booth and Bert was the first one off the stool. He said some-thing to John gesturing an invitation. He went over to the booth and started talking to the girls right away. John was still playing with the pencil and his head was low. He was drawing quick lines on the top and his lips were pinched to-gether. I could hear Bert laughing giddily with the girls and I saw him tell a story and then look at them waiting for them to laugh. They all did except Ellen. She smiled faintly and looked nervous. [89]She was really pretty, especially with the yellow light reflecting off her brown hair; she looked blond and timid. Bert kept talking and laughing loudly and I could see John looking into the mirror at their reflections. He was sitting there, then he jumped off the stool and knocked over a chair getting to Bert. He grabbed Bert by the coat and swung him around; his eyes were closed and he rammed his fist into Bert's face. Bert made a hissing noise and John slipped and fell back knocking another chair over. Bert stepped back, fists clenched. John got up and his shirt had blood on it. He squealed and lunged at Bert. Bert hit him in the forehead and John's head went back; he was crying. He grabbed Bert's coat, slipped and spun around hitting the booths with a shudder. He held on to the coat rack and covered his eyes; his chest heaved, then he looked at Ellen. [100]She was white; the veins stood out on her neck. [101]John's head was bruised and he was shaking; a muffled scream tried to get out but he turned and ran out. The aluminum door crashed closed.

Someone picked up the bottles that were rolling around on the floor; everybody sat down again. Bert said something; his eyes were wide and innocent. He rubbed the back of his hand across his face smearing the blood. The loud music blared even louder it seemed.

BRUCE GEARHEART

I LAY IN THE DARKNESS of the stiff, clean bed and listened to his weeping. [2]He was a boy, not more than fourteen, and he shouldn't have been in a sanitarium; but then perhaps no one should have.

He had arrived two days before they brought me in. Since we were to share the same room, we had spoken. We mumbled our first words, then grinned and silenced them for we feared to lose the refuge of anonymity. We exchanged no names and I soon escaped behind feigned sleep. I then watched him through half-closed eyes and began wondering why he was here. [8]He looked close to seventeen, with the firm, bulging muscles of a young wrestler. [9]He was neat in a hoodish sort of way, with a medium-high wave in his hair and a black polo shirt trimmed in white. He was reading a pocket novel and he kept putting it down as if to consider what he read. I felt he was using the book to avoid meeting my eyes until he looked up and smiled at me.

The next day we talked, awkwardly at first and then freely, pouring out the truths we had never accepted before the doctor told us they were very common. [13]He had also taken sleeping pills and, like me, had used a weak, commercial pill that hadn't proved fatal. He, too, wanted to run away. He just felt sorry for people all the time. He didn't know why. [17]He couldn't help it.

We finally exchanged names and Tommy began to show me around. I had talked to the doctor and had my meals but never left the room. Tommy opened the door and led me into a large green sitting room. This was called The Cellar. All new admits were placed on this floor first and if they showed no improvement, here they remained. The Cellar was the lounge for this floor and it was the only place the patients were allowed other than their own rooms.

[24]The sun glared into the room and revealed the vague lostness on nearly every face. Some were led by orderlies, others shuffled singly or in pairs, while others sat and stared blankly. Each wore a green and white striped seersucker robe over white pajamas. [27]Because they were allowed no belts, their sagging robes seemed to pull the weak forms into a defeated stoop. [28]I felt a sudden terror and then a nausea of disbelief. [29]I didn't belong here with these beings, these monsters. I turned and ran back into my room.

A few minutes later Tom returned with a companion. [32]She wasn't old and faded like the others, but big-boned and husky, with bulging arms and ankles, huge buttocks and matronly breasts. Her face, young and hard, was made harder by her hair. It had been bleached to a harsh yellow and now the dark roots were streaking out. Her make-up was cheap and heavy, caking open wide pores around her purpled lips. Although completely surrounded by mascara, it was her eyes that made her fierce. They were small and dark blue and blinked repeatedly between hateful glares. [38]Her name was Brenda and her wrists were taped.

[39]She was twenty and she didn't give a damn for this place. Yeah, she'd slashed her wrists—used her mother's car window. Her mother was a bitch and her old man drank and after Brenda had gotten her abortion they started getting a divorce. She'd tried her wrists before, but they caught her. This time she almost made it and when she got out, she'd do it again. How had I tried it?

I told her, shyly but rather proudly, how I had gone to a series of drug stores ordering a small quantity of a safe sleeping pill from each.

Humph, that was nothing. Her sister had copped the real thing from a doctor's office. They were the size of horsepills and three'd kill you sure. But it didn't matter, 'cause it was easy to see I didn't want to die anyway. I oughta go up to The Ward and then get out of this place. None of the doctors could help anybody anyway. But at least in The Ward I'd have visitors and could go for walks and then maybe get discharged. [53]Since we didn't have any cigarettes, Brenda would be back.

Brenda left and I began asking Tom about The Ward. [55]He explained that it was the next floor up and it was run like a regular hospital: it had recreation halls where you could have visitors, and you could walk around the grounds with student nurses. He had been scheduled to go up there the next day, but he wasn't so sure now. He got sad easy and if he got unhappy they'd keep him in The Cellar for a couple more days. [58]He picked up his book and began reading again.

I walked back to the lounge and sat down. [60]I forced myself to stare at the others and think what I was to do. [61]The thoughts were the same as always, but somehow I felt less afraid. Finally, I returned to the room and waited for the doctor.

[63]Now as I lay staring through the darkness to the weep-

ing boy I couldn't see, I felt at ease. [64]The doctor had
understood and agreed that I was ready to move upstairs.
[65]I had had visitors, but they weren't allowed on the first
floor. Yes, he knew they'd be back tomorrow and I could see
them. No, Tom wasn't ready to go upstairs yet, but he
probably would in a day or two. [68]If there was anything I
needed . . .

There was a lot I needed, and now I knew I was ready to
begin accepting the help and advice. Suddenly, I realized
Tom's weeping had stopped and that now he was standing
at the window. I wanted to speak, but could find no words.
He turned and walked back to his bed. [73]As he moved from
the window's light back into the darkness he said quietly,
"I'll see you upstairs."

ERNEST FOSTER

Commentary

The high points of narration usually shift to the mode of
drama, often marked plainly by quotation marks. But the
Xenophon, 15-24, even though it contains a dramatic exchange, is really just a shift to first-person narration. Only
in 25-32 does drama occur. In the Boccaccio, drama occurs
at the end of 14 and of 15; in the Thurber, 3, 6, 9, 12, 14,
18, 25, 27, 29, 33-38; in the Foster, 73. Drama also occurs
less plainly in the form of "indirect discourse" in the
Xenophon, 5; in the Boccaccio, in the address to the company, 1, and in 5 and 9; in the Austen, 2, 5 (in "obliged to
be attached"), 13, and increasingly in 16-20; and in the
Foster, 13-17, 39-53, 55-58, 65-68. As elsewhere, "indirect discourse" is here a way of minimizing the value of the conversation—which often strengthens it by ironic reversal.

Lower points in the narration are in the mode of description: in the Xenophon, 1-2; in the Thurber, 1; in the Foster,
8-9, 24-27, 32-38. The Gearheart is unusual in lacking drama,

and hence relying extensively on description, 4, 11, 24, 27, 30-34, 37-39, 56, 60-61, 89, 100. Reverie is also suggested in the Xenophon, 7; in the Boccaccio, 7, 10, 14, 15, 16-17; in the Thurber, 15; in the Foster, 28-29, 60-61, 63-64.

Abstractions occur here both plainly and not so plainly. Persuasion occurs in the Boccaccio, 2; in the Thurber, 41; but also less plainly in the Xenophon, 32; in the Foster, 2. The Austen has a bald definition, 4, and an implied process, 10, which is close to persuasion.

The enormous variety of narration is partly shown here. The Boccaccio and Austen are more like light tales emphasizing plot in their extended use of remote narration; the Gearheart and Foster are more like serious modern short stories emphasizing character in their extended use of minute narration. The Xenophon is written in a straightforward, bald, realistic narration which may remind modern readers of Hemingway; the Thurber by contrast is whimsically fabulous. All of them demonstrate the novelty of particular people doing particular things. When *else* could these things have happened, except to the people and on the occasions the writers have chosen?

Process

Process is abstract narration, just as narration is concrete process. A narrative is about particular persons, and happens once; a process is about a class of persons or things, and recurs. If you consider bodies in static suspension, abstraction or concretion appear simply in the nature of the bodies, concrete bodies resulting in description, abstract ones in definition. But if you consider bodies in action, in temporal succession, abstraction or concretion may appear both in the nature of the bodies and in the nature of their actions. Narration takes up concrete bodies in concrete actions; process, when fully differentiated from narration, takes up abstract bodies in abstract actions. There may be such exceptions of process as concrete bodies engaged in abstract or recurrent actions, or abstract bodies engaged in concrete actions. Perhaps the girl next door goes through exactly the same routine with her boyfriend every day; you see her as concrete but her actions as recurrent. Perhaps an economic or moral or physical event happens only once; though abstract it seems unique. Ordinarily, however, the choice of concrete or particular bodies will insure novel and unpredictable events, while the choice of abstract or general bodies will insure shared and recurrent events. If the girl does the same things every day, her actions are already not unique, and there are probably other girls in other streets doing about the same things; if a theoretical event happens once you can almost be sure it's a formula. Allegory is a recognized literary technique for mixing abstract and concrete, for passing off a process as a story: you tell a story of knights and ladies, but you mean a process of virtues and vices.

Whether processes exist at all is a matter of some philosophic dispute. The views of Mill and Bergson on the subject are conveniently polar. For Mill, the uniformity of the course of nature is axiomatic to induction, or science, and is itself an induction, perhaps the last and most telling one, when all other prior inductions have been tested and confirmed. (*System of Logic*, III, iii, 1) For Bergson, the course of nature is ever changing, never repeating, a cinematograph composed not of successive stills, but of figures in vital duration. (*Creative Evolution*, IV, iii) It might be said that Mill sees reality as process, Bergson as narration.

The disparity between the two views becomes more pronounced when you come to the rationale for process, causation. If events repeat themselves there must be a cause or causes to insure the repetition. For Mill, causation determines everything that happens, including human events. True, "the science of human nature . . . falls far short of the standard of exactness now realised in Astronomy; but there is no reason that it should not be as much a science as Tidology is." (VI, iii, 2) For Bergson, on the other hand, causation is a mere stratagem that science applies to inert matter with fair success but even there without strict legitimacy. As for human nature, "our personality shoots, grows and ripens without ceasing . . . . it is not only something new, but something unforseeable." (I, i) Keynes, an admirer of Mill, but embarrassed into accommodation of more recent disclaimers, observes that Mill's inductive hypothesis is indispensable to "the organon of thought," but is "neither a self-evident logical axiom nor an object of direct acquaintance." Still, he thinks, "We need not lay aside the belief that this conviction gets its invincible certainty from some valid principle darkly present to our minds, even though it still eludes the peering eyes of philosophy." (A *Treatise in Probability*, p. 264)

Whether or not process occurs in reality, it certainly occurs in rhetoric. An indispensable device of talking and teaching is how your experience may be expected to duplicate mine. Perhaps it never is exactly the same, but it may come close enough to offer you real guidance. The recipe is surely one of the oldest literary forms, and is used today for everything from soup to rockets: if you follow these steps, the result will be as follows. The popular "how-to" books are rhetorically the same as records of scientific experiments or proofs of geometrical theorems. The more abstract of these processes may seem more dependably recurrent, but as every elementary "lab" student can testify, it is often hard to duplicate the unmistakable process listed in the book.

Out of a review of the same series of events, in fact, a poet and a philosopher might come up, the one with a narrative, the other with a process; and treatises are needed no less than poems. A poet will seize, among the events passing before his attention, on those most novel and unexpected, and will relate a story of one man which may in the end comment on all men; a philosopher will seize, among the same events, on those he has observed or can imagine he might observe, in the same circumstances elsewhere, and will relate a process of a whole class of things or persons which may in the end comment on me. Perhaps process is an even more difficult mode than narration, for narration is simply a record of the most novel and unexpected features (as best they can be determined) of a series of events, while process is a record not simply of the commonest features of those events, but of those common features which are still special to the class of events under examination. The operation of the automobile engine shares many features with the operation of any machine, but unless those features are excluded you are recording the operation of all machines.

Whatever their differences, narration and process have much in common. The urge to write in either mode must be similar, for both attempt a perfection of reality. In fact process, by virtue of its typicality, or exclusion of the defects of particular things and events, may even more clearly than narration be seen as a means of perfecting reality. Poetry, as Aristotle says, (meaning narration and drama) tells what might happen or what should have happened instead of what did happen, as history does. Process tells what will always happen under given circumstances, and might also be considered nobler and more philosophic than history. Both modes capitalize on the sequentiality of discourse or literature, by offering an account which is temporal or successive in both the telling and in what is told about. The rhetorical structure of narration and process is identical: *avb then cv'd*, the verbs *v* and *v'* not static (like *to be*) but vivid (like *to hit*); only *a* and *c* are now typical members of a class rather than individual persons, and their complements *b* and *d* are common, not unique, objects of action: "He enters the room, then the camera photographs him."

Process is ordinarily in present tense, while narration is in past. Past tense is in fact uniquely suited to narration; present tense is needed for the two static modes, description and definition, as well as the abstract temporal mode, process. The static modes favor present tense for its implication of generality, and process favors present tense especially for its implication of recurrence. In languages whose present tense actually refers to present action (a requirement taken over in English by the "present progressive") another aorist means must be used for philosophic or theoretical discourse. But in English the present tense attached to the temporal formula *avb then cv'd* automatically renders a passage process.

While most comfortable in present tense, process may also occur in past or future tense, or in the "imperative mode." The past and future tenses do not by themselves suggest the recurrence necessary to process, and so, unless an occasional "always" or "often" or "whenever" is inserted, the passage will not be very clearly differentiated from narration. Past-tense processes may also make use of the periphrases *he used to go, he would go,* or *he kept going* instead of *he went.* Future-tense process is rare. Process in the "imperative mode" is very common, but perhaps I should say, since English lacks any distinctive imperative forms, that process may occur in either the first, second, or third persons. Regular second-person process is distinguished from "imperative" process only in a certain gratuitous addition of *you's:* "you turn the corner and put on your brakes" instead of "turn the corner and put on your brakes."

The rhetorical conduct of narration and process are almost the same. The following narrative formulas for two actions, *avb* preceding *cv'd,* are readily applicable to process, if the differences given above are observed: *avb then* (or *afterwards, later, next, thereafter*) *cv'd; after* (or *once, when*) *avb, cv'd; avb, before cv'd* (or *scarcely has avb when cv'd*). The following terms of concurrence serve equally for narration or process: *as, while, meantime.* The terms *since* and *till* in process, as in narration, contrast a single with a prolonged action, as follows: "since he has left, she works," and "she works till he leaves." (Observe that the leaving and the working are temporally as well as sequentially reversed here.) As in narration, the aspect and form of verbs is altered by the "function words" *have/has* and *are/is,* which govern the "past participle" and the "present participle" respectively. The following examples show the use of these aspects in a present context: "He has written the letter the day before," and, "When I come in he is writing." The latter verb is "present progressive," which here as elsewhere is more in-stantaneous than progressive.

There are, however, certain differences in the rhetorical conduct of narration and process, those resulting directly from the differences between the modes. Narration is sup-posed to be novel in beginning, middle, and end—the more novel in the beginning the better. Process, in order to insure a duplication of middle and end, may need to specify a be-ginning, a given or a statement of cause. There may need to be a list of ingredients; there may need to be a special place-ment or routine set up before the process can begin. Or occasionally the given may be slurred over with a mere "whenever . . ." clause. The extent of recurrence may also be shown at the beginning with the phrase *once a day* (or *second, century*), or the phrases *every day, each day*. The traditional narrative beginning *once upon a time* suggests on the contrary "only once out of all time."

In middles, so much novelty must be granted to Bergson even in process as to allow for some changes or differences of result, even if the process concerns machines or natural laws, but especially if it concerns persons. Bergson would probably insist that at any point of any so-called process the possibilities of development are infinite. But even among men anxious to observe recurrences, a process may, instead of moving in a single line, at certain points fork in different directions, according to new circumstances which come up along the way. The new directions are of course also re-current provided the same circumstances recur. Exceptions and alternatives may be accommodated by a structure bor-rowed from persuasive discourse: *if . . . then . . . .* In persua-sion these indicate a logical train of two thoughts; in process they occur at least in pairs and indicate a pair or more of alternatives to follow a given point: after *x*, if *a* then *b*; if *c* then *d*. And there may be more pairs of alternatives after each of those. Ordinarily in familiar prose these are only loosely taken account of by an *at times*, a *sometimes*, or an *often* at the head of each. Another way of indicating alternatives is with the "function word" *may/might*: "He may come back; he may stay home." Single, recurrent alternatives or extensions of a process may be more clearly accommodated with the structure *as often* (or *as many times*) *as avb, then cv'd*. Prolonged, recurrent alternatives or extensions may be accommodated by the structure *as long as avb, then cv'd*.

Like narration, process may be conducted by a minute or a remote view of the action, or of mixtures and switches back and forth. Minute passages recount brief single actions in close succession, remote ones more prolonged actions more widely separated in time. Compare "He enters the room then the camera photographs him" with "The people obey a tyrant for a time, then overthrow him." The focus between minute and remote appropriate to a given process, or to the parts of a process, arises simply from interest or prior knowledge. If a given process has heretofore been seen only from a particular focus, a more minute or remote focus might provide new insight. If a part of a process is well known it need only be presented remotely; and the minute inspection can be reserved for the parts previously unknown or unacknowledged.

Some authors, and some processes, may prefer as purely objective an account as possible, each stage or event recorded without comment. Other authors prefer, and other processes require, a running commentary, which in process as in narration, becomes an attribution of causes or motives. When all mention of causes is excluded there remains of course an implied commentary simply in the selection and progression of events. Why offer the events in this particular order, unless you suggest that one thing leads to another? Causes, motives, origins, or sources may be stressed, however, with the connectives *because, since, for, by reason of, on account of,* or the verbs *is due to, accounts for, gives rise to, brings about, leads to, explains, occasions, determines, influences,* and (as verbs) both *effects* and *causes*. Effects, results, or consequences may be stressed with the connectives *so, consequently*, or the connectives borrowed from persuasion, *thus, hence, therefore*.

Statements or implications of cause and effect may occur throughout a passage of process, but just as beginnings may feature causes, so ends may feature effects. At the end of a process you may wonder which process ordinarily follows this one, or how this one fits into other, larger processes. For, as Bergson would insist, there are no discrete, isolated events. Life is in continuous movement, and the isolation of one series of events from others is always a distortion, even though it is one the mechanical intellect needs. In fact my discussion here of the beginnings, middles, and ends of processes should not be taken to suggest that a process must be in a special form or length; that would be a violation of the process of process. For process, like other rhetorical modes, may last as long or proceed as fully as the writer likes.

Things more readily fall into processes than persons. Even Mill admits that a science of human nature is harder than other sciences, and Bergson would consider a human process laughable. In fact his celebrated formula for laughter, "something mechanical encrusted on the living," might be thought to point directly, in one of its paths, toward human process. Bergson says that "a really living life should never repeat itself" (*Laughter*, I, iv), but the rhetorical structure of process insists on repetition or recurrence. Duration was Bergson's answer to process, and laughter was his response to it: if he could not preach it, at least he could try to laugh it, out of existence. Two conclusions suggest themselves to Bergson's hypothesis: first to restrict process sensibly to things, to rocks, plants, and machines; or second to consider human processes of even greater, if only of satiric, interest and strength than others.

Many activities, even though human, are purely mechanical or physical skills, and are not subject to much variety. Breathing, eating, shaving, walking, swimming are activities nobody expects to change. Many other processes, such as games and other how-to activities, are pretty neutral, and thus exempt from satire. Your ability to compose in the mode of process may be very well tested by seeing how well you can recount a process like these, that everybody is familiar with, as if to someone who is completely unfamiliar with it. Beginners usually find, by the first sentence or two, that they have already depended on a full understanding of the process. This particular ability, the ability to begin at a recognizable beginning and proceed by clear and carefully defined stages through a process, without assuming the ending all along, is probably the most important ability a teacher can have, and it is the one deficient teachers are most deficient in.

Process is also seriously used in the synopsis of temporal works of art. A sonata, a novel, a movie, or a dance are reviewed in present tense, not because that makes the synopsis more vivid, but because present is the aorist, universal tense for any process. Any time you hear a sonata, this is how it will go. The use of the past tense for discussions of works of literature is a sign the writer mistakes Huck Finn or Gulliver for a historic personage like Caesar. Characters of literature, like musical themes, have an aorist, recurrent life which may be more real (or at least nobler and more philosophic) than historical reality.

But when you recount a process that human beings willingly and gratuitously engage in, you can hardly avoid suggesting a criticism of them. Presumably the rocks can't help forming their strata, but nobody forces human beings to lead routine lives. Even if your attitude toward the process is reverent (as toward religious rituals, perhaps) the careful, coldblooded enumeration of stages will suggest to readers the tone of the wry sociologist dutifully recording tribal dances. In the mode of process, human process, it is easier to be humorous than serious. A certain addition of concrete details within the abstract process will heighten the humor. However novel these details may seem, you suggest, they recur dependably in every occurrence of the process. Bergson, in a suggestion not very fully worked out, defines the method of humor this way: "we describe with scrupulous minuteness what is being done, and pretend to believe that this is just what ought to be done." (II, ii, 2) Non-human process is of course needed in many intellectual pursuits, though it always has a flavor of the textbook or encyclopedia. It is serious, and dull. Humans always prefer to read about themselves if possible, and process is doubtless most effective when the writer, aware of his virtual necessity to be funny, shows how people repeat themselves.

Now because the actions recorded in a process are common to a class of persons or things, it might also be thought that the actions have been commonly observed by everybody. But because recurrent, a process need not be trite. Gravitation had existed long before Newton recounted its process. Many other old processes in nature remain to be newly discerned. Many other effects are known, while their causes remain unknown or in dispute. As for human nature, new patterns are continuously appearing or old ones shifting. And there are local varieties everywhere: parties are different in Connecticut and in Florida. Originality may result from closer examination of particulars, or from a broader examination of universals. After all, American parties are not so different from classical Roman ones. Like other pieces of writing, a process will be most interesting when it records something new, something previously undiscerned, but something, after recorded, that seems true and valid to most readers. Nobody's definitions will be altogether satisfactory for your experience, and definitions are offered under a pretense that time can stand still. How much more variety of experience will appear if you set time in motion, which multiplies every static possibility infinitely.

THIS DIVERSION IS ONLY PRACTISED by those persons who are candidates for great employments and high favour at court. They were trained in this art from their youth, and are not always of noble birth, or liberal education. When a great office is vacant either by death or disgrace (which often happens) five or six of those candidates petition the Emperor to entertain his Majesty and the court with a dance on the rope; and whoever jumps the highest without falling, succeeds in the office. Very often the chief ministers themselves are commanded to show their skill, and to convince the Emperor that they have not lost their faculty. [5]Flimnap, the Treasurer, is allowed to cup a caper on the straight rope, at least an inch higher than any other lord in the whole empire. [6]I have seen him do the summerset several times together upon a trencher fixed on the rope, which is no thicker than a common packthread in England. My friend Reldresal, principal Secretary for Private Affairs, is, in my opinion, if I am not partial, the second after the Treasurer; the rest of the great officers are much upon a par.

These diversions are often attended with fatal accidents, whereof great numbers are on record. I myself have seen two or three candidates break a limb. But the danger is much greater when the ministers themselves are commanded to show their dexterity: for by contending to excel themselves and their fellows, they strain so far, that there is hardly one of them who hath not received a fall, and some of them two or three. [11]I was assured that a year or two before my arrival, Flimnap would have infallibly broke his neck, if one of the King's cushions, that accidentally lay on the ground, had not weakened the force of his fall.

There is likewise another diversion, which is only shown before the Emperor and Empress, and first minister, upon particular occasions. The Emperor lays on a table three fine silken threads of six inches long. One is blue, the other red, and the third green. These threads are proposed as prizes for those persons whom the Emperor hath a mind to distinguish by a peculiar mark of his favour. The ceremony is performed in his Majesty's great chamber of state, where the candidates are to undergo a trial of dexterity very different from the former, and such as I have not observed the least resemblance of in any other country of the old or the new world. The Emperor holds a stick in his hands, both ends parallel to the horizon, while the candidates, advancing one by one, sometimes leap over the stick, sometimes creep under it backwards and forwards several times, according as the stick is advanced or depressed. Sometimes the Emperor holds one end of the stick, and his first minister the other; sometimes the minister has it entirely to himself. Whoever performs his part with most agility, and holds out the longest in *leaping* and *creeping,* is rewarded with the blue-coloured silk; the red is given to the next, and the green to the third, which they all wear girt twice round about the middle; and you see few great persons about this court who are not adorned with one of these girdles.

JONATHAN SWIFT, *Gulliver's Travels,*
Bk. I, ch. 3

WHEN A WRITER has with long toil produced a work intended to burst upon mankind with unexpected lustre and withdraw the attention of the learned world from every other controversy or inquiry he is seldom contented to wait long without the enjoyment of his new praises. With an imagination full of his own importance he walks out like a monarch in disguise to learn the various opinions of his readers. [3]Prepared to feast upon admiration, composed to encounter censures without emotion, and determined not to suffer his quiet to be injured by a sensibility too exquisite of praise or blame, but to laugh with equal contempt at vain objections and injudicious commendations, he enters the places of mingled conversation, sits down to his tea in an obscure corner, and while he appears to examine a file of antiquated journals catches the conversation of the whole room. He listens but hears no mention of his book, and therefore supposes that he has disappointed his curiosity by delay, and that as men of learning would naturally begin their conversation with such a wonderful novelty they had digressed to other subjects before his arrival. The company disperses, and their places are supplied by others equally ignorant or equally careless. The same expectation hurries him to another place from which the same disappointment drives him soon away. His impatience then grows violent and tumultuous. He ranges over the town with restless curiosity, and hears in one quarter of a cricket match, in another of a pickpocket; is told by some of an unexpected bankruptcy, by others of a turtle feast; is sometimes provoked by importunate inquiries after the white bear, and sometimes with praises of the dancing dog. He is afterwards entreated to give his judgment upon a wager about the height of the Monument, invited to see a foot-race in the adjacent villages, desired to read a ludicrous advertisement, or consulted about the most effectual method of making inquiry after a favourite cat. [10]The whole world is busied in affairs which he thinks below the notice of reasonable creatures, and which are nevertheless sufficient to withdraw all regard from his labours and his merits.

[11]He resolves at last to violate his own modesty and to recall the talkers from their folly by an inquiry after himself. He finds everyone provided with an answer. [13]One has seen the work advertised, but never met with any that

had read it. Another has been so often imposed upon by specious titles that he never buys a book till its character is established. A third wonders what any man can hope to produce after so many writers of greater eminence. The next has inquired after the author, but can hear no account of him and therefore suspects the name to be fictitious. [17]And another knows him to be a man condemned by indigence to write too frequently what he does not understand.

[18]Many are the consolations with which the unhappy author endeavours to allay his vexation and fortify his patience. He has written with too little indulgence to the understanding of common readers. He has fallen upon an age in which solid knowledge and delicate refinement have given way to low merriment and idle buffoonery, and therefore no writer can hope for distinction who has any higher purpose than to raise laughter. He finds that his enemies, such as superiority will always raise, have been industrious, while his performance was in the press, to vilify and blast it, and that the bookseller whom he had resolved to enrich has rivals that obstruct the circulation of his copies. [22] He at last reposes upon the consideration that the noblest works of learning and genius have always made their way slowly against ignorance and prejudice, and that reputation which is never to be lost must be gradually obtained, as animals of longest life are observed not soon to attain their full stature and strength.

[23]By such arts of voluntary delusion does every man endeavour to conceal his own unimportance from himself.

SAMUEL JOHNSON, Rambler 146

THE IDLE MANNER OF IT was this:—
Toward the end of September, when school-time was drawing near and the nights were already black, we would begin to sally from our respective villas, each equipped with

a tin bull's-eye lantern. The thing was so well known that it had worn a rut in the commerce of Great Britain; and the grocers, about the due time, began to garnish their windows with our particular brand of luminary. [4]We wore them buckled to the waist upon a cricket belt, and over them, such was the rigor of the game, a buttoned top-coat. [5]They smelled noisomely of blistered tin; they never burned aright, though they would always burn our fingers; their use was naught; the pleasure of them merely fanciful; and yet a boy with a bull's-eye under his top-coat asked for nothing more. The fishermen used lanterns about their boats, and it was from them, I suppose, that we had got the hint; but theirs were not bull's-eyes, nor did we ever play at being fishermen. The police carried them at their belts, and we had plainly copied them in that; yet we did not pretend to be policemen. Burglars, indeed, we may have had some haunting thoughts of; and we had certainly an eye to past ages when lanterns were more common, and to certain story-books in which we had found them to figure very largely. But take it for all in all, the pleasure of the thing was substantive; and to be a boy with a bull's-eye under his top-coat was good enough for us.

[10]When two of these asses met, there would be an anxious "Have you got your lantern?" and a gratified "Yes!" That was the shibboleth, and very useful too; for, as it was the rule to keep our glory contained, none could recognize a lantern-bearer, unless (like the polecat) by the smell. [12] Four or five would sometimes climb into the belly of a ten-man lugger, with nothing but the thwarts above them—for the cabin was usually locked, or choose out some hollow of the links where the wind might whistle overhead. [13] There the coats would be unbuttoned and the bull's-eye discovered and in the checkering glimmer, under the huge windy hall of the night, and cheered by a rich team of toasting tin-ware, these fortune young gentlemen would crouch together in the cold sand of the links or on the scaly bilges of

the fishing-boat, and delight themselves with inappropriate talk. [14]Woe is me that I may not give some specimens— some of their foresights of life, or deep inquiries into the rudiments of man and nature, these were so fiery and so innocent, they were so richly silly, so romantically young. But the talk, at any rate, was but a condiment; and these gatherings themselves only accidents in the career of the lantern-bearer. The essence of this bliss was to walk by yourself in the black night; the slide shut, the top-coat buttoned; not a ray escaping, whether to conduct your footsteps or to make your glory public: a mere pillar of darkness in the dark; and all the while, deep down in the privacy of your fool's heart, to know you had a bull's-eye at your belt, and to exult and sing over the knowledge.

ROBERT LOUIS STEVENSON, "The Lantern Bearers"

THE FIRST DANCING LESSON usually comes about by chance. Lured by the offer of one free lesson, with no obligation involved, the prospective student gathers courage and enters the studio. [3]The receptionist, a self-assured, stylishly dressed young woman, greets her with deference and respect, and after taking down her name and other information, assures her that Mr. Romano, who is to conduct her lesson, will be with her in a moment. [4]The prospect settles down in one of the pink leather-covered chairs and begins looking through a pamphlet which extolls the benefits of knowing how to dance.

In a short time, Mr. Romano arrives. [6]Though not exceptionally handsome, he is immaculately groomed, his dark hair carefully combed and his manner polished and sophisticated. He, like the receptionist, is deferential and respectful, almost obsequious, as he conducts the prospect on a tour of the studio. [8]Guiding her gently by the elbow, he shows her through bare-floored lesson rooms which have one wall completely mirrored, small carpeted offices, well furnished, dimly lit lounges, and a large ballroom with a highly polished floor. As they proceed, he introduces her to various teachers and students. The teachers are very attentive and express the hope that she will soon join the happy group. After the tour, Mr. Romano, clutching her by the hand as if afraid this prospect might evade his grasp, shows her into one of the mirrored lesson rooms where a few other couples are dancing. [12]He explains that the first lesson is actually a dance analysis, to determine the student's ability and knowledge. By flipping a switch on the wall, he selects the type of music he wants, and they proceed through all the currently popular dances. [14]Mr. Romano, after each dance, makes mysterious symbols and checks in the alloted spaces in a large white leaflet, and repeatedly assures the prospect, in a very flattering and charming manner, that she is a natural dancer, has excellent rhythm, and learns very quickly.

At the lesson's end, he again takes her hand and leads her to one of the offices. Here his manner becomes more brisk and businesslike, and he begins his sales talk in earnest. [17]He explains to her the meaning of the marks in the leaflet, which show her strong and weak points in dancing, and estimates the number of lessons needed, offering his personal guarantee that at the end of the prescribed course the student will be an accomplished dancer. [18]When the prospect inquires about fees, he produces a chart listing the rates, and points out that the greater number of lessons taken, the cheaper the cost per hour. If the prospect remarks that the rates seem high, he has a number of arguments. There are easy terms available, and also a special offer being made at this time, and the prospect should keep in mind all the fringe benefits—the parties, refreshments and outings, not to mention the congenial company. [21]Surely these are more than worth the money involved. He hands the prospect a pen and a contract and urges her to sign immediately. If she does so, she goes on to become a full-fledged student.

[24]If, however, she says that she would like to think the matter over and return the next day, she is politely informed that the special rates will no longer be in effect. Realizing that he has a recalcitrant prospect, Mr. Romano summons the supervisor for support and backing. [26]The supervisor points out all the advantages of being a good dancer. The prospect is assured that not only will she meet people and have a wonderful time, but will become more popular and sought-after by the opposite sex, will have more self-assurance and poise, a sense of achievement, and a means of fulfillment. Mr. Romano and the supervisor are shocked when the prospect appears doubtful that all this can be derived from knowing how to dance. Seeking a reason for this inexplicable reluctance, they inquire into her private affairs, social activities, and job, and are appalled at the monotony and emptiness of her life. [30]They console her with the assurance that there is still hope; a dancing course will immediately change all this, and she will be swept up in a gay social whirl.

If, in spite of the increased entreaties, the prospect still refuses to sign, their manner becomes decidedly colder. [32]Mr. Romano takes this refusal as a personal affront, abetted by the supervisor, who insinuates that this reluctance can be only because the prospect does not think Mr. Romano's lessons are worth the money. When this appeal makes no impression on the prospect, the supervisor finally gives up and stalks haughtily from the room. Mr. Romano, wearing an injured expression, conducts the prospect to the door in icy disapproval. [35]He has been unforgivably insulted, he informs her at parting, and one day she will regret turning her back on the golden opportunity he so generously extended.

LEILA DAGHIR

PROMPTLY AT FIVE O'CLOCK at the four corners of Exchange St. and Main in Rochester, all the law offices close down for the night and spill out all the expensive legal talent in Rochester's Bench and Bar circles. But the practice of law continues in circles around benches and bars. Two things determine which bar a lawyer will patronize: one is rank, the other proximity.

The lesser and the younger up-and-coming go to local pubs in their own neighborhoods, where, disguising their knowledge (or rather lack of it) under legal nomenclature and phraseology, they can hold forth to the laymen and totally ignorant with finesse, savoir-faire, and downright incorrectness, knowing that in the unfamiliarity of their subject to their subjects, they will never be caught, overruled, or have their opinions contested, no matter how wrong they are. They supply their cronies (just buy him a drink) with legal advice all the way from how to fix a speeding ticket to whom to sue for how much at what time. Should any of their clients take a bona fide law suit to their small offices in the large corporations, they will undoubtedly hear their lawyer say, after the summation, deliberation, and smoke have cleared, "There's always the appeal." [7]They have either yet to arrive or will never arrive.

But the aristocrats, those who have their after-work cocktails in the *real* legal bars, patronize either the Il Re or, even more elite, the Cafe D'Or of the Powers Hotel. There is one decisive reason why the Il Re is less established—proximity. If one's office is near the Il Re on the right hand side of State Street (heading north), one has to cross two streetcorners in order to get to the Court House Building. This, to a lawyer whose time is often worth $30 per hour, is a dreadful inconvenience. They can't yet afford the high rent district of the Powers Building (on Main Street across from the Court House, but with special crosswalk in the middle of the block privileges) or the Union Trust Building, right next to the Court House Building. There is one building, the Times Square Building, which is on the right side of the street, wrong end of the street. Walking time from one's office there to the Court House is about three minutes longer, or about $1.50 shot to hell.

One of the distinct advantages of the Powers Hotel is a small buffet table. [16]Not just a cheese bowl with some crackers, not just a few measly bowls of peanuts strewn around the bartop, but real honest-to-God hors d'oeuvres. Of course this attracts some riffraff, who come, order one draft beer, and sip it while they camp at the table uninhibitedly having a full six course meal. There are others, who want a free meal, but because of inhibitions never get their fill. They meander back and forth, back and forth, from the bar to the table, taking a small bite every time. They spend so much time and energy walking back and forth that you quite often wonder if the food they get is worth the spent energy.

But this is only a side show. The main ring is to watch a few of the lawyer laureate spew forth years of experience and knowledge to the newly-arrived, who stand in small self-conscious circles around the old guard. They are slightly hunched towards the middle of the circle, leaning to catch every golden-bound word on such divers matters as: how to plead a case, what their opinions are of a certain tacky legal problem, what Oliver Wendell Holmes's opinion was of a certain tacky legal problem. [24]And it is indeed fitting and just that they lean forward to catch every word, because are they not in a real sense still in law school, only it is a graduate graduate law school?

WILLIAM MALONEY

THE SOPHISTICATED WOMAN allows herself to be seated by the headwaiter. She smiles, with just enough warmth, at her escort. He is a Sophisticated Man. [4]He orders the wine with particular attention to vintage. The Sophisticated Woman secretly eyes the neighboring tables. She is satisfied that her escort is noticed. She unfolds her napkin and places it on her lap.

And then it starts. At first it is just a teasing itch on her right thigh. She hardly notices it. Unconsciously she smooths her skirt, but the itch is not appeased. As it persists, the proper smile becomes fixed. [13]Briefly she longs for the anonymity of a hot-dog stand, but the itch angrily reminds her of the carpeted surroundings. [14]She hesitates, her fork poised over her shrimp cocktail, and then, with determination, she begins to eat.

The Sophisticated Woman shifts her position, and her movement is accompanied by subtle lowering of her right hand to her thigh. Her thumb-nail presses into the itch, bisecting it and momentarily forming two itches. [17]She thinks of the privacy of the Ladies Room. [18]Her roast duckling arrives. [19]A retreat now would be too embarrassingly abrupt. [20]The Sophisticated Man would too politely excuse her. Readjusting her napkin, she makes a stab at the itch with her index finger.

The itch is growing. It seems to be spreading. Its intensity is making her toes grow rigid. Its importance is shutting out the taste of food and the sound of voices. Her entire attention is devoted to the itch.

She improvises a rapid series of table to thigh movements. Sighing at her escort, she lowers her hands to her lap in helpless femininity. She laughs with her escort and slaps her thigh. Demurely she wipes the corners of her mouth with her napkin and lowers it to her lap. She vigorously straightens her skirt. [32]Her mind heaves erratically. Speed, she thinks. Sleight of hand. Move so quickly the eye can't follow. [36] Distract the Sophisticated Man.

[37]The Sophisticated Woman picks up her purse, smiles wickedly, and pitches it at her escort's left foot. She murmurs apologies for her silly carelessness. As he bends to pick it up, she hoists her skirt to front-page-tabliod heights. Nearby tables are hushed. Her fingers claw for the itch, but

her dinner ring catches in the hem of her skirt. She can't reach the itch. She can't loosen the ring. Frantically she tears it free, disregarding the accompanying rip of the dress. Below her chair, like a flag on a breezeless day, hangs the hem. Returning the purse, the Sophisticated Man smiles his icy concern. The itch victoriously magnifies itself. But just then a waiter nears her chair and passes within inches. Thanks to his clumsiness, she spills a small bit of food on her dress. He comes to her assistance, but with a panicky laugh she gestures him away. Carefully she moistens her napkin. [52] With concentration and dedication, she scrubs and scrubs the soiled spot.

The Sophisticated Woman is at ease. Smiling a proper smile at her escort, she studies the menu and chooses dessert.

HILDRETH SMITH

Commentary

As in narration, the high points of process often shift to a mimetic mode, which may seem dramatic but is more like dialogue in its suggestion of recurrence. Dialogue occurs in the Johnson, 13-17; in the Stevenson, 10; in the Daghir, 12, 14, 17, 18-21, 24, 26-30, 32, 35. Definition is suggested (with a hint of gloomy persuasion) in the Johnson, 23; in the Maloney, 7 and 24. Some hints of a mental mode, a reverie-persuasion, occur in the Johnson, 3, 10, 11, 18-22; in the Stevenson, 14; in the Smith, 13, 17, 19-20, 32-36.

Concrete effects here as in other abstract modes wittily suggest that, however novel, they are nevertheless recurrent. Description occurs in the Stevenson, 4-5; in the Daghir, 3-4, 6, 8; in the Maloney, 16. Narration occurs in the Swift (with no sign of recurrence), 5-6, 11; and it is suggested in the concrete effects of the Stevenson, 12-13; and the Smith, 4, 14, 18, 37-52.

Process is not necessarily restricted to human action, but

all of these are, which gives them all a satiric flavor. The satire ranges from the acid denunciations of Swift to the nostalgic playfulness ("What fools we were!") of Stevenson. The Swift differs from the others in utilizing allegorical fantasy: he says that they were, but he means that courtiers might just as well be, jumping rope. The other examples are all varyingly realistic. Their applicability does not differ so greatly as may at first appear. The Maloney is restricted to one modern city, but has a wider application; the Johnson is just as clearly restricted to eighteenth-century London, though it too has a wider application. Even the Stevenson is reminiscent of boyhood games in other times and places. The target of satire does differ, for the Johnson and Smith are directed at an individual, the Stevenson and Maloney at a group, the Swift and Daghir at an institution (or racket). All are alike in tracing a temporal foible in human affairs.

THE
MIMETIC
MODES

Plato in the third book of the Republic will not endure this music. He dislikes the Lydian harmony because it is high and suitable for lamentation. Indeed they say it was originally devised for that purpose, for Aristoxenus tells us in his first book on music that Olympus started it by playing a Lydian elegy on the flute over the Python. But some say that Melanippides began this kind of music. And Pindar in his paeans says that the Lydian harmony was first brought in by Anthippus in an ode on the marriage of Niobe. But others say that Torrhebus first used it, as Dionysius the Iambus relates.

PLUTARCH, On Music, 15

Drama

Pantomime is representation essentialized in gesture
alone. The special pleasure of pantomime comes
from your secure disbelief that the staircase is really there,
that the girl is really on the park bench, or the tiger really
in the cage. That is the imitation of life in quotation marks.
In the production of plays the art of pantomime may be
refined away and separately regarded, and is generally called
staging, the business, the properties and apparatus, the movement and shifting and kissing and killing of actors—as distinct from the words they speak. A performed play is then
pantomime plus drama, or an acted script. Perhaps it is the
constant implication of pantomime even in the script that
is the characteristic of drama (confirmed by its derivation
from *dran,* to do), but a thorough precedence of gesture
results in cheap melodrama, the words set to the actions,
as in television westerns you can be sure of guns and fights
at the three-quarters mark.

Drama is words, and words in present exchange between
persons. In fact, there is a certain pedantic unreality about
the use of words for anything but drama—a dry exchange

between a lone scholar and his "audience." For discourse is devised in the first place to handle the burden of drama, human talk. Modern linguists wisely prefer drama to any other mode of discourse as a source of the actual form of the language: Fries studied 50 hours of telephone conversations for his *Structure of English*. The human experience behind a description, a story, or a reverie was not in words, and so you must strain words to report those experiences. But if you overhear a conversation, the very words of the speakers might be used in your report. This equation between experience and report is the basis of drama, and explains both its strengths and dangers.

Drama is strongest in performance, but performance is not necessary to drama as a mode of discourse, any more than it is to polyphony as a mode of music: even today both dramatic and lyric poetry can be recited, as they were in Greece. Because performance adds a strength of its own, perhaps the basic strength of drama can be seen aside from performance, placing drama in Spartan competition with other discourse. But even on the page drama has certain typographical accouterments other discourse is denied. In plays (and movie- or television-scripts) there are character-tags, colons, and passages of present-tense description and narration (stage-directions); in the "scenes" of novels there are indentations, quotation marks, and passages of past-tense description and narration.

Perform an additional operation, then, transform the page, omit the stage-directions and signs of speakers, and string the successive statements along, as in other discourse, justifying the right as well as the left margin. If a whole play were thus printed, for how many lines would the attribution of persons be in doubt? Students reduced to this maneuver for a page or two—a pure and unassisted view of dramatic progression for once—can generally distinguish successive speakers and lines. Editors of Greek and Roman or Elizabethan plays may also be sometimes unsure of the speaker.

> Come, my Lord, away.

The Quarto attributes this line (in *Lear* II, ii, 146) to Regan as addressed to Cornwall; the Folio to Cornwall as addressed to Gloucester. You may choose between considering it a routine exit-line for Regan, or a means of characterizing Gloucester's sympathetic reluctance to leave Kent.[1] But the rarity of such legitimate ambiguities, even in the colossal butcheries that Shakespeare's texts have suffered, shows that dramatic progression is generally discernible in itself.

Any statement, in any rhetorical mode, can be conceived as uttered by one person to another, but those places are not uniquely dramatic. Drama is characterized by certain knots or conflicts or violations of ordinary, that is, of univocal or non-dramatic, rhetorical succession, which prevent you from making sense of the passage otherwise than by positing several different voices. The simplest condition of discourse, non-dramatic discourse, being successive variety (the words will be different as they follow one another), it follows that repetition is the simplest form of conflict. But it is at best a probable sign of drama.

> *The heads of the maids.*
> *Ay, the heads of the maids.*

The next condition of discourse is the maintenance of the same focus of person and tense, unless an integral shift is required which calls for a smooth transition or modulation. An unmodulated shift of such focus, especially when the other elements of the statement are very nearly repeated, is a fair sign of drama.

> *I strike quickly being moved.*
> *But thou art not quickly moved to strike.*

---

1. For a clarification of this issue I am indebted to a review by Leo Kirschbaum of George Ian Duthie's *King Lear*, in the *Review of English Studies*, April 1951, p. 172.

These may come from a single speaker distinguishing himself from a second person present, the focus remaining constant, but if the same person is meant in both statements (Sampson in *Romeo and Juliet*, I, i, 8-9), there is a shift of focus in person, and a sign of two speakers. The next condition of discourse is the absence of interrogation, at least of the kind clearly requesting some information which is immediately supplied. Questions and answers are a fair sign of drama.

> *Do you bite your thumb at us, sir?*
> *I do bite my thumb, sir.*

The last condition of discourse, and perhaps the crucial one, is a smoothness of logical progression and an absence of unresolved contradiction.

> *I'll not endure him.*
> *He shall be endured.*

If the two statements had been connected by "but," a single speaker might be thought to acknowledge his contradiction. The lack of "but" leaves the conflict standing, and dramatic. Even in its most basic line-by-line progression, then, drama is marked by various conflicts, systematized into several distinct voices in opposition to each other. Idealized drama is stichomythia, in which you watch like a spectator at a tennis-match the interplay of lines by unmistakably opposite dramatic persons.

Plato offers a different analysis of drama (*Republic* 393)— and Aristotle follows him closely (*Poetics* 3)—when he distinguishes, in Homer, between *diegesis* (narration) and *mimesis* (imitation): in the one the poet speaks "in his own person," in the other he "hides himself" and pretends to be someone else. This analysis results in three divisions of poetry (394): the purely mimetic, tragedy and comedy; the purely non-mimetic, in the poet's own voice, the best example of which is lyric poetry; and the mixed sort, epic. These match modern rhetorical types: drama; lyric and narrative; and fiction, which mixes the dramatic and narrative modes— which includes, says Plato of epic, "both speeches and passages between speeches."

As for the speeches themselves, the drama itself, Plato locates it simply in the impossibility of attributing the passage to the poet himself, or, to carry it one step further, to the actor himself.

> You know the beginning of the Iliad, where the poet says that Chryses begs Agamemnon to release his daughter, and when the other gets angry, he, having failed, curses the Achaians before God? . . . Well, you know, up to these words: "and he appealed to all the Achaians, but most to the two Atreides, commanders of the people," the poet speaks himself, and does not undertake to mislead us into the belief that someone other than himself is the speaker. But after that he speaks as if he is Chryses himself and tries his best to make us think that the speaker is not Homer, but the aged priest.   (Republic 392E)

As a poet, Homer achieves drama when he "quotes" Chryses; as an actor, Thespis achieves drama when he makes a bargain with his audience to be mistaken for Ajax, or Oedipus. In the first, lyric half of the *Agamemnon*, the chorus is represented as "quoting" Agamemnon (ll. 206-217), rehearsing the action which has occurred before the opening of the play, Agamemnon's dilemma of killing his daughter or betraying the fleet. Of course you cannot tell how this passage was played, whether recited by the whole chorus, or by one member who stood apart, or even by the same actor who later enters as Agamemnon himself. But you can probably assume that here is a clearly differentiated example of rhetorical drama without theatrical drama.

The misdeed of both poet and player, which results in drama and is consequently outlawed from Plato's Republic, is impersonation. Censorship, not of all poetry, but of drama, rhetorically determined, is what Plato dictates. In the ideal state men shall know their persons and not pretend to be somebody else. The indulgence of drama is equally disastrous, according to Plato, whether viewed by its effect on the poet, who must stoop to represent unworthy characters (396C), or on the actor, who soon becomes morally and physically marked by the roles he plays (395D), or on the audience, who grow excessively doleful or clownish according to the entertainment. (606A)

But the occurrence of impersonation—some considerable distance between speaker and author—is difficult to determine by rhetorical means. If the speaker in a poem is a woman, it is by means outside the poem that John Donne is known to be the author, and impersonation therefore to have taken place. When Browning's "The Bishop Orders his Tomb" specifies its place and time as "Rome, 15—," it is by biographical extension that the author's place and time are known to be England, 1845. Since no composition can ever be a pure job of either impersonation or introspection, there must be more reliable means of specifying drama. If Browning's "monologues" are then in any real sense more "dramatic" than Donne's, it must be by the suggestion of such devices as I have offered above. Though only one voice is speaking, others are suggested or quoted, and responded to.

> Ye mark me not! What do they whisper thee,
> Child of my bowels, Anselm? Ah, ye hope
> To revel down my villas while I gasp . . .   (ll. 63-65)

Numerous other local disturbances, largely syntactical, of smooth rhetorical progress, conclude the evidence by which Browning's poems may be considered more "dramatic" than others, or a soliloquy, considered in isolation, anything but a lyric. Drama itself may be detected by the major dislocations of progress listed above.

Aristotle's observation that tragedy, as distinct from epic, tries to limit its action to one revolution of the sun (*Poetics* 5:8)—later solidified into the "unity of time"—has a simpler meaning than its abuse into exhortation has permitted. Drama, I have said, equates experience and report; when performed it also equates the performance and the perception of it, in quality and in time. While narration may compress time and include the passage of several years in a sentence, and while reverie may well expand time and cover a moment in a page, drama will either actually or by illusion equate the spectator's wristwatch with the clock on the stage. Dr. Johnson says: "The time required by the fable elapses for the most part between the acts; for of so much of the action as is represented, the real and poetical duration is the same." (*Preface to Shakespeare*) But even when years are presumed to have passed between acts, the illusion of the theater, the gathering together of the audience for an evening's performance, will suggest that the action is encompassed and rounded off at a sitting, like the movements of a symphony.

So relentless indeed is this equivalent succession of time that authors and directors must strain their ingenuity for means of breaking off its march when necessary. In Greek drama the chorus often serves, by introduction of the mode of lyric, to imply the passage of more or less time than its own recitation takes. On the Elizabethan stage there is the page bearing a sign of time and place. In the modern theater there are intermissions, curtains, blackouts. In movies and television there is the gratuitous closeup of a clock, or the riffling of calendar pages. Even when modern playwrights set out to distort times within an act, there must be some indication, if only musical, of a shift of time, and until a new shift occurs, an equivalence is once more implied. Of course the equivalence need not be actual, only illusory. The battle in *Lear* V, ii lasts a half dozen lines. But when Shakespeare's scenes thus show by analysis the passage of more or less time than any reading of the lines will justify, the discrepancy is usually smoothed over by his superior manipulation of the spectator's illusion.

Not only is the spectator's time equal to the actor's in duration, but it is the same time; or, to put it otherwise, drama creates an equivalence for the spectator in both time and space. "The time is the present" is redundant, since drama is always now, and here. The various arrangements of audience and stage—the fourth wall removed, or the playing to three or four sides—compete in their invitation to the audience to participate in the action. And though the successive statements in drama may occur in any tense, the real time, even in historical plays, is the present. Performance renders this effect especially acute, but even the reading of plays or "scenes" in fiction has a presence that narration and other rhetorical modes cannot offer. This perhaps accounts more fully than mere impersonation for the dangerous power Plato found in drama, and banned. The equation of played and observed time and action results for the observer simply in accrued experience, like any other, and basis for further action. You may think of Plato's concern over the improper entertainments of the young when you see the current rock-and-roll movies. Teenagers sensibly disregard the "moral" appearing in type at the beginning and end, and profit from the real moral: that brutality wins the respect of the gang, and the adoration of the girl—and so leave the theater, switchblades poised.

The special presence of drama implies special distinctions for the use of narrative and drama in the composition of fiction, or epic. Narration will serve the widest spatiotemporal needs. It may put as great a space and time between action and spectator as it chooses, or it may come closer and closer to putting the spectator in the scene, and making his experience equivalent to the action. But when it aspires to total equivalence it must break out in drama, in the voices of the characters themselves. The wise author therefore estimates the interest and import of his story at every turn with care, putting the dullest and most readily predictable sections in the most remote narration, the sections of further interest in more minute narration, and reserving for drama the most heightened and crucial times. You may complain, when the novelist offers routine conversation, that he has not bridged the gap with narration: "They greeted each other." You may similarly complain, when he slips over a crucial scene by narration, that he has left out the best part. The climax of *Pride and Prejudice*, of which the development has been so largely dramatic, may be said to suffer from this weakness:

> *Elizabeth, feeling all the more-than-common awkwardness and anxiety of his situation, now forced herself to speak, and immediately, though not very fluently, gave him to understand that her sentiments had undergone so material a change since the period to which he alluded, as to make her receive with gratitude and pleasure his present assurances. The happiness which this reply produced was such as he had probably never felt before, and he expressed himself on the occasion as sensibly and as warmly as a man violently in love can be supposed to do. (Ch. 58)*

A whole composition in dramatic progression, a play, is then a more pretentious form than a novel, for drama professes a continuously relevant and revelatory view of character and conflict, avoiding all but the most heightened and complex psychological moments. This may largely account for Aristotle's preference of tragedy over epic: "its vividness holds both in reading it and in performance." (26:11) Its only means of exclusion is an abrupt halt of time, a curtain; otherwise even routine conversation must be mimetic and not narrative. The chief problem in composing drama is therefore to make every word, every moment count. If the distinct feature of dramatic progression is a series of rhetorical conflicts, you may complain, if very many speeches pass without it, that narration or some other rhetorical mode has been arbitrarily divided up between the speakers. Johnson says: "Narration in dramatic poetry is naturally tedious, as it is unanimated and inactive and obstructs the progress of the action; it should therefore always be rapid, and enlivened by frequent interruption." The most embarrassing misuse of drama is for passages of crude "exposition," the gathering of several persons on the stage to review information well known to them all ("You remember what happened yesterday, John . . ."), in order to make certain communications to the audience. If a passage is not discernibly many-voiced by other than typographical means, it is not fully dramatic.

The rhetorical conflicts analyzed above in discourse as it passes reach their full dimension in the major psychological conflicts on which the action of the whole play is based. Drama equates the conflicts, as it equates the times, of author, actor, and spectator. At this level the exploration of dramatic conflict is as complex surely as the study of psychology. Here I take conflict to be simply any disparity between two or more represented characters. Even two people in love will express their love disparately, if they are caught at the right moments and not when they are simply small-talking.

Aristotle's celebration of Aeschylus for raising the number of actors from one to two at a time, and Sophocles from two to three (4:13-14), has commonly seemed extravagant, even if the chorus occasionally speaks singly as an additional dramatic element. Surely the modern stage may teem with characters. The hard thing, you may feel, must have been the switch from lyric to impersonation, as Plato defines it; once that innovation arrived, the addition of characters seems an obvious extension. But it is as a matter of fact remarkable that the modern theater has not significantly increased the number of actors. Most scenes continue to be played between two or three persons, and additional dramatic voices tend to become choric. How many persons can be comprehended in present verbal exchange? The answer lies not so much in dramatic convention as in the elementary psychology of small numbers. The simplest and starkest human confrontation is always between two persons, two being, as they say, company, and three a crowd. Three is an invitation for two to gang up against one, and perhaps for numerous switches of two against one, reducing the dramatic elements once more to two. But if three elements may occasionally function in precarious balance, four is a real crowd, or chorus.

This normal dramatic limit of three persons, that is, a first, a second, and a third person, seems to be confirmed by Indo-European grammar: *I*, *you*, and *he*. The order here is not arbitrary, whether you think philosophically of man in his universe, or psychologically of a baby in his crib: the *I* being everywhere prior; the *you* second in immediate perception, mama; the *he* the remainder, others, daddy hovering at the door. Even the third person becomes somewhat blurred. The forms *luei* and *amat* and *macht* apply indiscriminately to all remaining persons after *I* and *you*; *he* very nearly becomes an indeterminate *they*; and *they* is very nearly equivalent in usage to *one* or *anyone*. Thoreau says: "I had three chairs in my house; one for solitude, two for friendship, three for society." (*Walden*, ch. 6)

Of the three persons, the second seems most distinctive of drama. Every line of drama is spoken by someone who thinks of himself as *I*, but what he says will be spoken to *you*. While any mode may use any person, apparently reverie is reflection and prefers *I*, narration is reference and prefers *he*, drama is address and prefers *you*. There is also an alliance between the present time which is crucial to drama, and the second person. E. S. Dallas says: "in speaking to You, it is evidently implied that You are present; and in speaking of

Him it is evidently implied that He is absent and gone."
(*Poetics: an Essay on Poetry*, p. 101) In some modern languages it is considered rude to use the third instead of the
second person for someone present; to do so implies a com-
plicity between speaker and the person spoken to against the
person spoken of.

These rudimentary distinctions, applied to the relationship between audience and actors, suggest an identification
with the chief sympathetic person represented, and an attitude toward the remaining persons identical to his. Drama,
then, also equates the sympathy of author, actor, and spectator. But assuming that in skillful drama the balance of
sympathy may occasionally shift, all *he's* eventually becoming
I's, *t*he spectator may be asked to keep in mind not only the
two initial attachments between the first *I* with its *you* and
he, but the four resulting from these and a switch of his
attitude toward the other two, and the twelve resulting from
each of the three persons becoming *I*, and a further switch
of attitude. When Hamlet turns from Gertrude to Claudius,
Claudius changes from *he* to *you*, and Gertrude from *you*
to *she*; at other times Claudius or Gertrude may become
I and similarly turn from one to the other. These twelve
possible attachments, though only three persons are involved, generally offer plenty of dramatic complexity or confusion.

Most drama can be readily comprehended as a series of
such confrontations of two or three persons. By confrontation I mean any significant grouping of several persons, and
the stretch of drama resulting from their talk. Between confrontations may be curtains, or simply transitional passages,
the entrance of a maid, a call offstage, any pretext for a re-
arrangement of persons, though a break may also occur by a
major readjustment of dramatic sympathy between the same
persons. The notion of "scene" in the classical French theater
was based on an understanding of this sort, but was absurdly
solidified into the insistence on a new scene at any minor

stage-entrance. Clearly the division of confrontations must be as free and easy as drama itself. The theater of Chekhov, which challenges the division of confrontations as fully as may be, often seems, especially in *The Cherry Orchard*, a patchwork of transitional passages, with no or few dramatic confrontations between persons paying attention to each other.

> *Time, I say, passes.*
> *And it smells like patchouli here.*
> *I'm going to bed. Good night, Mama.*[2]

This technique of irrelevance is even more pronounced in recent playwrights such as Beckett and Ionesco. Actually even here you can trace a loose sequence of confrontations between a few persons, with others walking on.

Now the whole play, often thought to be formed in accordance with its inherent dramatic development, is also governed externally by the limit an audience can be expected to suffer, anything over three hours being a long play. The act, which doubtless also makes its own form, is governed by the necessity for intermission, or wide gaps in stage-time. Only the confrontation is completely free of external necessity and remains the reliable unit of dramatic discourse. The priority of the confrontation as a unit is readily seen when plays are transformed to movies, which must, in respect to the greater spatiotemporal fluidity of the cinema, do considerable violence to their originals. Here, speeches readily transferable from one speaker to another are by definition expository. What, if anything, will be respected is the confrontation itself, when all else, what seemed the orderly development of the act or play—the sequence of confrontations—has been violated out of all recognition. For new confrontations mean a new play.

---

2. The translation is by Stark Young, *Best Plays by Chekhov*, Modern Library, p. 235.

Plato's hypothetical dismissal of the poet carries a heavy burden of poetic guilt: "we will send him away to another city, after pouring myrrh over his head and crowning him with wool." (*Republic* 398A) Later he invites poetry "to come back, defending herself in lyric or some other meter." (607D) If Aristotle's *Poetics* is in part an answer to this invitation, his suggestion that the poet needn't represent ignoble people (26:7) seems lame, for poets will notoriously represent the whole range of human degradation and glory, and will approve or disapprove just as they please. Indeed Plato's arguments are unanswerable in their own terms. And perhaps the only excuse for drama, for the equation it ignites between the conflicts, the time, and the sympathy of author, actor, and spectator is Aristotle's earlier pronouncement on the nature of mankind: "Imitation is inborn in men from childhood." (4:2)

AWAY, I DO BESEECH YOU, both away. I'll board him presently.
O, give me leave.

> *Exeunt King, Queen and Attendants.*

How does my good Lord Hamlet?

Hamlet Well, God-a-mercy.

Polonius Do you know me, my Lord?

Hamlet Excellent well; you are a fish-monger.

Polonius Not I, my Lord.

Hamlet Then I would you were so honest a man.

Polonius Honest, my lord?

Hamlet [12]Ay, sir; to be honest, as this world goes, is to be one man picked out of ten thousand.

Polonius That's very true, my lord.

Hamlet For if the sun breed maggots in a dead dog, being a good kissing carrion—Have you a daughter?

Polonius I have, my lord.

Hamlet Let her not walk i' th' sun: conception is a blessing, but as your daughter may conceive—Friend, look to 't.

Polonius [*Aside.*] [19]How say you by that? Still harping on my daughter: yet he knew me not at first; 'a said I was a fishmonger; 'a is far gone; and truly in my youth I suffered much extremity for love; very near this. [21]I'll speak to him again.—What do you read, my lord?

Hamlet Words, words, words.

Polonius What is the matter, my lord?

Hamlet Between who?

Polonius I mean, the matter that you read, my lord.

Hamlet [27]Slanders, sir; for the satirical rogue says here that old men have grey beards, that their faces are wrinkled, their eyes purging thick amber and plum-tree gum, and that

153

they have a plentiful lack of wit, together with most weak hams: all which, sir, though I most powerfully and potently believe, yet I hold it not honesty to have it thus set down; for yourself, sir, shall grow old as I am, if like a crab you you could go backward.

Polonius [*Aside.*] [28]Though this be madness, yet there is method in 't.—Will you walk out of the air, my lord?

Hamlet Into my grave?

Polonius Indeed, that is out of the air. [*Aside.*] [32]How pregnant sometimes his replies are: a happiness that often madness hits on, which reason and sanity could not so prosperously be delivered of. [33]I will leave him, and suddenly contrive the means of meeting between him and my daughter.—My lord, I will take my leave of you.

Hamlet [35]You cannot, sir, take from me anything that I will not more willingly part withal—except my life, except my life, except my life.

Polonius Fare you well, my lord.

Hamlet These tedious old fools!

WILLIAM SHAKESPEARE, *Hamlet*, II ii

CHARMING DAY it has been, Miss Fairfax.

Gwendolen Pray don't talk to me about the weather, Mr. Worthing. Whenever people talk to me about the weather, I always feel quite certain that they mean something else. And that makes me so nervous.

Jack I do mean something else.

Gwendolen I thought so. In fact, I am never wrong.

Jack And I would like to be allowed to take advantage of Lady Bracknell's temporary absence. . . .

Gwendolen I would certainly advise you to do so. Mamma has a way of coming back suddenly into a room that I have often had to speak to her about.

Jack [*nervously*] Miss Fairfax, ever since I met you I have

admired you more than any girl . . . I have ever met since
. . . I met you.

Gwendolen Yes, I am quite aware of the fact. And I
often wish that in public, at any rate, you had been more
demonstrative. For me you have always had an irresistible
fascination. Even before I met you I was far from indifferent to you. [*Jack looks at her in amazement.*] [17] We live,
as I hope you know, Mr. Worthing, in an age of ideals.
[18]The fact is constantly mentioned in the more expensive
monthly magazines, and has reached the provincial pulpits,
I am told; and my ideal has always been to love some one
of the name of Ernest. There is something in that name that
inspires absolute confidence. The moment Algernon first
mentioned to me that he had a friend called Ernest, I
knew I was destined to love you.

Jack You really love me, Gwendolen?

Gwendolen Passionately!

Jack Darling! You don't know how happy you've made
me.

Gwendolen My own Ernest!

Jack But you don't really mean to say that you couldn't
love me if my name wasn't Ernest?

Gwendolen But your name is Ernest.

Jack Yes, I know it is. But supposing it was something
else? Do you mean to say you couldn't love me then?

Gwendolen [*glibly*] [31]Ah! that is clearly a metaphysical speculation, and like most metaphysical speculations
has very little reference at all to the actual facts of real life,
as we know them.

Jack Personally, darling, to speak quite candidly, I don't
much care about the name of Ernest. . . . I don't think the
name suits me at all.

Gwendolen It suits you perfectly. It is a divine name.
It has a music of its own. It produces vibrations.

Jack Well, really, Gwendolen, I must say that I think

there are lots of other much nicer names. I think Jack, for instance, a charming name.

Gwendolen   Jack? . . . No, there is very little music in the name Jack, if any at all, indeed. It does not thrill. It produces absolutely no vibrations. . . . I have known several Jacks, and they all, without exception, were more than usually plain. Besides, Jack is a notorious domesticity for John! And I pity any woman who is married to a man called John. She would probably never be allowed to know the entrancing pleasure of a single moment's solitude. The only really safe name is Ernest.

Jack   Gwendolen, I must get christened at once—I mean we must get married at once. There is no time to be lost.

Gwendolen   Married, Mr. Worthing?

Jack [*astounded*]   Well . . . surely. You know that I love you, and you led me to believe, Miss Fairfax, that you were not absolutely indifferent to me.

Gwendolen   I adore you. But you haven't proposed to met yet. Nothing has been said at all about marriage. The subject has not even been touched on.

Jack   Well . . . may I propose to you now?

Gwendolen   I think it would be an admirable opportunity. And to spare you any possible disappointment, Mr. Worthing, I think it only fair to tell you quite frankly beforehand that I am fully determined to accept you.

Jack   Gwendolen!

Gwendolen   Yes, Mr. Worthing, what have you got to say to me?

Jack   You know what I have got to say to you.

Gwendolen   Yes, but you don't say it.

Jack   Gwendolen, will you marry me? [*Goes on his knees.*]

Gwendolen   Of course I will, darling. How long you have been about it! I am afraid you have had very little experience in how to propose.

Jack My own one, I have never loved any one in the world but you.

Gwendolen Yes, but men often propose for practice. I know my brother Gerald does. All my girl-friends tell me so. What wonderfully blue eyes you have, Ernest! They are quite, quite blue. I hope you will always look at me just like that, especially when there are other people present.

OSCAR WILDE, *The Importance of Being Earnest*, Act I

PAGE 121 . . . lines eleven and twelve. Here it is. [*Reads*] "If you ever, ever need my life, come and take it.". . .

Arkadina [*Looking at her watch*] The horses will be here soon.

Trigorin [*To himself*] If you ever, ever need my life, come and take it.

Arkadina I hope you are all packed.

Trigorin [*Impatiently*] Yes, yes. . . . [*In deep thought*] [8]Why is it I seem to feel sadness in that call from a pure soul, and my heart aches so with pity? If you ever, ever need my life, come and take it. [*To Madame Arkadina*] Let's stay just one more day. [*She shakes her head.*]

Trigorin Let's stay!

Arkadina Darling, I know what keeps you here. But have some self control. You're a little drunk, be sober.

Trigorin You be sober, too, be understanding, reasonable, I beg you; look at all this like a true friend. . . . [*Presses her hand*] You are capable of sacrificing. Be my friend, let me be free.

Arkadina [*Excited*] Are you so infatuated?

Trigorin I am drawn to her! Perhaps this is just what I need.

Arkadina The love of some provincial girl? Oh, how little you know yourself!

Trigorin Sometimes people talk but are asleep. That's how it is now . . . I'm talking to you but in my dream see her. I'm possessed by sweet, marvelous dreams. Let me go . . .

Arkadina [*Trembling*]   No, no, I'm an ordinary woman like any other woman, you shouldn't talk to me like this. Don't torture me, Boris. It frightens me.

Trigorin   If you wanted to, you could be far from ordinary. There is a kind of love that's young, and beautiful, and is all poetry, and carries us away into a world of dreams; on earth it alone can ever give us happiness. [33] Such a love I still have never known. In my youth there wasn't time, I was always around some editor's office, fighting off starvation. [35] Now it's here, that love, it's come, it beckons me. What sense, then, is there in running away from it?

Arkadina [*Angry*]   You've gone mad.

Trigorin   Well, let me!

Arkadina   You've all conspired today just to torment me. [*Weeps.*]

Trigorin [*Clutching at his breast*]   She doesn't understand. She doesn't want to understand.

Arkadina   Am I so old or ugly that you don't mind talking to me about other women? [*Embracing and kissing him*] Oh, you madman! My beautiful, my marvel . . . you are the last chapter of my life. [*Falls on knees*] My joy, my pride, my blessedness! [*Embracing his knees*] If you forsake me for for one hour even, I'll never survive it, I'll go out of my mind, my wonderful, magnificent one, my master.

Trigorin   Somebody might come in. [*Helps her to rise*]

Arkadina   Let them, I am not ashamed of my love for you. [*Kisses his hands*] My treasure! You reckless boy, you want to be mad, but I won't have it, I won't let you. [*Laughs*] You are mine . . . you are mine. This brow is mine, and the eyes mine, and this beautiful silky hair, too, is mine. You are all mine. You are so talented, so intelligent, the best of all modern writers; you are the one and only hope of Russia . . . you have such sincerity, simplicity, healthy humor. In one stroke you go to the very heart of a character or a scene; your people are like life itself. Oh, it's impossible to read you without rapture! Do you think this is only in-cense? I'm flattering you? Come, look me in the eyes . . . Do I look like a liar? There you see, only I can appreciate you; only I tell you the truth, my lovely darling . . . You are coming? Yes? You won't leave me?

Trigorin   I have no will of my own . . . [65]I've never had a will of my own. Flabby, weak, always submitting! [67]Is it possible that might please women? Take me, carry me away, only never let me be one step away from you.

Arkadina [*To herself*] [69]Now he's mine. [*Casually, as if nothing had happened*] However, if you like you may stay. I'll go by myself, and you come later, in a week. After all, where would you hurry to?

Trigorin   No, let's go together.

Arkadina   As you like. Together, together then. [*A pause. Trigorin writes in notebook*] What are you writing?

Trigorin   [77]This morning I heard a happy expression: "Virgin forest." [78]It might be useful in a story. [*Yawns*] So, we're off. [80]Once more the cars, stations, station buffets, stews and conversations!

ANTON CHEKHOV, The Sea Gull,
Act III, transl. Stark Young

THE MARVELLOUS THING is that it's painless," he said. "That's how you know when it starts."

"Is it really?"

"Absolutely. I'm awfully sorry about the odor though. That must bother you."

"Don't! Please don't."

"Look at them," he said. "Now is it sight or is it scent that brings them like that?"

[11]The cot the man lay on was in the wide shade of a mimosa tree and as he looked out past the shade onto the glare of the plain there were three of the big birds squatted

obscenely, while in the sky a dozen more sailed, making quick-moving shadows as they passed.

[12]"They've been there since the day the truck broke down," he said. "Today's the first time any have lit on the ground. [14]I watched the way they sailed very carefully at first in case I ever wanted to use them in a story. That's funny now."

"I wish you wouldn't," she said.

"I'm only talking," he said, "It's much easier if I talk. But I don't want to bother you."

"You know it doesn't bother me," she said. "It's that I've gotten so very nervous not being able to do anything. I think we might make it as easy as we can until the plane comes."

"Or until the plane doesn't come."

"Please tell me what I can do. There must be something I can do."

"You can take the leg off and that might stop it, though I doubt it. Or you can shoot me. You're a good shot now. I taught you to shoot didn't I?"

"Please don't talk that way. Couldn't I read to you?"

"Read what?"

"Anything in the book bag that we haven't read."

"I can't listen to it," he said. "Talking is the easiest. We quarrel and that makes the time pass."

"I don't quarrel. I never want to quarrel. Let's not quarrel any more. No matter how nervous we get. Maybe they will be back with another truck today. Maybe the plane will come."

"I don't want to move," the man said. "There is no sense in moving now except to make it easier for you."

"That's cowardly."

"Can't you let a man die as comfortably as he can without calling him names? What's the use of slanging me?"

"You're not going to die."

"Don't be silly. I'm dying now. Ask those bastards."

[52]He looked over to where the huge, filthy birds sat, their naked heads sunk in the hunched feathers. A fourth planed down, to run quick-legged and then waddle slowly toward the others.

"They are around every camp. You never notice them. You can't die if you don't give up."

"Where did you read that? You're such a bloody fool."

"You might think about some one else."

"For Christ's sake," he said, "That's been my trade."

He lay then and was quiet for a while and looked across the heat shimmer of the plain to the edge of the bush. [62]There were a few Tommies that showed minute and white against the yellow and, far off, he saw a herd of zebra, white against the green of the bush. [63]This was a pleasant camp under big trees against a hill, with good water, and close by, a nearly dry water hole where sand grouse flighted in the mornings.

"Wouldn't you like me to read?" she asked. She was sitting on a canvas chair beside his cot. "There's a breeze coming up."

"No thanks."

"Maybe the truck will come."

"I don't give a damn about the truck."

"I do."

"You give a damn about so many things that I don't."

"Not so many, Harry."

"What about a drink?"

"It's supposed to be bad for you. It said in Black's to avoid all alcohol. You shouldn't drink."

"Molo!" he shouted.

"Yes, Bwana."

"Bring whiskey-soda."

"Yes Bwana."

"You shouldn't," she said. "That's what I mean by giving up. It says it's bad for you. I know it's bad for you."

"No," he said. "It's good for me."

ERNEST HEMINGWAY, "The Snows of Kilimanjaro"

IT'S RAINING.

Linda   Is it?

Jenny   Has been for about an hour. [4]The air was so calm and still, no hint of a storm. Then all at once, it came down in buckets. I was out in it when it started, of course. Started running and made it to the Gallery. [8]Then I got a cup of coffee and sat up front by the window so that I could watch the rain and the people. [9]Strange about people in the rain. [10]Some run, then some just walk along, faces up, glorying in the wetness.

Linda   You used to do that. You used to love the rain.

Jenny   Funny, now I run like most of the others.

Linda   He called again, Jenny.

Jenny [*after a pause, guardedly*]   What did he want?

Linda   You know perfectly well what he wanted. He still wants to see you. Jenny, I really think you should—

Jenny   Why can't he leave me alone? Doesn't he get the message? And you. You're always pushing me. "Jenny, see him. Jenny, feel sorry for him." I thought you were on my side. I thought you understood. But no, you just meddle in things that . . . sorry. I really am. I'm a bit edgy, I guess. I honestly didn't mean to fly at you like that.

Linda   I know. But you must realize that if it's something worth getting upset about it must be pretty important.

Jenny   We have nothing to talk about.

Linda   Don't be an idiot. You have everything to talk about. Until you see him you will always be afraid of meeting him. For twenty-three years he's been with you, hounding you. And he will always be there until you meet him face to face.

Jenny   What would I say to him? "Hello, my dear Mr.

Lawrence. So nice to see you after all these years. I've heard so much about you." Then he'd get all choked up and say something revolting about "his little girl." He tried that the first time he called. It made me sick. I could feel all the cruel things I'd been saving these many years on the tip of my tongue, so I hung up. Why didn't I just say them and get it over with? [48]Maybe I just don't want to hurt him. [49]That used to be important to me, but perhaps it isn't any more.

Linda   So why not see him?

Jenny   Because he'd bait me, like he did on the phone, with the loving father bit. He must know what I feel when he starts out. He's trying to punish himself. He'll force me to give out with all of the things that I've felt all my life, then slowly walk away dejected, defeated; yet he will have appeased his conscience. I may not want to hurt him, but I haven't mellowed enough to want to humor him. That would be a lovely, noble gesture. But no thank you.

Linda   Okay, okay. Sometimes you really try my patience. You're like that too often. I can't follow you and I'm beginning to think you deliberately plan it that way. You'll pull that with Matt one time too many and you'll lose him. You get so wrapped up in your own petty problems you can't think of anyone else. People have always been drawn to you and you never fail to hurt them. Unfortunately, they keep coming back for more.

Jenny   Look, I said no! Now, please, let's drop it.

[*There is an uncomfortable pause.*]

Linda   Bill came by earlier and we went looking for a living room suite. You know I wanted something in gold. But I started thinking about keeping it clean. I couldn't find anything I liked, within reason, anyway. I do wish we had more money to start with, but with me working, I guess we'll make out.

Jenny   It won't be long now.

Linda   No, just two more months, then I'll be Mrs.—

Jenny Hum? Oh! No, I mean until it stops raining. It's beginning to let up.

Linda You didn't hear anything I said, did you? Really, Jen, you exasperate me sometimes! You're never completely with anyone. Matt said the same thing the other night.

Jenny [84]It's not safe to ever be completely with any-one else. [85]Don't you ever want to keep part of your-self—well, protected, I guess? . . . No, I guess not. Don't mind me. I'm just in a mood. The rain probably.

Linda Sometimes I really feel I don't know you at all.

Jenny [*lightly, mood changes*] What's for supper? I'm starved.

Linda Well, I thought we'd fix a roast. Then we'd have leftovers for sandwiches later in the week.

DONNA QUENAN

THAT'S THE WAY it happened.

Eric Well, I knew your feeble mind would get you in trouble sooner or later. I would never get in such a situation.

Ted And why not?

Eric Because I like myself too much to be associated with that type surrounding.

Ted I *could* take that remark as an insult.

Eric I guess you could. It is an insult.

Ted Well, I'm not trying to impress you. Just love me or leave me. Anyway, who the hell are you? The big eccentric with the platinum ring and the Sears and Roebuck wallet. *Would*n't get yourself in such a situation.

Eric Correct. I can repress such desires when it is wise that I do so.

Ted You're a goddam liar. You would have done the same thing. I know you would have. Say you would.

Eric That is where you're wrong.

Ted I've seen you when you've been loaded and you cer-tainly let your inhibitions fly.

Eric   Yes, I do, but I still contain myself. I do common things. Things *every*one does when they've had enough to drink—not including chasing thirteen-year-olds around.

Ted   Now, don't start that crap. I told you how it happened.

Eric   I told you a long time ago you would do something stupid on one of your binges. And I know why it happened —because I was not there to stop you. You've sprouted wings recently and left me behind. Now you are beginning to pay and you come to me for help. Well, I am not your nurse-maid now.

Ted   Be quiet! I don't like you when you're sober. You don't talk this way to me when you are drinking, do you? You're nicer then. That's when you like to talk and philos-ophize and try that hypnotic crap.

Eric   I do it within my own limits and bring harm to no one.

Ted   Okay, okay. Will you give me the money or not? I could do you harm if you refuse me.

Eric   And how may you do me harm?

Ted   That hypnotic business. [43]I've remembered that night many times. It was close to Christmas. I was stone drunk and you were rubbing my shoulders and telling me to relax. [46]I passed out then. How the hell do I know what you did? I could dramatize the evening a little.

Eric   That wouldn't be a bit fair.

Ted   No, it wouldn't. Get out the scotch.

Eric   Okay.

RICHARD DEWEY

Commentary

Drama switches to reverie for special revelations, such as the asides in the Shakespeare 19-21, 28, 32-33; and in the Chekhov, 69. Reverie also occurs when a speaker permits

himself to reflect aloud without the privacy of the aside, as
in the Chekhov, 8, 65-67, 77-78; and in the Quenan, 48-49,
51-57. Lower points in the drama are in the modes of description or narration. Description occurs here in the Hemingway,
11, 52, 62-63. Narration occurs here in the Chekhov, 33-35;
in the Hemingway, 12-14; in the Quenan, 4-8; in the Dewey,
43-46.

Of the abstract modes, definition occurs, with some suggestion of thematic persuasion, in the Shakespeare, 12 and 27
(a concrete-abstract "character"); in the Wilde, 17-18 and
31; in the Chekhov, 80; in the Quenan, 9-10 and 84-85.

The excitement of these examples, as of all drama, is that
you seem to be overhearing a conversation so novel it could
not possibly recur. Trite, flabby drama sounds like the same
old stuff everybody has heard on or off stage. Each of
these is a conversation between two people, one of whom is
somehow trying to get the better of the other, and some
psychological movement takes place in the course of the
conversation. But the movers in the Shakespeare, Hemingway, and Quenan are largely unsuccessful, and those unmoved become eloquent in their refusal to be moved. In the
other three pieces, the Wilde, Chekhov, and Dewey, the
movers are variously successful, least of all in the Dewey,
overwhelmingly and comically in the Wilde and Chekhov.
The Wilde in fact poses a trite foppish hero against a heroine
so jaded that the proposal seems as much hers as his. The
Chekhov poses a foolish egotistical hero against a consum-
mate actress who wins him back so resoundingly that she
can risk her success at the end by offering to withdraw it.
The first three of these examples are light, though *Hamlet* is
a tragedy, as you are reminded at the end of 35; the latter
three are serious, though more suggestive of "problem plays"
than tragedies.

Dialogue

Dialogue is abstract drama, just as drama is concrete dialogue. Conversation includes both, but usually refers to the actual happening rather than the literary perfection of either. People talk, not only about whether they love or hate each other, but about what love and hate are in themselves. The subjects of their conversations, that is, may be concrete or abstract; but so may the sequence of their conversations. It is not only Chekhov's plays which proceed by almost haphazard, concrete intrusions of conflicting personalities. All drama is concrete in both substance and sequence. The whole play may exhibit the abstract form and order appropriate to any work of art, but local passages are spontaneous if they are dramatic at all. Plays are illogical or psychological; dialogues are logical and proceed by ideal and typical stages, which are at least theoretically recurrent. Any time you want to examine love and hate from these points of view, a dialogue suggests, here is how you must go about it.

The Socratic dialogues of Plato, by their beauty, skill, and precedence, have exercised a needless tyranny over the rhetorical mode of dialogue. The special Socratic elenchus, the examination of a false contention by a succession of simple questions and answers so well put that by the last answer your opponent refutes his own contention, has often seemed the only conduct possible for a dialogue. There are many studies of dialectic, none of dialogue. Of the dialogues written many betray a bondage not only to the mode, but also to the whimsical preferences of Plato. In no other mode of rhetoric has anything comparable happened. Imagine the mode of narration forever restricted to beginning *in medias res*, with a flashback, a descent to the underworld, gods, and twenty-four books—simply because Homer did it that way.

The study of dialogue must then be an attempt to rescue the mode from the bonds imposed on it by its master. Such a study might proceed by stripping the Socratic dialogues of whatever seems peculiar to them by way of Socrates' personality or Plato's style. An alternate procedure, however, is to see when and how ordinary abstract, one-voiced discourse (an essay) differs from many-voiced discourse, or dialogue. The simplest sign of dialogue is gratuitous repetition, for ordinary discourse varies as it proceeds.

> *So it seems*
> *So it seems to us.*   (*Charmides* 159D)

The next sign of dialogue is a shift of person or tense uncalled for by the argument.

> *For health comes as a good thing to us, if you admit this.*
> *I admit it.*   (165D)

Apparently the "I" and the "you" above refer to the same person, and so there seem to be two persons present. The next sign of dialogue is a question with its answer.

> *Are you speaking of him or of someone else?*
> *I mean both him and someone else.*   (174A)

A single speaker may put a question to himself and then answer it, but this question seems to request an answer from another, which the other then supplies. The final sign of dialogue, and a more telling one than the last, is a standing disagreement between two statements.

> *Well, didn't we, he said, make the right admission?*
> *I don't think so, I said.*   (172E)

The disagreement may sometimes be more restrained than this one—in fact Socrates tries to conceal his disagreement whenever possible.

> *I think, he said, what you are asking about is in a word quietness.*
> *I wonder, I said, whether you are right there?*   (159B)

The combination of such violations of ordinary discourse, progressively sustained in two or more voices or attitudes results in dialogue, as distinct from essay.

Socratic dialogue may already be considered eccentric, in its preference of the third sign of dialogue (questions and answers) over the fourth sign (disagreement). For disagreement occurs in a Socratic elenchus only twice: at the beginning, when it is veiled by Socrates' profession of ignorance; and at the end, when the line of questioning has demanded a withdrawal of the original contention. But Socratic questioning is always enlivened by your assurance that the false contender will in the end be proven wrong, and that every step brings you closer to this goal. Still every elementary reader of Plato has felt some boredom with the respondent's easy, almost mechanical agreement along the way: "I agree," "By all means," "Certainly, Socrates," or just "Yes." Some translators follow the suggestion of Plato himself and omit some of the respondent's agreement, permitting Socrates to carry on without interruption. Except when the respondent makes an intellectual contribution—registers a qualification or alters his original contention or tries to browbeat the questioner—the Socratic dialogue may be regarded essentially as a lecture in the form of questions, leading to a *quod non erat demonstrandum*, followed by the respondent's admission of his error.

Catechism is also dialogue in the form of questions and answers, but now the answerer, not the questioner, is the master; the questioner is a novice or catechumen, who only asks, never disagrees. Every question requests knowledge which its answer immediately supplies.

> *What do we mean when we say that God is infinitely perfect?*
> *When we say that God is infinitely perfect we mean that He has all perfections without limit.*[1]

From this point of view a catechism is nothing but a lecture in which every statement is made twice, first as question, then as answer—a repetition useful for learners of the dogma, tiresome and unnecessary for others. In fact questions in composition are often suspect: if the writer has no answer he is engaging in aimless mystification; if he is about to supply an answer the question is usually superfluous; only if the question cannot easily be assumed from the answer need it be given. The third is the case R. G. Collingwood is thinking of when he says, "you cannot tell whether a proposition is 'true' or 'false' until you know what question it was intended to answer." (*Autobiography*, p. 38) To give the question for every proposition will result in arid catechism, but to omit all questions will, especially in later ages, baffle the reader. If Collingwood is right in thinking that only by reconstructing the unasked questions can you rightly interpret a writer, it would follow that only by giving you his questions in advance (or writing a dialogue) does a writer leave a valid record of his thought.

Hegel's dialectical triad is both a definition of dialogue and an account of all experience. Certainly many dialogues,

---

1. Baltimore Catechism, no. 11.

possibly all, exhibit the overall triadic progression from a thesis to its antithesis and finally to a synthesis which somehow harmonizes them. Rhetorically, this definition liberates dialogue from the bondage of the elenchus, but it imposes another bondage, in its insistence on a synthesis. Not every dialogue, or every passage of dialogue, will end in a resolution agreeable to the disputants. Perhaps if they cannot agree, something like a synthesis nevertheless occurs as a whole in the reader's mind. But rhetoric is more interested in parts or "passages" than in wholes, and the difference between dialogue and other modes in passing is the relationship of thesis and antithesis which I have called disagreement. As for the broader implications of the Hegelian triad, no grander status for dialectic can be conceived, since it is the basis of everything.

There is a Hegelian dialectic, but no Hegelian dialogues. Hegel thought of everything except his own ideas dialectically: "I know," he said, "that my method is the only true one." (Introduction to *The Science of Logic*) What chiefly differentiates dia- from mono-logue is disagreement; what chiefly differentiates dialogists from monologists is uncertainty. There is no necessity to write a dialogue rather than an essay unless the writer is of at least two minds on a subject. Simple irresolution is a good motive for writing nothing; mixed resolution is the right motive for dialogue. The writer of dialogue will know more, not less, than enough to write an essay. And a writer who habitually composes dialogues will have a mind like Plato's, constantly tentative and searching, not simply curious and unresolved. A hypothetically ideal dialogue might be between two peers each coming up with an equal half-victory; but most writers will not resist the temptation to prefer one argument. The dialogist must constantly frame not only his own opinions, but those contrary to his own, and this practice usually makes him something of an ironist as well. Irony could be defined as the impersonation of a character dumb enough to believe the

opposite of the truth. Plato, Lucian, Erasmus, Dryden, Wilde
are remembered for irony as well as dialogue, and often for
irony within dialogue. But if a writer tries to frame the contrary opinion as persuasively as possible, he may find he can
agree with it better than he thought, like Dryden, who
between *Religio Laici* and *The Hind and the Panther* became
persuaded of the "wrong" opinion. If the writer has no
respect at all for the contrary opinion he will make of the
second speaker a mere straight man feeding opportunities
for punch lines to the star. No opinion in a dialogue should
be thoroughly contemptible, not even Ion's or Thrasy-
machus', and every statement should seem at least momentarily superior to the last one. Hugh Blair states the case
persuasively:

> But the greatest part of modern dialogue writers have no
> idea of any composition of this sort; and bating the out-
> ward forms of conversation, and that one speaks and an-
> other answers, it is quite the same as if the author spoke
> in person throughout the whole. He sets up a Philotheus,
> perhaps, and a Philatheos, or an A and a B; who, after
> mutual compliments, and after admiring the fineness of
> the morning or evening, and the beauty of the prospects
> around them, enter into conference concerning some grave
> matter; and all that we know farther of them is, that the
> one personates the author, a man of learning, no doubt,
> and of good principles; and the other is a man of straw,
> set up to propose some trivial objections, over which the
> first gains a most entire triumph, and leaves his skeptical
> antagonist, at the end, much humbled, and generally, con-
> vinced of his error. This is a very frigid and insipid manner
> of writing; the more so, as it is an attempt toward some-
> thing, which we see the author cannot support. It is the
> form, without the spirit, of conversation. The dialogue
> serves no purpose, but to make awkward interruptions;
> and we should with more patience hear the author con-
> tinuing always to reason himself, and remove the objections
> that are made to his principles, than be troubled with the

*unmeaning appearance of two persons, whom we see to be
in reality no more than one.*

      (*Lectures on Rhetoric and Belles Lettres*, lect. 37)

Blair's antidote to the abuses of dialogue is "natural and
spirited representation of real conversation," and so he prefers Plato (despite his lapses into "allegory, fiction, enthusi-
asm, and the airy regions of mystical theology") above all
writers of dialogue. But the characteristic Socratic elenchus,
as I have tried to show, requires two speakers only at the beginning and end, or at major transitions of the argument;
along the way it would seem, according to Blair's analysis, "a
very frigid and insipid manner of writing." If conversation becomes too natural and spirited it is not dialogue at all, but
drama. A certain elegance or elevation (I mean by way of simplicity, not pomposity) may be considered becoming to the
ideality of dialogue. What is needed to make dialogue is genu-
ine intellectual, not emotional—or abstract, not concrete—
discord from one speech to the next.

Drama is always present in its effect, but utilizes any tense
along the way; dialogue by comparison has a plagal remote-
ness of effect, but is written almost exclusively in present
tense, the general aorist tense of most philosophic discourse.
A dialogue in fact has no real time or place, only an ideal
abstraction of both. The speakers of a dialogue customarily
begin, as Blair says, "after admiring the fineness of the
morning or evening, and the beauty of the prospects around
them"—which are ideal even if real places and times are
mentioned. "Let us turn aside," says Socrates to Phaedrus,
"and go by the Ilissus; we will sit down at some quiet spot."
"Can there be," says Philonous to Hylas, "a pleasanter time
of the day, or a more delightful season of the year?" In
dialogue no water pipes burst, and in-laws never arrive for
the weekend—those events are from the concrete world of
drama. The speakers in a dialogue are at their ease, and
though interested in their subject, also disinterested. A

husband and a bachelor are more likely to have a dialogue on marriage than a husband and a wife, whose talk is usually drama.

Compared with drama, dialogue is elegant but remote; compared with definition or process, dialogue is lively, maybe even, as Blair says, "natural and spirited representation of real conversation." Abstract discourse, if it stays static, or even becomes temporal, has a scholarly standoffishness, which dialogue, though also abstract, is exempt from. Fifty pages of Plato is an easier and pleasanter assignment than ten pages of Aristotle. Definition occurs at no time or in any time; process engages time but condenses it to a shorter period than actual on-the-spot observation; persuasion may well expand time and give a moment of the author's thought in several pages. Of abstract discourse only dialogue actually equates the times of the speakers and the reader, and achieves something of the directness of drama. But occurrences of dialogue are not restricted to works self-consciously labeled dialogues, with their Q's and A's or their Philothei and Philatheoi. Almost any "expository" or persuasive work will break out here and there in dialogue, if you accept the definition of dialogue offered here. Even Aristotle is not above a little lively controversy.

> . . . Epic, they say, is aimed at a cultivated audience who do not need gestures; and tragedy at the vulgar. If then it is unrefined, it must be worse.
> Now first, the criticism applies to the art, not of poetry, but of acting. . . . Then, tragedy has all the elements of epic—it can even use epic meter—and has the not minor addition of music and acting, by which its pleasures are vivified; and this vividness holds both in reading it and in performance. (Poetics, 26: 5-11)

Attach "he said" (instead of "they say") to the first statement and "I said" to the second, or "Philepicus" to the first and "Philotragicus" to the second, and the passage makes perfectly acceptable dialogue.

Just as drama is reserved for the most crucial and critical moments of description and narration, so dialogue may be introduced to heighten and enliven abstract discourse. Whenever a contrary opinion is entertained and answered dialogue has been used, however briefly. Some writers occasionally introduce questions or objections as put to them by a hypothetical opponent, and often employ quotation marks and exclamation points as well—these are unmistakable occurrences of dialogue. The right spots for dialogue in expository or persuasive prose are those where the author feels closest to being of a mixed mind on the subject—or where he should. Maybe much of his argument can be conducted in safe reliance on his opponent's agreement; the touchy spots are those where the opponent's argument comes closest to being better than his. A composition wholly in dialogue professes to be continuously touchy; long speeches by the preferred speaker and long silences by the other show a temporary or permanent betrayal of the mode of dialogue.

Aristotle's *Topics* is a handbook of dialogue, a sort of Robert's Rules of Order for two. But it tells how to carry on a dialogue rather than how to write one, and it too seems hamstrung by the precedent of Plato. This is shown by his calling the two speakers questioner and answerer or, even more revealingly, subverter (*anairon*) and contender (*kataskeuazon*). (IV, iii, 7) There seems no actual necessity of restricting the speakers of dialogue to two, unless an elenchus is the object. But as in drama, a single passage of dialogue can hardly support more than three speakers or attitudes, and the basic confrontation, elenchus or not, is always between two speakers. Of course the two speakers will not be crudely *pro* and *con*, as in school debating societies: if the issue is worth dignifying with dialogue both or all speakers will be mixed *pro* and *con*—assuming in the first place that the issue is simple enough to submit to such division. "Controversial subjects" with their standard oppositions are those least fruitful of interesting controversy; the trick is to take a subject that had not seemed controversial and show that it deserves to be. Nor are there two but countless sides to most subjects worth talking about; and unless the speakers mechanically repeat their initial position ("I am for—" and "I am against—"), they will go on to expand, amplify, and alter their positions.

For the province of dialectic, as Aristotle says, is not fact but opinion. A scientific demonstration is not open to doubt or discussion; it commands belief in itself and not through the arguments of others. But a dialogue is an exchange of probabilities. Logical propositions may be converted to dialectical problems by adding "whether or not" to them, but not all propositions are suited to this conversion. No one in his right mind would question some propositions, and others are so doubtful there isn't much to talk about. A man who questions whether snow is white lacks sense; a man who questions whether the world is everlasting is wasting his time. The remaining problems are those which appear probable to all, or to most, or to the wise. (See *Topics*, I, i, x, xi.)

The area of conversation most immediately open to probabilities rather than certainties is human affairs. Not every scientific issue is resolved, but the sciences of human nature would seem more productive of uncertainty. From this point of view it is no accident that Plato's dialogues are almost exclusively on ethical themes. A dialogue is after all an exchange, not between machines or animals, but between men, whose favorite subject is themselves. Though the speakers are not particular persons but typical representatives of their classes, their longings and complaints will usually be human, even when abstract. The study and composition of dialogue is consequently more humane than those of definition or process, for things may be conceived in space or time, but only people are worth arguing about.

In fact the matter of drama and dialogue may come very close to overlapping. Aristotle, in his *Poetics* (6) places ideas (*dianoia*) third after plot and character in order of importance for drama; and judging by the theater of Shakespeare or Chekhov ideas would seem last in order of importance, after even style and spectacle. But judging by some of Ibsen or Shaw ideas are paramount, the actions and characters thin exemplifications of a theme. In fiction the abstract, elevated conversations of Ivy Compton-Burnett seem as close to the dialogues of Plato (or Wilde) as to the talk of a concretely blooded novelist, for example Hemingway. Normally the "theater of ideas" does not seem worth staging or screening, and *Pygmalion* will continue to be played, over Shaw's dead body, while *Back to Methuselah* is read in the study. The current flurry over "absurd" plays is bound to pass, showing them to be, when stripped of their shocks and symbols, little more than staged sermons in two voices. If you go to the theater you have a right to expect live drama; if you want live dialogue, instead of reading Plato to yourself, you can always invite your friends over for a talk.

Aristotle lists three advantages of engaging in dialogue, which are also advantages of writing or reading it: skill on every subject; aptness of opinions; and readier perception of the true and the false. (I, ii) Reading and writing dialogues, and engaging in them, satisfy each of Bacon's recommendations: "Reading maketh a full man; conference a ready man; and writing an exact man." (*Of Studies*) As an instrument of teaching, dialogue has always been unsurpassed, from the "Socratic method" to the new teaching machines, which ask of the student, Socrates-like, a series of questions the answers to which are obvious and implied by former questions and answers, but in the end reward him only with information, not wisdom. The virtues of the Socratic method in the classroom have often been urged, especially by the German philosopher Leonard Nelson:

> The lecture, too, can stimulate spontaneous thinking, particularly in more mature students; but no matter what allure such stimulus may possess, it is not irresistible. Only persistent pressure to speak one's mind, to meet every counter question, and to state the reasons for every as-

sertion transforms the power of that allure into an irresistible compulsion. The art of forcing minds to freedom
constitutes the first secret of the Socratic method.

(*Socratic Method and Critical Philosophy*)[2]

Perhaps the secret of dialogue's success in stimulating
thought is that it is constantly aspiring toward reflection or
persuasion, the free abstract activity of the mind. "Are not
thought and speech the same, except that the unspoken dialogue of the soul with herself has been called thought?"
(*Sophist* 263E) It is not only Yeats who writes a Dialogue of
Self and Soul. When a dialogist, or even a playwright, is accused of representing characters who are all simply versions of
himself he might well respond, Whose else could they be? A
certain shadow-boxing of the mind, by engaging in or composing dialogue, forces you to be constantly aware of the keenest
objections to your opinions—and there can be no better intellectual training than that. Many a view remains ludicrous
when it is put forth in disregard of the objections to it, but
might become brilliantly original when it has overcome them.

Aristotle too sets great store by originality, and seems to
prefer, among dialectical problems, those he calls *theses*,
paradoxical judgments of those celebrated in philosophy. (I,
xi) Elsewhere he says that a syllogistic argument is most
acute, if from things which appear especially probable, a
person can subvert what is especially probable—if, that is,
he can persuade you of an unlikely opinion by perfectly acceptable means. (*Sophistical Elenchi*, xxxiii, 2) The speakers
in a dialogue speak not merely for themselves but for their
class, and the course of their dialogue is also typical of what
may ensue when any two such speakers are brought together
—but that does not mean the dialogue has to be trite. A
skillful dialogist will in the end alter your vision, and along
the way he will successively startle you with striking abstract
exchanges, each apparently victorious over the last.

---

2. The translation is by Thomas K. Brown III, p. 15.

I SUPPOSE, LYSIS, I said, that your father and mother love you very much.

Certainly, he said.

Then they would like you to be as happy as possible?

Yes, of course.

[5]But do you consider a man to be happy, enslaved and unable to do anything he wishes?

[6]No sir, not me, he said.

Then if your father and mother love you and wish you to be happy, it is quite clear that they are eager to promote your happiness.

Yes, of course, he said.

Then they must let you do what you like, and never scold or prevent you from doing as you wish?

Yes sir, they do, Socrates; there are a great many things they stop me from doing.

How's that? I said. They want you to be content and yet prevent you from doing what you like? [13]But tell me this: if you wanted to mount one of your father's chariots, and take the reins at a race, they would not allow you but prevent you?

No sir, they certainly would not allow me, he said.

[15]But whom would they?

[16]There is a charioteer, in my father's pay.

How's that? They trust a hireling to do what he likes with the horses rather than you? and in addition pay him a salary?

Why, of course, he said.

[20]But I imagine they trust you to lead the mule-cart, and if you wish to take the whip and lash out they will let you?

Let me! he said. Certainly not.

What then, I said, may no one lash the mules?

Oh yes, he said, the muleteer.

And is he a slave or a free man?

A slave, he said.

So it seems they value a slave more than you their son, and entrust him with their property rather than you, and let him do what he likes but prevent you? And tell me more now: do they let you rule over yourself or don't they trust you in that either?

They certainly don't, he said.

But someone does rule over you?

There, my tutor, he said.

And is he a slave?

Why of course, he is our slave, he said.

How strange, I said, a free man ruled over by a slave! And how does he go about ruling over you?

He takes me to school.

You don't mean to say that your teachers also rule over you?

Of course they do.

Then your father is willing to inflict many lords and masters on you. [40]But when you come home to your mother, she will let you do what you like to make you content, either with the wool or the loom, when she is weaving? [41]I don't suppose she prevents you from handling her batten or her comb or any other of her spinning implements.

And laughing he said, I assure you, Socrates, not only does she prevent me, but I would be beaten if I were to handle them.

Great Scott, I said, it couldn't be that you have done some wrong to your father or your mother?

No sir, not me, he said.

But what reason have they for so strangely preventing you from being happy and doing what you like; and for keeping you all day long ruled over by somebody, and in a word doing nothing you wish to do; so that you, as it seems, benefit neither from their great possessions, which everybody rules over rather than you, nor from your own fair person, which is also tended and taken care of by another; while you, Lysis, rule over nobody, and can do nothing you wish?

[46]I suppose, he said, because I am not of age, Socrates.

That can hardly stop you, son of Democrates, since there are some things, I imagine, that both your father and mother entrust to you and do not wait until you are of age. For when they'd like something read or written, you, I imagine, are the first person in the house set to it, aren't you?

Certainly.

[50]Then you are allowed to write whichever letter you like first and whichever second, and are allowed to read the same way; and when, as I imagine, you take up the lyre neither your father nor your mother prevents you from tightening or loosening the strings, or from strumming or striking with the plectrum; or do they prevent you?

Oh no.

Then whatever can be the reason, Lysis, I said, that they do not prevent you in these, while in those things we were just speaking of they do?

[53]Because, I suppose, he said, these I understand, but not those.

[54]Very well, I said, my friend, then it is not your age your father is waiting for to entrust you with everything; but on the day when he considers you to reason better than himself—on that day he will entrust you with both himself and his possessions.

I imagine so, he said.

PLATO, *Lysis*, 207D-209C

WE TALKED OF DRINKING WINE. [*Johnson*] 'I require wine, only when I am alone. I have then often wished for it, and often taken it.' [*Spottiswoode*] 'What, by way of a companion, Sir?' [*Johnson*] 'To get rid of myself, to send myself away.

[6]Wine gives me great pleasure; and every pleasure is of itself a good. It is a good, unless counterbalanced by evil. A man may have a strong reason not to drink wine; and that may be greater than the pleasure. [9]Wine makes a man better pleased with himself. I do not say that it makes him more pleasing to others. Sometimes it does. [12]But the danger is, that while a man grows better pleased with himself, he may be growing less pleasing to others. Wine gives a man nothing. It neither gives him knowledge nor wit; it only animates a man, and enables him to bring out what a dread of the company has repressed. It only puts in motion what has been locked up in frost. But this may be good, or it may be bad.' [*Spottiswoode*] [17]'So, Sir, wine is a key which opens a box; but this box may be either full or empty.' [*Johnson*] [18]'Nay, Sir, conversation is the key: wine is a pick-lock, which forces open the box and injures it. [19]A man should cultivate his mind so as to have that confidence and readiness without wine, which wine gives.' [*Boswell*] 'The great difficulty of resisting wine is from benevolence. For instance, a good worthy man asks you to taste his wine, which he has had twenty years in his cellar.' [*Johnson*] 'Sir, all this notion about benevolence arises from a man's imagining himself to be of more importance to others, than he really is. They don't care a farthing whether he drinks wine or not.' [*Sir Joshua Reynolds*] 'Yes, they do for the time.' [*Johnson*] [25]'For the time!—if they care this minute, they forget it the next. And as for the good worthy man; how do you know he is good and worthy? No good and worthy man will insist upon another man's drinking wine. As to the wine twenty years in the cellar,—of ten men, three say this, merely because they must say something;—three are telling a lie, when they say they have had the wine twenty years;— three would rather save the wine;—one, perhaps, cares. I allow it is something to please one's company: and people are always pleased with those who partake pleasure with them. But after a man has brought himself to relinquish

the great personal pleasure which arises from drinking wine,
any other consideration is a trifle. To please others by drinking wine, is something, only if there be nothing against it.
[32]I should, however, be sorry to offend worthy men:—

> "Curst be the verse, how well so e'er it flow,
> That tends to make one worthy man my foe." '

[Boswell] 'Curst be the *spring*, the *water*.' [Johnson] 'But let
us consider what a sad thing it would be, if we were obliged
to drink or do any thing else that may happen to be agreeable
to the company where we are.' [Langton] 'By the same rule
you must join with a gang of cut-purses.' [Johnson] 'Yes, Sir:
but yet we must do justice to wine; we must allow it the
power it possesses. To make a man pleased with himself, let
me tell you, is doing a very great thing:

> "Si patriæ volumus, si Nobis vivere cari." '
> ['If we could make our life of value to our country and to
> ourselves.'   HORACE, Epistles i, 3. 29, Wickham]

I was at this time myself a water-drinker, upon trial, by
Johnson's recommendation. [Johnson] 'Boswell is a bolder
combatant than Sir Joshua: he argues for wine without the
help of wine; but Sir Joshua with it.' [Sir Joshua Reynolds]
'But to please one's company is a strong motive.' [42][John-
son] (who, from drinking only water, supposed every body
who drank wine to be elevated,) 'I won't argue any more
with you, Sir. You are too far gone.' [Sir Joshua] 'I should
have thought so indeed, Sir, had I made such a speech as
you have now done.' [Johnson] (drawing himself in, and,
I really thought blushing,) 'Nay, don't be angry. [46]I did
not mean to offend you.' [Sir Joshua] 'At first the taste of
wine was disagreeable to me; but I brought myself to drink
it, that I might be like other people. The pleasure of drinking wine is so connected with pleasing your company, that
altogether there is something of social goodness in it.'

[*Johnson*] 'Sir, this is only saying the same thing over again.'
[*Sir Joshua*] 'No, this is new,' [*Johnson*] 'You put it in new
words, but it is an old thought. This is one of the disadvan-
tages of wine. It makes a man mistake words for thoughts.'
[*Boswell*] 'I think it is a new thought; at least, it is in a new
attitude.' [*Johnson*] 'Nay, Sir, it is only in a new coat; or
an old coat with a new facing. (Then laughing heartily,)
It is the old dog in a new doublet.—An extraordinary instance
however may occur where a man's patron will do nothing
for him, unless he will drink: *there* may be a good reason
for drinking.'

I mentioned a nobleman, who I believed was really uneasy
if his company would not drink hard. [*Johnson*] 'That is
from having had people about him whom he has been ac-
customed to command.' [*Boswell*] 'Supposing I should be
tête-a-tête with him at table.' [*Johnson*] 'Sir, there is no more
reason for your drinking with *him*, than his being sober with
you.' [*Boswell*] 'Why, that is true; for it would do him less
hurt to be sober, than it would do me to get drunk.' [*Johnson*] 'Yes, Sir; and from what I have heard of him, one would
not wish to sacrifice himself to such a man. If he must always
have somebody to drink with him, he should buy a slave,
and then he would be sure to have it. They who submit to
drink as another pleases make themselves his slaves.' [*Boswell*] 'But, Sir, you will surely make allowance for the duty
of hospitality. A gentleman who loves drinking, comes to
visit me.' [*Johnson*] 'Sir, a man knows whom he visits; he
comes to the table of a sober man.' [*Boswell*] 'But, Sir, you
and I should not have been so well received in the Highlands
and Hebrides, if I had not drunk with our worthy friends.
Had I drunk water only as you did, they would not have been
so cordial.' [*Johnson*] [72]'Sir William Temple mentions
that in his travels through the Netherlands he had two or
three gentlemen with him; and when a bumper was necessary, he put it on *them*. Were I to travel again through the
islands, I would have Sir Joshua with me to take the

bumpers.' [*Boswell*] 'But, Sir, let me put a case. [75]Suppose Sir Joshua should take a jaunt into Scotland; he does me the honour to pay me a visit at my house in the country; I am overjoyed at seeing him; we are quite by ourselves, shall I unsociably and churlishly let him sit drinking by himself? [76]No, no, my dear Sir Joshua, you shall not be treated so, I *will* take a bottle with you.'

JAMES BOSWELL, Life of Johnson,
Tuesday, 28 April 1778

I WISH I COULD SEE through you, Mr Boanerges. But I have not your sort of cleverness. I can only ask you to be frank with me.

Boanerges [*now convinced that he has the upper hand*] You mean about the crisis. Well, frank is just what I have come here to be. And the first thing I am going to tell you frankly about it is that this country has got to be governed, not by you, but by your ministers.

Magnus   I shall be only too grateful to them for taking a very difficult and thankless job off my hands.

Boanerges   But it's not on your hands. It's on your ministers' hands. [10]You are only a constitutional monarch. [11] Do you know what they call that in Belgium?

Magnus   [12]An indiarubber stamp, I think. Am I right?

Boanerges   You are, King Magnus. [15]An indiarubber stamp. [16]Thats what you have got to be; and dont you forget it.

Magnus   Yes: thats what we are most of the time: both of us.

Boanerges [*outraged*]   What do you mean? both of us?

Magnus   [19]They bring us papers. We sign. You have no time to read them, luckily for you. But I am expected to read everything. I do not always agree; but I must sign: there is nothing else to be done. For instance, death warrants. [25]Not only have I to sign the death warrants of persons who in my opinion ought not to be killed; but I may not even issue death warrants for a great many people who in my opinion ought to be killed.

Boanerges [*sarcastic*]   Youd like to be able to say "Off with his head!" wouldnt you?

Magnus   Many men would hardly miss their heads, there is so little in them. Still, killing is a serious business: at least the person who is to be killed is usually conceited enough to think so. I think that if there were a question of killing me—

Boanerges [*grimly*]   There may be, someday. I have heard it discussed.

Magnus   Oh, quite. I have not forgotten King Charles's head. Well, I hope it will be settled by a living person and not by an indiarubber stamp.

Boanerges   It will be settled by the Home Secretary, your duly constituted democratic minister.

Magnus   Another indiarubber stamp, eh?

Boanerges.   At present, perhaps. But not when I am Home Secretary, by Jingo! Nobody will make an indiarubber stamp of Bill Boanerges: take that from me.

Magnus   Of course not. Is it not curious how people idealize their rulers? [42]In the old days the king—poor man! —was a god, and was actually called God and worshipped as infallible and omniscient. That was monstrous—

Boanerges   It was silly: just silly.

Magnus   But was it half so silly as our pretence that he is an indiarubber stamp? The ancient Roman emperor-god had not infinite wisdom, infinite knowledge, infinite power; but he had some: perhaps even as much as his ministers. He was alive, not dead. What man has ever approached either a king or a minister and been able to pick him up from the table and use him as one picks up and uses a piece of wood and brass and rubber? Permanent officials of your department will try to pick you up and use you like that.

Nineteen times out of twenty you will have to let them do it, because you cannot know everything; and even if you could you cannot do everything and be everywhere. But what about the twentieth time?

Boanerges The twentieth time they will find they are up against Bill Boanerges, eh?

Magnus Precisely. The indiarubber stamp theory will not work, Mr. Boanerges. The old divine theory worked because there is a divine spark in us all; and the stupidest or worst monarch or minister, if not wholly god, is a bit of a god—an attempt at a god—however little the bit and unsuccessful the attempt. [56]But the indiarubber stamp theory breaks down in every real emergency, because no king or minister is the very least little bit like a stamp: he is a living soul.

Boanerges A soul, eh? You kings still believe in that, I suppose.

Magnus I find the word convenient: it is short and familiar. [60]But if you dislike being called a soul, let us say that you are animate matter as distinguished from inanimate.

Boanerges [*not quite liking this*] I think I'd rather you called me a soul, you know, if you must call me anything at all. I know I have too much matter about me: the doctor says I ought to knock off a stone or two; but there's something more to me than beef. Call it a soul if you like; only not in a superstitious sense, if you understand me.

Magnus Perfectly. [65]So you see, Mr Boanerges, that though we have been dealing with one another for less than ten minutes, you have already led me into an intellectual discussion which shews that we are something more than a pair of indiarubber stamps. [66]You are up against my brains, such as they are.

Boanerges And you are up against mine.

Magnus [*gallantly*] There can be no doubt of that.

GEORGE BERNARD SHAW, *The Apple Cart*, Act I

A MAN OUGHT to have more than just two sides to sleep on,"
declared Simple. "Now if I get tired of sleeping on my left
side, I have nothing to turn over on but my right side."

"You could sleep on your back," I advised.

"I snores on my back."

"Then why not try your stomach?"

"Sleeping on my stomach, I get a stiff neck—I always have
to keep my head turned toward one side or the other, else I
smothers. I do not like to sleep on my stomach."

"The right side, or the left side, are certainly enough sides
for most people to sleep on. I don't know what your trouble
is. But, after all, there are two sides to every question."

"That's just what I am talking about," said Simple.
[12]"Two sides are not enough. I'm tired of sleeping on
either my left side, or on my right side, so I wish I had
two or three more sides to change off on. Also, if I sleep
on my left side, I am facing my wife, then I have to turn
over to see the clock in the morning to find out what time
it is. If I sleep on my right side, I am facing the window
so the light wakes me up before it is time to get up. If I
sleep on my back, I snores, and disturbs my wife. [17]And my
stomach is out for sleeping, due to reasons which I mentioned.
In the merchant marine, sailors are always talking about
the port side and the starboard side of a ship. A human
should have not only a left side and a right side, but also a
port side and a starboard side."

"That's what left and right mean in nautical terms," I
said. "You know as well as I do that a ship has only two
sides."

"Then ships are bad off as a human," said Simple. "All a
boat can do when a storm comes up, is like I do when I
sleep—toss from side to side."

"Maybe you eat too heavy a dinner," I said, "or drink too
much coffee."

"No, I am not troubled in no digestion at night," said
Simple. "But there is one thing that I do not like in the

morning—waking up to face the same old one-eyed egg Joyce has fried for breakfast. [27]What I wish is that there was different kinds of eggs, not just white eggs with a yellow eye. [28]There ought to be blue eggs with a brown eye, and brown eggs with a blue eye, also red eggs with green eyes."

"If you ever woke up and saw a red egg with a green eye on your plate, you would think you had a hang-over."

"I would," said Simple. [32]"But eggs *is* monotonous! No matter which side you turn an egg on, daddy-o, it is still an egg—hard on one side and soft on the other. Or, if you turn it over, it's hard on both sides. [34]Once an egg sets in the frying pan, it has only two sides, too. [35]And if you burn the bottom side, it comes out just like the race problem, black and white, black and white."

"I thought you'd get around to race before you got through. You can't discuss any subject at all without bringing in color. God help you! And in reducing everything to two sides, as usual, you oversimplify."

"What does I do?"

"I say your semantics make things too simple."

"My which?"

"Your verbiage."

"My what?"

"Your words, man, your words."

[46]"Oh," said Simple. [47]"Well, anyhow, to get back to eggs—which is a simple word. For breakfast I wish some other birds besides chickens laid eggs for eating, with a different kind of flavor than just a hen flavor. Whatever you are talking about with your *see-antics*, Jack, at my age a man gets tired of the same kind of eggs each and every day —just like you get tired of the race problem. [50]I would like to have an egg some morning that tastes like a pork chop."

"In that case, why don't you have pork chops for breakfast instead of eggs?"

"Because there is never no pork chops in my icebox in the morning."

"There would be if you would put them there the night before."

[54]"No," said Simple, "I would eat them up the night before—which is always the trouble with the morning after —you have practically nothing left from the night before— except the race problem."

LANGSTON HUGHES, "Two Sides Not Enough"

[1]LOOK, DISCURSA, at the blue jays flying across the pale sky. [2]And below that see the striking reds and yellows of the rainbow. It seems as if nature were created to be beautiful to man, and its beauty makes me wonder how I can find the truth so that I can live harmoniously with it.

D   My friends and I have just been considering the same question, Reflexa.

R   I have been thinking about it alone. [6]The solution to any problem requires thought, and clear thought requires solitude.

D   But if you don't talk to other people what can be the object of your thought? Truth involves everyone; you should seek out other minds and see how they work.

R   Have you forgotten that you have a mind yourself? [10]Introspection is surely the most reliable method for discovering truth. It provides thoughts free from the deceits which cloud words between men.

D   But I can never know from introspection alone whether someone else has an idea I should know about in order to discover truth. Through discourse I can see how mens' minds differ and how they are the same.

R   Since you want to know how mens' mind work, you should read; you don't have to uncloud deceits to discover the author's meaning.

D   [15]Even supposing an author's words to be always

explicit, I think that many an author, because he thinks he must be dogmatic when he writes, omits any doubts or indecisions he may have had. Were I to know these omissions, I might consider them very pertinent to his discussion. Omission is surely more deceitful than any deceit practiced by a man facing me, whom I can cross-question until discovering whether he contradicts himself.

R   What one author omits another includes.

D   [19]But if an author omits something, I will never know his mind well. And the conversations books record are far away. [21]When a person is before me I can relate his words to present life and thus be able to evaluate them more sensibly.

R   [22]Suppose, Discursa, that a person you are talking to justifies an action which is contrary to your own moral beliefs. You cross-question him and find that he is in earnest. [24]You might consider him misled, perhaps even immoral, but I doubt that you would waste more time getting to know his mind.

D   You seem to forget, Reflexa, that an author might also be immoral. By talking to a person I can discover what in his past might cause his different beliefs. You are merely seeking corroboration and prestige for your own opinions. Another person might well have an opinion that would change your entire perspective of life.

R   And an author is most likely to have such a notion. Unthinking conversations reveal nothing but triteness.

D   Don't you think that what often seems trite, with a little closer investigation, brings valuable revelation? Perhaps what you consider trite is merely so imbedded in a mind that it more nearly approaches the unquestionable, the true. You have no faith in your fellow man, Reflexa. Ah well, I fear I am getting nowhere. I must be off to find my friends.

R   And I must be off to the library. Surely anyone with valuable thoughts will be in such a place while you are out seeking the revelations of mediocrity.

BONNIE REID

I SIMPLY CAN'T UNDERSTAND why you have so much trouble making up your mind about things.

B   Don't you ever have that difficulty?

A   No, I just don't allow myself to waste the time agonizing over decisions. It seems so stupid.

B   Oh, come now; look at the classic example: Hamlet. He was a man of extraordinary intelligence, a genius, so the critics say.

A   Okay, but haven't you heard the story about the moron who had the egg-sorting job? He had to put the brown eggs in the brown baskets and the white eggs in the white baskets, and he complained, "The decisions I have to make!"

B   [9]Well that doesn't prove anything; the feeble-minded have trouble with any mental process. My difficulty in making decisions is that I perceive the alternative courses too clearly.

A   That's no excuse; there are always alternatives. I just choose the one I think is best.

B   [13]But I can see definite advantages in each course. There are not only possibilities but also probabilities in every venture and they should all be examined very closely. It's all very well to make snap judgments, if that's what you pride yourself on. I feel I must weigh each side on the scales.

A   Sure, and then you keep on rationalizing until the scales balance. Then you're paralyzed; you don't do anything.

B   [19]No, then I'm sure I haven't analyzed the problem thoroughly enough. I refuse to take the easy way out; the eeny-meeny-miny-mo routine doesn't require intelligence.

A   [21]I don't think intelligence has much to do with it; it's more a matter of discipline. You've never tried to train yourself to make firm decisions.

B   I was brought up to believe that it's better to think things out carefully rather than to act on an impulse. When we wanted to do something on our own, our parents always sat down with us and discussed the pros and cons of the idea.

A   [25]Well, the family conference can be overdone; you would have been better off if they'd let you get a few bruises finding out for yourself if it was a good idea. Instead of experiencing trial and error, you got in the habit of questioning the merits of every move you make.

B   At least I'm not as likely to make mistakes that way.

A   [28]But you get yourself so hopelessly tied up in mental knots you have to beg for advice; then you never take it. If you can't trust your own judgment, I should think you'd have the sense to trust someone else's.

B   [30]Well, what happens is that when someone suggests a course of action, I feel tremendously relieved one minute, but the next minute I'm haunted by the thought that the other person doesn't really understand the intricacies of the situation.

A   You and Hamlet, huh? I hope you never have to sort eggs together.

BARBARA BALDING

Commentary

Crucial speeches of dialogue, or just long ones, usually grow reflective or persuasive, as in the Plato, 53-54; in the Boswell, 19, 25-32; in the Shaw, 65-66; in the Hughes, 54; in the Reid, 6 and 10; in the Balding, 21 and 25. Definition occurs in the Plato, 5-6; in the Boswell, 6, 17-18; in the Shaw, 10-12, 42, 56, 60; in the Hughes, 35; in the Balding, 9. Process occurs in the Plato, 13, 20, 40-41, 50; in the Boswell, 9-12, 72; in the Shaw, 19-25; in the Hughes, 12-17, 32-34; in the Reid, 15, 19-21, 22-24; in the Balding, 13-19, 28-30.

Of the concrete modes, description occurs in the Reid, 1-2. Narration is suggested hypothetically in the Boswell, 75-76. Drama occurs clearly in the Boswell, 42-46. Reverie occurs in the Hughes, 27-28, 47-50.

The Socratic elenchus is much more clearly shown here

in the Shaw than in the Plato. Socrates does not manage to browbeat Lysis into a false contention until 46, close to the end; Boanerges obliges with a false contention in 15-16; and both of these are refuted at the end. The Hughes is more of a one-sided conversation from Simple with the other as straight man. It is also unusual for its informality and its symbolism: he says sides and eggs but he means races. The Boswell, Reid, and Balding are more fluid in progression, and more even in victory. Boswell gets the last, and no doubt best, word, but Johnson has shined throughout. Discursa and A seem to prevail, but only slightly. In every example the less favored opinion has a likely enough sound. Nobody would be considered foolish for believing that boys are not trusted until they come of age; that soberness, especially in company, is commenndable; that modern monarchs are rubber stamps; that every question has two sides; that books are the best source of knowledge; that indecision is one mark of intelligence. It takes a sophisticated argument, therefore, to prefer opinions different from these.

THE
MENTAL
MODES

The Mixolydian too is pathetic and suitable to tragedy. And Aristoxenus says that Sappho was the first to hit on the Mixolydian, and that from her the tragic poets learned it. In taking it they coupled it with the Dorian, since the one gives grandeur and dignity and the other pathos, for tragedy is a mixture of these.

PLUTARCH, On Music, 16

Reverie

Every age proposes its own solution to the mystery of the mind, while smiling at former ones. Already the Freudian drama of the ego, super-ego, and the id has acquired a medieval charm, and seems hardly more daring or fruitful than the Hippocratic drama of blood, phlegm, choler, and melancholy. But while views of how the mind actually works, and especially of how it plays, are forever subject to improvement, the limitations of human discourse, the necessity of words succeeding each other, impose a certain permanence on literary representations of the mind. Reverie is a word used for this play of the mind, and also for a writer's attempt to mind or re-mind you of this play of the mind.

The modern works of Joyce and others have restricted rather than amplified the mode of reverie—as it were an invention of the twentieth century, as if there were a special reason for honoring the mind today. Now it is of interest to see what is distinctive about modern reverie; it is also of interest to see what is not distinctive about it, what it shares with any reverie. Was Dorothy Richardson, or even Laurence Sterne, the first to attempt reverie?

Reverie, they say, "is subjective, proceeds from one individual; has to do, not with events, but with feelings." There "is represented the inward life alone . . ." and ". . . things are what they seem." The thinker "is out of sight in a moment. He gets up into the clouds; becomes so abrupt in his transitions; so eccentric and irregular in his motions, and of course so obscure, that we essay in vain to follow him, or to partake of his raptures." Reverie expresses an "unknown, dark *psychic material.*" "Like the soliloquy, it represents character, and character under excitement moving from the expression of one emotion to another." In reverie you can make out "an oracular, meditative, irregular, unpredictable, and essentially discontinuous rhythm." Again, reverie "is an associative rhetorical process, most of it below the threshold of consciousness, a chaos of paronomasia, sound-links, ambiguous sense-links, and memory-links very like that of the dream." But all these definitions have been proposed, not of reverie, but of lyric.[1]

The traditional division of literature into epic, drama, and lyric results in a confusion of genre (shape of the whole), prosody (metrical patterns of lines and stanzas) and rhetorical mode—three quite separate concerns. As Northrop Frye complains, epic becomes a jargon term for any long poem, lyric for any short one (*Anatomy of Criticism*, p. 246); and plays are presumably scripts well marked for stage performance. Then you must make the awkward admission that all three, as genres, exist in prose as well as verse. But Plato, who originated this division, offers it as elementary rhetoric, according to whether the author has adhered to his own voice: in lyric the poet speaks in his own voice; in drama in others' voices; and in epic both in his own and in others'

---

1. The quotations are from Francis B. Gummere, A *Handbook of Poetics*, p. 40; E. S. Dallas, *Poetics: an Essay on Poetry*, p. 146; Hugh Blair, *Lectures on Rhetoric and Belles Lettres*, lect. 39; T. S. Eliot quoting Gottfried Benn, *On Poetry and Poets*, p. 110; George Lansing Raymond, *The Representative Significance of Form*, p. 339; Northrop Frye, *Anatomy of Criticism*, p. 271; and *Ibid.*, p. 272.

voices. Plato's complaint is against disguises of the voice, as
in drama, and so he censors all drama, and the dramatic parts
of Homer. Unfortunately he gives no means of determining
the author's fidelity to his own voice.

Plato's scheme nevertheless appears a satisfactory review
of the concrete rhetorical modes, except for its signal exclusion of description. Perhaps Horace's snubbing of "purple
patches" issues from a pervasive classical rejection of description from the realm of poetry. Lessing states this rejection
more fully, though without denying that description, in both
verse and prose, does exist. Beyond description, surely epic,
as defined by Plato, is the rhetorical mode of narration;
surely drama is drama; surely lyric is reverie.

The earliest lyric does not differ markedly from the most
streamlined stream of consciousness.

> Some Saian dotes on my shield, that I
> had to leave innocent behind a bush.
> Still I escaped death, myself. Let the
> shield go. I'll get another no worse.
>
> (ARCHILOCHUS 6)

Notable here is the persistence of the first person, but this
is a feature shared with first-person narration. What is additionally notable here is the rapid shifting of tenses: of five
verbs the first is a present, the second and third are in past
tense, the fourth is an imperative, and the fifth a future. In
a short space you have covered all times. The separate statements are logically or substantively connected only by apparent or unapparent mental associations. The first statement may be ambiguously considered an unattached speculation, or a response to a present visual stimulus, which recalls
the circumstances under which the shield was lost. The self-
pity implied by this statement is then balanced with a
matter for self-satisfaction, which in turn outweighs the loss
previously lamented over. And the matter is resolved with
an appropriate decision for the future.

Such progressions are widely observable outside the twentieth-century novel. In the following passage the second, not the first, person is adhered to, but without other rhetorical difference. If reverie represents the mind talking to itself, it may be defined as the mode in which the first and second person have a common referent.

> *Yesterday you was still too jocular and talked of yourself, particularly of your whoring, which was shameful; however, you continue your plan of study, and you make no great deviations. Lesser things must come by degrees. Try firmly this week never once to speak of yourself. It will be great. Go to the French church. Then home and read Xenophon and bring up journal clear today.*
>
> (Boswell in Holland, p. 51)

There can be no rhetorical objection to attributing this passage to Leopold Bloom. Harry Levin has also quoted a passage from Fanny Burney's diary which, he says, asks "demurely for comparison with the last words of Molly Bloom." (*James Joyce*, 2nd ed., p. 84)

Choral lyric, as it flowers in Greek tragedy, serves as a review of past action, a commentary on present action, and a foreshadowing of future action. Temporally, then, it is reverie, but its use of the first person is sparse and impersonal, and it usually lacks the revelatory privacy of reverie. Greek drama more clearly verges on reverie when the speaker, by madness or despair, loses touch with those present—loses touch, that is, with the special presence of drama—and lets his mind roam into all times.

> *Ah what a fire it is! It comes upon me.*
> *Apollo, Wolf-Destroyer, pity, pity . . .*
> *It is the two-foot lioness who beds*
> *Beside a wolf, the noble lion away,*
> *It is she will kill me.*
>
> (Agamemnon, ll. 1256-60)[2]

---

2. The translation is by Louis MacNeice.

Soliloquy, as in the watchman's speech at the opening of *Agamemnon*, is also in the mode of reverie.

In Elizabethan drama, not only the soliloquy but the aside are conventions for appropriating the mode of reverie to the stage.

> How say you by that? Still harping on my daughter: yet he knew me not at first; 'a said I was a fishmonger; 'a is far gone; and truly in my youth I suffered much extremity for love; very near this. I'll speak to him again.
>
> (*Hamlet*, II, ii, 88-93)

Polonius here explores all times through mental association; he responds to a stimulus and determines on an action.

Such examples as these are sometimes cited by commentators on the modern novel in order to insist on their marked differences from recent streams of consciousness. But the only real differences adduced are discontinuity and incoherence.[3] And such commentators forget Ophelia's "They say the owl was a baker's daughter," and the Bishop's "Saint Praxed at his sermon on the mount." From this point of view it might be said that the distinctiveness of modern reverie is in making madness attractive. Septimus Warren Smith is by no means the only character of modern fiction, though he may be the most obvious, that earlier ages would consider too mad to bother about. But even if discontinuity and incoherence were measurable, only stylistic, not rhetorical, differences would have been established between recent and earlier reverie. If an obscure passage communicates to anybody it can do so only by participating in recognizable linguistic patterns, and by suggesting mental associations according to information somewhere available. Even that *reductio ad absurdum* of reverie, *Finnegans Wake*, must decide whether it is discourse or gibberish. If it is discourse

---

3. See Leon Edel, *The Modern Psychological Novel*, p. 17; and Robert Humphrey, *Stream of Consciousness in the Modern Novel*, p. 32.

at all it is in the mode of reverie as defined here.

John Locke observes that all ideas come from sensation or reflection. If this is a just analysis, the transcription of the mind to the page ought to follow it; and the various effects of reverie can indeed be distinguished as responses to immediate stimuli, and as associations or reflections or anticipations of previous or present or future responses. A modern behaviorist might object that these two processes do not deserve to be so distinguished. Reflection may be nothing more than a comparison of present with past and future sensations. If the mind adds anything to what it gets from sensation it might be wondered where it gets it. Even its trick of association, however complex it becomes, may be based on previous strings of sensations that the mind has learned and now abstracted. Or a modern intuitionist might object that these two processes are not nearly complicated enough, that they divide the mystery of the mind into crude halves. Whatever its validity for psychology, however, Locke's distinction is handy for rhetoric.

All things can be thought, and in any succession, including those things and successions characteristic of the simpler rhetorical modes. Through sensation the mind records what it sees and hears and smells and tastes and touches in space before it—and that is description. Through sensation the mind records the succession of events happening in time before it—and that is narration. Through sensation the mind hears what is addressed to its person and formulates a response—and that is drama. The three modes appear here in three successive sentences, as if filtered through Steven's consciousness by reverie.

> *She was red in the face. Mr Dedalus rooted with the*
> *carvers at the end of the dish and said:*
> *—There's a tasty bit here we call the pope's nose.*
>   (A Portrait of the Artist as a Young Man, ch. 1)

If one of these modes is pursued for very long the sense of

reverie is lost, and you simply have a passage of description, narration, or drama. But even if they are generously mixed, you have only mixtures of these three modes, no clear indulgence of reverie. At most you are offered no more than what a particular person there might perceive through sensation: a single "point of view" is maintained.

The special effects of reverie are achieved only through reflection. Reflection sends the mind drifting from the present to the past and future by its private associations—the process defined above as reverie. But reflection does not exist apart from sensation, except in moments of relative passivity, for instance Molly Bloom or H. C. Earwicker in bed. From this point of view psychoanalysis, the patient's regular visit to the couch, may be defined, like sleep, as the periodic cleansing of sensation from reflection—or inspected daydreaming. The patient's ramblings, if ever they are fully purified of dramatic exchange with the analyst, if ever they occur in a space-proof, time-proof setting, are pure reverie, however inartistic, just as overheard or taped conversation is pure, or at least raw, drama. For in ideal passivity the procession of images or ideas can only be determined by association, never by fresh stimulus. "The fancy," says Coleridge, "is, indeed, no other than a mode of memory emancipated from the order of time and space. . . . But . . . the fancy must receive all its materials ready made from the law of association." (*Biographia Literaria*, ch. XIII)

Associations appear to be either sensory or substantive, or perhaps I should say, concrete or abstract. Any of the five senses may provide a concrete memory-link with another time and place. There is Proust's celebrated crumb of "madeleine" thoughtlessly dipped in tea, which recalls a whole establishment of his childhood. There is Prufrock's "perfume from a dress/ That makes me so digress." The associations of sights are, I take it, even more vivid and influential. Sounds provide associations not only between noises but between voices and words—verbal associations and puns. Substantive associations differ from these in abstracting some quality from the stimulus, or from the last thought, and adding another instance substantively similar though spatio-temporally unrelated. This results in a kind of primitive metaphorizing. Bloom says: "A corpse is meat gone bad. Well and what's cheese? Corpse of milk." (*Ulysses*, ch. 2) Such abstract associations do occur in reverie, though concrete ones are clearly more frequent and appropriate.

The associations between thoughts may be more interesting and revealing than their substance. Surely the analyst does not deserve his name if he can only repeat his patient's thoughts and cannot explain why one follows another. There is a parlor game of association which provides for an amusing communal analysis: around the room everyone must say a word, revealing his first association with the previous word. In literary reverie the reader's grasp of how images are associated may provide his keenest insight, as it does the analyst's, into human character.

The sequence of concrete rhetorical modes may in fact be said to proceed constantly closer to the mystery of character, or mind. The sequence of personal pronouns most appropriate to each mode shows an increasing intimacy of character: description—*it*; narration—*he*; drama—*you*; reverie—*I*.[4] You proceed here from outside inside the human mind, the reverse of the grammatical sequence of persons. And as this psychological rank of persons suggests, there is some general hierarchical dominance in the sequence of modes. In mixed description and narration, story dominates. In mixed narration and drama, scene dominates. In a literary genre permitting all concrete modes (the novel) reverie usually dominates. You filter all occurrences through Emma Bovary even if, out of context, many passages might seem objective.

Each successive mode also reduces the time referred to, permitting constantly closer inspection of character. De-

4. Dallas, p. 99 offers a correspondence between drama and *you*; epic and *he*; lyric and *I*.

scription normally deals with things, not persons, in space; in its neglect of time for space, it really refers indiscriminately to all times. Narration deals with persons, not things, in one unit of time, but the unit is considerably longer than the time it takes to read about it: the forty days of the *Odyssey* can be read in much less time. In drama the actors confront, not only each other but the audience, so that both their times are equal: between curtains Hamlet's time passing is equal to my reception of it. Now in reverie even less time of reference passes than in drama; there is what Beach calls an "infinite expansion of the moment." (*The Twentieth Century Novel*, p. 409) The eighteen hours of *Ulysses* may take the reader eighteen days or eighteen years to read—though of course the book did not grow so big without appropriating many other times and places to its eighteen hours. Actually, the question of how much time it might take Leopold Bloom to think what is on one page of Ulysses is a question for psychology, not rhetoric. And it might be more just to say that reverie annihilates both space and time in order to permit the character at last full freedom and scope.

But reverie labors under a serious handicap, which drama is singularly free from, and which the other modes do not share equally with reverie. Art is not life, and the description of a place does not, as Lessing complains, equal the experience of it. Still, if someone wants to know what the place is like I can try to tell him. Similarly, the experience of events is different from the narration of them, but still I can tell a story. Now when you come to drama there is a curious equation: the medium by which you experience it and the medium by which you represent it are identical—words; in fact, words may be said to be devised specifically to handle the burden of drama, human talk. This gives drama a rhetorical strength over every mode. But words are not so inadequate to description and narration, for a part of what people talk about—in dramatic exchange—is the places they see and the stories they experience. The stream of consciousness, however, only now and then occurs in words; still the medium of reverie, as of other modes, must always be words. You cannot tell your thoughts except by hypothesizing an imaginary dramatic exchange, an answer to someone's offer of a penny for your thoughts. Poor words are never so twisted as in their attempt to represent the fretful and intractable mind of man.

Movies make a convenient analogy with discourse. Even before the introduction of sounds (among others, discourse) movies could describe, narrate, dramatize, and even reflect. Perhaps it would be truer to say that simple photography (stills), like painting, could describe; movies made possible the other modes. The highest achievements of silent movies were probably in the mode of narration; the lowest (remember those awkward, fine-lettered dialogue-cards intruding on the action) in the mode of drama. Talkies, as is clear from their name, were to magnify drama. Perhaps it is a testimony to the strength of drama that even in a medium where picture may prevail over word, pictorial drama instead of dramatized picture is the result.

The technique which permitted such startling success in silent movies was montage, the connecting of disparate film-strips in order to heighten and speed up the action. As in narration, important stretches could be lingered over minutely, and unimportant stretches could be bridged by remote control. Then it became clear that the connected strips need not be chronological or any-logical in sequence, and movies verged on reverie, as several critics have noted. Montage frees movies from any spatiotemporal bondage, and may suggest the roamings of the mind by association of ideas.

Because the stream of consciousness may include either words or pictures, but is restricted to neither, it seems that montage-movies and literary reverie are in fair competition

to represent the mind. Both report the sensations and reflections of a consciousness by casting new sensations and
reflections on the consciousness of the perceiver. Their
relative success (or potential for success) might be established by a psychological experiment showing whether the
stream of consciousness is more often pictorial or verbal.
Obviously the ratio varies with perceivers. Shakespeare will
prove verbal, Michelangelo pictorial.

A new Lessing might insist that movies make a more
direct and vivid appeal to the eye than literature does to
any sense, that more mental effects are translatable to pictures than words, that movies may anyway now include
words whenever they feel like it. This argument might be
answered by saying that literature, though its appeal to the
eye is indirect, can make an indirect appeal to all the senses
through the mind, and that such indirect mental associations
are the very substance of the stream of consciousness. Or it
might be admitted that while movies are obviously superior
in representing the sensations of the mind, reverie is obviously superior in representing its reflections, which may or
may not be visual. The experience of reading a book, looking
and turning the pages, is like a dream (or a reflection) in its
exclusion of distracting sensations: a hidden voice telling
the least you must know to govern your reflections—what
Molly Bloom thinks as she lies in bed, for example. The
experience of watching a movie is more like a waking dream,
despite the darkness of the theater: a magic window showing
a constantly changing series of sensations—what Leopold
Bloom sees as he walks down the street, for example. If any
attempt at reflection occurs in movies it too must be through
sensation. But the necessity of constantly filling the window
with sights may result in irrelevance as well as vividness. Mrs.
Dalloway may have had a ludicrous hair-style without your
knowing it; Greta Garbo's you see.

Twentieth-century excitement over the mind and its operations has resulted in a certain experimentalism in both

reverie and montage, which may occasionally render them incoherent, at least by the standards of earlier or simpler modes. Almost any jumble of words or pictures is open to some interpretation, and the mind is amazingly able to find connections and progressions no matter how dense the thicket. This may, though not so often as the public suspects, leave the artist open to the charge of fraud. There is the joke about the monkey at the typewriter who eventually composes *Hamlet*. You have only to change his letter-machine to a word-machine or a syllable-machine to render his product almost recognizable reverie, a page at an arbitrary opening of *Finnegans Wake*. Plato, who naïvely assumed that an indulgence of the first person committed the author to a dignified portrayal of his own personality, and that impersonation could only occur in drama, would be startled to find that the most extravagant impersonations of the twentieth century, rhetorically the same as his lyric, deserve the description he gives of the worst abuses of drama. (*Republic* 396-7) Surely it would seem to him impossible that an author should present ravings, near those of an idiot (Benjy, for instance) in the first person, perhaps to be mistaken for his own. Recently the borderline between reverie and idiocy or gibberish may seem thin, and you may even be led to the dangerous conclusion that the most complex and worthwhile literary effects are found on the fringes of nonsense. But post-Joycean reverie will probably never venture so far, and most of the literature of reverie remains well within the limits of comprehensibility or sanity.

Perhaps it is no accident of social history that the stream of consciousness is a contemporary of the ouija board. There may seem a certain sentimentality in all the breathless tracing out there has been of Bergson's *élan vital* and James's stream of consciousness—an attempt heroically difficult, and forever mysteriously doomed to failure. "The attempt at introspective analysis," says William James, ". . . is . . . like seizing a spinning top to catch its motion, or

trying to turn up the gas quickly enough to see how the
darkness looks." (*Principles of Psychology*, vol. I, p. 244)
Perhaps, you may now think, it is not so hard as all that.
Virginia Woolf, a laborer in the stream of consciousness, was
nevertheless able to see that the mystery and the wonder
of it all might here and there be subject to humor: "the
most ordinary movement in the world," she says, "such as
sitting down at a table and pulling the inkstand toward one,
may agitate a thousand odd, disconnected fragments, now
bright, now dim, hanging and bobbing and dipping and
flaunting, like the under-linen of a family of fourteen on a
line in a gale of wind." (*Orlando*, ch. 2) The homeliness of
the image may bring you up short from Orlando's exquisite
inkstand and its meanderings.

Just as drama is reserved for the most heightened moments
of narration, so perhaps reverie should be reserved for the
most heightened moments of drama. Might it be that minds
are not always worth investigating? It is at crises that the
mind is startled by its own operations and begins tracing
them out. A whole novel in reverie may necessarily result
in the humdrum clichés of Leopold Bloom. Who would
want to find one of Tennessee Williams' characters in real
life and tape his conversations for the day? Perhaps a machine for reproducing reverie would give no better results.
At least John Locke, who started all the furor over reverie,
thought so. "Thus, methinks," he says, "every drowsy nod
shakes their doctrine who teach that the soul is always
thinking." (*Essay*, II, i, 13) Even Joyce nods.

HAD THIS VOLUME been a farce, which, unless every one's life and opinions are to be looked upon as a farce as well as mine, I see no reason to suppose—the last chapter, Sir, had finished the first act of it, and then this chapter must have set off thus.

Ptr. .r. .r. .ing—twing—twang—prut—trut—'tis a cursed bad fiddle.—Do you know whether my fiddle's in tune or not?—trut. .prut. .—They should be fifths.—'Tis wickedly strung—tr. . .a.e.i.o.u.-twang.—The bridge is a mile too high, and the sound post absolutely down,—else—trut. .prut— hark! 'tis not so bad a tone.—Diddle diddle, diddle diddle, diddle diddle, dum. [8]There is nothing in playing before good judges,—but there's a man there—no—not him with the bundle under his arm—the grave man in black—'Sdeath! not the gentleman with the sword on. [9]—Sir, I had rather play a Capriccio to Calliope herself, than draw my bow across my fiddle before that very man; and yet I'll stake my Cremona to a Jew's trump, which is the greatest musical odds that ever were laid, that I will this moment stop three hundred and fifty leagues out of tune upon my fiddle, without punishing one single nerve that belongs to him—Twaddle diddle, tweddle diddle,—twiddle diddle,—twoddle diddle,— twuddle diddle,—prut trut—krish—krash—krush. [10]—I've undone you, Sir,—but you see he's no worse,—and was Apollo to take his fiddle after me, he can make him no better.

Diddle diddle, diddle diddle, diddle diddle—hum-dum-drum.

—Your worships and your reverences love music—and God

has made you all with good ears—and some of you play de-
lightfully yourselves—trut-prut,—prut-trut.

[13]O! there is—whom I could sit and hear whole days,—
whose talents lie in making what he fiddles to be felt,—who
inspires me with his joys and hopes, and puts the most hidden springs of my heart into motion. [14]If you would borrow five guineas of me, Sir,—which is generally ten guineas
more than I have to spare—or you Messrs. Apothecary and
Tailor, want your bills paying,—that's your time.

LAURENCE STERNE, *Tristram Shandy*, V, xv

[1]RASKOLNIKOV'S THOUGHTS were in a whirl. [2]He was in
terrible exasperation.

"The worst of it is they don't disguise it; they don't care
to stand on ceremony! [4]And how if you didn't know me
at all, did you come to talk to Nikodim Fomitch about me?
So they don't care to hide that they are tracking me like a
pack of dogs. They simply spit in my face." [7]He was
shaking with rage. [8]"Come, strike me openly, don't play
with me like a cat with a mouse. It's hardly civil, Porfiry
Petrovitch, but perhaps I won't allow it! [10]I shall get up
and throw the whole truth in your ugly faces, and you'll see
how I despise you." [11]He could hardly breathe. [12]"And
what if it's only my fancy? What if I am mistaken, and
through inexperience I get angry and don't keep up my
nasty part? Perhaps it's all unintentional. All their phrases
are the usual ones, but there is something about them. . . .
[16]It all might be said, but there is something. Why did
he say bluntly, 'With her?' Why did Zametov add that I
spoke artfully? Why do they speak in that tone? Yes, the
tone. . . . Razumihin is sitting here, why does he see nothing? That innocent blockhead never does see anything!
Feverish again! Did Porfiry wink at me just now? Of course
it's nonsense! What could he wink for? Are they trying to
upset my nerves or are they teasing me? Either it's all fancy

or they know! Even Zametov is rude. . . . Is Zametov rude? Zametov has changed his mind. I foresaw he would change his mind! He is at home here, while it's my first visit. Porfiry does not consider him a visitor; sits with his back to him. They're as thick as thieves, no doubt, over me! Not a doubt they were talking about me before we came. Do they know about the flat? If only they'd make haste! When I said that I ran away to take a flat he let it pass. . . . I put that in cleverly about a flat, it may be of use afterwards. . . . Delirious, indeed . . . ha-ha-ha! He knows all about last night! He didn't know of my mother's arrival! The hag had written the date on in pencil! [45]You are wrong, you won't catch me! There are no facts . . . it's all supposition! You produce facts! [48]The flat even isn't a fact but delirium. I know what to say to them. . . . Do they know about the flat? I won't go without finding out. What did I come for? But my being angry now, maybe is a fact! Fool, how irritable I am! Perhaps that's right; to play the invalid. . . . He is feeling me. He will try to catch me. Why did I come?"

[59]All this flashed like lightning through his mind.

FYODOR DOSTOEVSKY, *Crime and Punishment*, III, v, transl. Constance Garnett

HOW MANY! All these here once walked round Dublin. Faithful departed. As you are now so once were we.

Besides how could you remember everybody? Eyes, walk, voice. Well, the voice, yes: gramophone. Have a gramophone in every grave or keep it in the house. After dinner on a Sunday. Put on poor old greatgrandfather Kraahraark! Hellohellohello amawfullyglad kraark awfullygladasseragain hellohello amarawf kopthsth. Remind you of the voice like the photograph reminds you of the face. Otherwise you couldn't remember the face after fifteen years, say. For instance who? For instance some fellow that died when I was in Wisdom Hely's.

Rtststr! A rattle of pebbles. Wait. Stop.

[20]He looked down intently into a stone crypt. Some animal. Wait. There he goes.

[24]An obese grey rat toddled along the side of the crypt, moving the pebbles. An old stager: greatgrandfather: he knows the ropes. [26]The grey alive crushed itself in under the plinth, wriggled itself in under it. Good hidingplace for treasure.

Who lives there? Are laid the remains of Robert Emery. Robert Emmet was buried here by torchlight, wasn't he? Making his rounds.

Tail gone now.

One of those chaps would make short work of a fellow. Pick the bones clean no matter who it was. Ordinary meat for them. A corpse is meat gone bad. Well and what's cheese? Corpse of milk. I read in that *Voyages in China* that the Chinese say a white man smells like a corpse. Cremation better. Priests dead against it. Devilling for the other firm. Wholesale burners and Dutch oven dealers. Time of the plague. Quicklime fever pits to eat them. Lethal chamber. Ashes to ashes. Or bury at sea. Where is that Parsee tower of silence? Eaten by birds. Earth, fire, water. Drowning they say is the pleasantest. See your whole life in a flash. But being brought back to life no. Can't bury in the air however. Out of a flying machine. Wonder does the news go about whenever a fresh one is let down. Underground communication. We learned that from them. Wouldn't be surprised. Regular square feed for them. Flies come before he's well dead. Got wind of Dignam. They wouldn't care about the smell of it. Salt white crumbling mush of corpse: smell, taste like raw white turnips.

[66]The gates glimmered in front: still open. Back to the world again. Enough of this place. Brings you a bit nearer every time. Last time I was here was Mrs Sinico's funeral.

Poor papa too. The love that kills. And even scraping up the
earth at night with a lantern like that case I read of to get at
fresh buried females or even putrefied with running grave-
sores. Give you the creeps after a bit. [75]I will appear to
you after death. You will see my ghost after death. My ghost
will haunt you after death. There is another world after
death named hell. [79]I do not like that other world she
wrote. No more do I. Plenty to see and hear and feel yet. Feel
live warm beings near you. Let them sleep in their maggoty
beds. [84]They are not going to get me this innings.
[85]Warm beds: warm fullblooded life.

JAMES JOYCE, Ulysses, II

MRS. DALLOWAY SAID she would buy the flowers herself.

For Lucy had her work cut out for her. The doors would
be taken off their hinges; Rumpelmayer's men were coming.
[4]And then, thought Clarissa Dalloway, what a morning—
fresh as if issued to children on a beach.

What a lark! What a plunge! For so it had always seemed
to her, when, with a little squeak of the hinges, which she
could hear now, she had burst open the French windows
and plunged at Bourton into the open air. [8]How fresh,
how calm, stiller than this of course, the air was in
the early morning; like the flap of a wave; the kiss
of a wave; chill and sharp and yet (for a girl of eighteen
as she then was) solemn, feeling as she did, standing there at the open window, that something awful was
about to happen; looking at the flowers, at the trees with the
smoke winding off them and the rooks rising, falling; standing and looking until Peter Walsh said, "Musing among the
vegetables?"—was that it?—"I prefer men to cauliflowers"
—was that it? He must have said it at breakfast one morning
when she had gone out on to the terrace—Peter Walsh.
[10]He would be back from India one of these days, June or
July, she forgot which, for his letters were awfully dull; it

was his sayings one remembered; his eyes, his pocket-knife,
his smile, his grumpiness and, when millions of things had
utterly vanished—how strange it was!—a few sayings like this
about cabbages.

VIRGINIA WOOLF, Mrs. Dalloway

DAMN LANDLADY, she's probably watching me go by . . . what
a nosy bastard. It was a nice apartment though; Timmy
would have been able to call it his first home if we stayed
a month longer . . . the nosy one would probably want to
know how many times we changed his diapers. Dianne and
I made our big adjustment to married life in only a few
weeks . . . only a few rooms too. Probably could have adjusted a lot faster if it wasn't for Thelma. I should have
kicked . . . well for God's sake, that's her . . . sure enough,
that's her watching me. I should stop and kick her ass just
for general principles . . . [7]Boy, I came close to doing
some fancy kicking that afternoon when we painted . . .
you're putting the paint on too thick—my walls—you'll ruin
them—oh it's too thick. Her old man must turn over in the
grave every time she opens her big mouth . . . [9]Everyone
raved over the color scheme Dianne selected. [10]Dad and
I sure celebrated when we finally got that last window
painted . . . those beer cans on the shelf reminded me the
next morning why my head was about to split . . . come
to think of it, Thelma never did bark about that night . . .
probably forgot to check the garbage cans the next day for
the dead soldiers . . . [11]Oh, that night I came home with
$9 in tickets for parking around school that week and Dianne
walks in with her $10 pay check because of being sick the
week before . . . handed me my hat tipped upside down
and said to start calling on our neighbors. [12]Thelma would
have had a nervous breakdown over the next month's rent
if she knew what we were laughing so hard for. . . . How do
you like that; first time I drive past the old homestead in a

year and a half and there she is, nose out the window. Could be a coincidence. . . . No, not that bastard. [16]Why, I knew she was going into the apartment while we were away . . . then that night when I called her up and showed her the potato chips that I had placed under the light throw rugs that morning . . . she had the nerve to say that it was the weight of the rugs that broke them; not anyone stepping on them. [17]Bet she was a big pig in her day . . . walks right in while I'm in my undershorts . . . mumbled something about seeing many guys in the raw when I threw her out. I bet all our furniture wouldn't fit in those three rooms now . . . doesn't take long for things to start accumulating. [19]Dianne had her first drink there on her birthday . . . lay down on the sofa and drank it for fear it would knock her down. [20]Thelma must have seen me come home with the bottles . . . claimed the whole neighborhood complained over the drunken brawl in our apartment. [21]I'll never forget our first little home . . . hope I never meet a bastard like her again.

ROBERT FLAHERTY

I WAS SO AFRAID she wouldn't die. They say things happen in threes and already there was Aunt Elizabeth, Aunt Caroline, and Aunt Jane. All in one winter. [4]But she finally did, and all alone too. Funny how everyone had left for just a minute. Then breathing slowly . . . faster, faster, faster. Nothing. [8]Breathing slowly . . . faster, faster, nothing . . . nothing . . . in a minute . . . it does this sometimes, called Cheyne-Stokes. Nothing. Forever nothing. Cheyne-Stokes, funny name. Reminds me of a locomotive. That's how I remember it. Cheyne rhymes with train. Stokes—like stoking a fire in a steam engine. My children will never remember real steam engines. She taught me how to put a penny on the tracks for a train to flatten. [18]Copper discs as thin and flat as her luster ware. Transluscent. Beautiful. Deli-

cate. [22]Made in England years and years ago maybe in
the England of David Copperfield. Now it's mine. She
always said I was the type to have the demitasse set. Sarah's
to have the punch set. That fits Sarah. High-spirited and
carefree like the punch. Demitasse is so correct. So prim.
How horrible, but how true. Maybe if she had decided when
I was little that I was to have the punch set, and Sarah was
to have the demitasse, Sarah would be more like me and I
would be more like her. Strange to change places with her. Six
places more to be set at the table. So much food. We shall
have to write hundreds of thank you notes. Bake things to
send back in all these dishes. Those baked beans we had
for lunch from Mrs. Butler—just a couple of cans of Grandma
Brown's Baked Beans opened and stuck in a casserole dish.
I recognize the flavor. Unopened bean cans would be better.
No dish to return. Should be more charitable. Of course
she only sent something because it's a social custom. I'll
send her back an apple kuchen. Homemade, too. Silly pride.
Social conventions. Table's ready. She starched the cloth
last time. Made on the island of Madeira. She showed me
a map when I was small. So many things she knew. Used
both the demitasse cups and the punch bowl. [53]A combined temperament. Wise. We are only parts. [56]The
whole is gone.

                                                        BARBARA MILLER

Commentary

Description occurs here in the Sterne, 8; in the Joyce,
66; in the Woolf, partly in 8 and in 10; in the Miller, 18-22.
Narration occurs in the Joyce, 20, 24, 26; in the Dostoevsky,
1-2, 7, 11, 59; in the Flaherty, 10, 11-12, 16, 17, 19-20; in the
Miller, 4-8. The quotation marks in Dostoevsky are almost an
apology for reverie; later writers mix narration and reverie
without any signals. Drama is suggested in the Sterne, 9,

10, 14; in the Joyce, 75-79; in the Dostoevsky, 4, 8-10, 45-48; in the Woolf, partly in 8; in the Flaherty, 7.

Hints of abstraction may be found in the Sterne, 13-14, on the power of music; in the Joyce, 84-85, on the assertion of life over death; in the Dostoevsky, 12-16, on the nature of fear; in the Woolf, 4, on the excitement of the day; in the Flaherty, 21, on first setting up housekeeping; in the Miller, 53-56, on the inadequacy of descendants.

Each of these examples uncovers a character peculiar enough in his succession of concrete thoughts to be considered unique. Dull reverie results from vague and trite thoughts, from typical characters in familiar situations. Each of these has some narrative basis, as does all reverie—if it is only that the thinker is asleep. Here you find thinkers fiddling between acts at a play, visiting police who are looking for a murderer, leaving a cemetery after a funeral, going out for a walk, passing a former residence, setting the table after a funeral. Nothing much happens in the course of the reverie, except that the thinker juxtaposes some past and future thoughts against his present ones. Of these the Sterne seems mainly present, the Flaherty mainly past, and the others pretty well mixed. Most of the thinkers are largely at peace, except of course for Raskolnikov, whose agitation makes his reverie the most serious one here. The Sterne, Joyce, and Flaherty seem light by comparison, and the Woolf and Miller balanced or serene.

Persuasion

Persuasion is abstract reverie, just as reverie is concrete persuasion. If reverie is what the mind privately talks itself into, persuasion is what the mind publicly talks others into. Not that persuasion need be oratorical; I mean to include within persuasion any abstract succession of thoughts, from the most casual, speculative meditations to the most formal, ratiocinative argumentations. It is public because recurrent. Reverie offers you secret, never-to-be-repeated thoughts, and in unique succession; persuasion offers you the general deliberations of mankind. It invites you to match wits, to see whether you could possibly have different, or better, thoughts, or in any other order. Reverie is for poets, who cherish their individuality; persuasion for philosophers, who reveal only those thoughts they can reasonably expect others to share, and repeat.

Like definition, persuasion has suffered rhetorically from being overdefined by logicians. The distinction between concrete and abstract thought they do not recognize, or obscure out of a desire to seem lively; and so their examples usually seem as appropriate to reverie as to persuasion. Consider whether Socrates is mortal, or (to take two recent examples) whether Jones needs quinine, or Harry is a British subject, and you will just as easily be led to think about the particularities of Socrates, Jones, or Harry, as about the generalities of mortality, malaria, or citizenship. Surely abstraction is more suited to the ideal schemes of logic than the haphazard quirks of particular cases.

The customary logical analysis of persuasion is of course the syllogism, composed of a major premise, a minor premise, and a conclusion: "All men are mortal; Socrates is a man; therefore Socrates is mortal." A passage of persuasion (or argument) is then thought to be a series of syllogisms, leading to four "modi" or four "dilemmas" in *if—then* patterns, or to a series of syllogisms called a sorites. For rhetoric a looser analysis seems more serviceable, not of premises and conclusions, but of protases (*if*-clauses) and apodoses (*then*-clauses): "If Socrates is a man, then he is mortal." But the syllogism about Socrates, if it has any interest for rhetoric, may be reduced to a single statement: "Even Socrates is mortal." As a formula for persuasion it lacks an apodosis, a thesis, a stand or claim to argue or reason about. I supply one here, which I will use as an example of persuasion: "If all men are (or if even Socrates is) mortal, then we should give up all pretensions of immortality."

As for the utility of the syllogism even to logic, Toulmin at least feels that "the apparently innocent forms used in syllogistic arguments turn out to have a hidden complexity." (*The Uses of Argument*, p. 108). And so he prefers, as a perfectly candid analysis for actual arguments, a formula using six instead of three items—datum, warrant, backing, qualifier, rebuttal, claim. This is his example: "Harry was born in Bermuda (D); so, since a man born in Bermuda will generally be a British subject (W), on account of the following statutes and other legal provisions (B), presumably (Q), unless both his parents were aliens, or he has become a naturalized American (R), Harry is a British subject (C)." (p. 105) An extension of my own abstract argument into this pattern might run as follows: "All men are mortal (D); so, since it is vain to pretend to impossibilities (W), on account of the nature of reality (B), probably (Q), unless we can settle for the immortality of our children or works (R), we should give up all pretensions of immortality (C)." Of course not all rhetorical arguments, or parts of them, can be made to yield these six items so conveniently. Some items will be omitted, submerged, or combined; others may be extended almost beyond recognition. The actual contingencies of persuasion may well require fewer or greater subtleties than these.

Logicians are not primarily committed to discourse, and so they are more interested in the relations between propositions than in the terms that signal those relationships. Recent logicians especially prefer unambiguous symbols to the connectives of discourse, which remain, however, the primary commitment of persuasion as a rhetorical mode. These connectives occur in all discourse, but they are more frequent and more appropriate in persuasion. Drama and reverie may well (as in the examples from logicians) make concrete, and dialogue certainly makes abstract, use of logical progression. But there, as in the static or temporal modes, the use of logical connectives usually indicates at least a passing persuasive interest. In the examples below I use p and a for the protasis and apodosis of my example: "If all men are mortal, then we should give up all pretensions of immortality." I will try to show how this example can be adapted to the various logical connectives. Of course these terms are also used to connect words and phrases; here I am considering them only as the connectives of statements.

There are several families of logical connectives in English. The *if p then a* formula looks like a condition, but there is not necessarily any doubt about the truth of p, which can be offered simply as a justification or proof of *a*. The "subjunctive" conditional ("If all men were immortal, we would not need to give up all pretensions of immortality") offers a condition clearly untrue. The "general" conditional ("If men die, others replace them") is a conditional relationship between recurrent actions, most appropriate to the mode of process. The relationship of *p* and *a* in my example is actually that of cause and effect, as is shown by the connectives that can replace *if* and *then*, without materially altering the logical relationship. The terms *because, since,* and *on account of* can certainly replace *if*, usually without the *then*, which is not really needed in the *if—then* pattern either; otherwise there is no change in the statement. *Because* and *since* call slightly greater attention to the cause; the *if—then* pattern would be chosen, as I have here, to show that the statement functions in a series of logical statements, or to show that the writer has a lingering doubt about the *p*. Several common replacements of *because* are reserved for slightly different cases than my example suggests, but they too could conceivably occur here: *supposing,* which is not necessarily likely; *in case,* only if; and *provided* or *on condition that,* if the following can be agreed to in advance. If these terms are called causal, the last term certainly shows that causal and conditional connectives in English are not materially different. All of these terms head the *p*, which need not come first: you may have *a if* (or *because*) *p*. One term, *for*, can also replace these, but only in this reversed sequence, *a for p; for* always adds a justification or explanation of an effect already stated.

A distinction is commonly made between causal and illative connectives (*so* and company), but the only difference is in which half of the formula they attach to. There is no difference of relationship, and the *p* could just as easily be called pre-illative, or the *a* effective. The following terms must attach to the *a*, which must also follow the *p*: *p so a*. In this pattern the following terms can replace *so: hence,*

thus, therefore, accordingly, consequently, then. The last
term (with or without *if* attached to the *p*) should make
clear that all the terms mentioned so far provide only varia-
tions of the same formula. All of the illative terms except *so*
will fit as easily (and more gracefully) within the *a* as before
it: "we should conseqently give up all pretensions of immortality" but "so we should . . ." There is very little difference of meaning between them except for *therefore*, which
has a mathematical or logical flavor, and suggests a stricter
consequence coming up than otherwise; *hence* and *thus* are
slightly old-fashioned; between the rest the choice is, as
between *because* and *since*, chiefly according to rhythm or
euphony, or personal preference.

So far my example has remained intact, the only changes
being the terms heading each half. The term *but* requires
further change; it is commonly called "adversative," meaning opposing or contradicting. Though sometimes loosely
used in place of *and*, or for slight contrasts, its real utility
in English is to signal a full contradiction, both halves
of which are nevertheless insisted on. My example shows the
opposite relationship, between two statements so harmonious
that one seems to entail he other; and so the example can
only accommodate *but* by negating one of the two halves:
"All men are mortal but we should (still) not give up all
pretensions of immortality" or "All men are immortal but
we should (still) give up all pretensions of immortality." A
logician interested only in "truth value" argues: "When one
chooses 'but' or 'although' in favor of 'and', it is only for
rhetorical purposes; 'but' is ordinarily used to emphasize a
contrast, and 'although' is used when the contrast attains
such proportions as to cause surprise." (Quine, *Elementary
Logic*, p. 18) From a rhetorical point of view, however,
the difference between affirmation and negation, as between
if p then a and *p but not-a*, certainly seems a logical difference.

Numerous terms can replace *but* in this pattern, notably

yet, still and *only*, which, like *but*, head the second half: "All men are mortal, yet we should not give up all pretensions of immortality." The term *still* will replace *but* here, but it can also be used optionally to emphasize another term of contradiction, as in the examples above. The term *only* has a slightly different suggestion than the other terms, and minimizes the point following: "it's just that . . ." The following terms can also replace *but*, and are arranged here roughly in ascending order of length and pomposity: *however, nevertheless, all the same, none the less, notwithstanding, on the contrary, on the other hand*. The merit of these terms (the only merit) is that they will fit as easily (and much more gracefully) within the statement they are attached to. In my apodosis, any of these terms will fit in any of the places marked by asterisks here: *we should* give up*all pretensions* of immortality*. Of these places, the head is the most awkward and the place most often chosen. If any term is to head a statement it might better be *but* or *yet*, which are brief and can only go there. Contrary to the traditional rule, *but* and *and*, when used as connectives between statements, can only go at the beginning of a sentence or main clause.

In my example the two contradictory statements cannot very easily be reversed. Usually they can (Consider *I stayed but he left* and *He left but I stayed*), and then the term moves, and always heads the second statement. Several other terms also signal a contradiction, but may head either action, and often come first: *though* or *although p*, (*yet* or *still*) *a*. The term *while* can replace *though*, and is reserved for concessions: "I grant you that . . ." The term *despite* (*the fact that*) will also fit here, and has a slightly more polemical flavor.

The term *or*, or the pattern *either—or*, signals alternatives, but if taken as exclusive alternatives (one or the other but not both), the two halves must, as in the "adversative" examples above, be contradictory; if *but* is used, both halves are insisted on; if *or*, only one: "Either all men are mortal, or we need not give up all pretensions of immortality" or "Either all men are immortal or we should give up all pretensions of immortality." Inclusive alternatives (one or the other or both) will not apply to my example without considerable change: "Either all men are mortal or all dogs are mortal." This inclusiveness is sometimes indicated by the legalistic "and/or" at the head or by "or both" at the tail of the second half, either of which seems too high a price to pay for a distinction rarely needed. The pattern *neither—nor* shows a double denial, say, of *p and a*, or *if p then a:* "Neither are all men mortal nor should we give up all pretensions of immortality." Unlike *either—or* it offers no alternatives, but states a consistent negation to somebody's affirmation.

The term *unless* is in English the only way to signal the relationship shown in Toulmin's formula above (rebuttal), which may be applied to my example thus: "Unless all men are mortal, we need not give up all pretensions of immortality." This is, as Quine observes (p. 18), equivalent to the *either—or* pattern, for example the one just above: "Either all men are mortal, or we need not give up all pretensions of immortality." It is chosen over the *either—or* pattern to show, as Quine says, that the half not headed by *unless* is more likely to be true than the other; the half headed by *unless* offers the only hindrance to belief in the other. The term *unless* is also equivalent to *if—not*, as here: "If all men are not mortal, then we need not give up all pretensions of immortality." This term also usually accompanies statements in future tense, or recurrent, or subjunctive, or, as here, "a modest or polite volitive," (Curme, *Syntax*, p. 397) as distinct from "imperative"—*we should give up* as distinct from *give up!*

If these logical patterns appearing in pairs of statements also appear in larger structures, you might decide that all passages of persuasion fall into three classes. The *if p then a* pattern, which is the same as the *p so a* pattern, proceeds from the more known and agreed upon to the less. Each successive apodosis would then be more surprising or original than the last, and the "thesis" would not come till the "conclusion," the end. Certainly the majority of logical connectives in English are heading in this direction, which suggests that possibly the better place for the thesis is not, according to the handbooks, at the beginning, but at the end. Must only storytellers save the best till last? Nor is it to be expected that good writers, or speakers, restrict themselves to one thesis; many writers offer theses by the paragraph, if not by the sentence. The thesis at the beginning is the pattern *a for p*, which is a successive backing up of the thesis with more and more reasons and justifications. It provides a respectable if duller structure.

The third pattern, *p but not-a* or *either p or not-a*, is suggestive of a mind fond of alternatives, not to say of contradictions or paradoxes. It is hard to imagine a very extended passage of persuasion based on this structure, for the writer would probably begin construing his successive oppositions along double lines and would soon adopt dia- rather than mono-logue. Generally a writer of persuasion will be satisfied with one or two spots of opposition, or dialogue.

According to classical precedent, the study of rhetoric is restricted to persuasion. But a full view of persuasion itself involves all the other modes, for persuasion is of all abstract modes, as reverie is of all concrete modes, the most inclusive; and passages of definition and process, as well as dialogue, will often occur, in subservience to the overall thesis. In lively essayists, concrete passages of description, narration, or drama, also occur, and sometimes, as in E. B. White, leave you in some doubt whether to call the result "essay" or "story." How do you distinguish between a thematic story and a narrative essay? I call the result persuasion, and essay, if the major progressions are the logical and abstract ones listed here.

But the mere presence of a thesis in generally abstract writing will make the result seem persuasive even if the logical structures are few. For there is some general hierarchical dominance in the sequence of abstract, as of concrete, modes. In passages of two or more modes, process will prevail over definition, dialogue over both, and persuasion over all. I differentiate the thesis from the other statements and propositions of discourse, in common with other analysts of persuasion, as a recommendation or at least an anticipation, however remote or indirect, of general action. After all, if I merely define something, I am arguing against other definitions: but I am only arguing that you alter your view of reality to suit mine. The writer of persuasion asks you to do something about it.

The sequence of modes in fact shows a temporal progression toward action. The static modes, description and definition, offer a static identity, in no time, with no action; the temporal modes, narration and process, offer a record of past actions, even if the tense of process is usually present; the mimetic modes, drama and dialogue, offer a discussion of present actions, even if the tenses shift considerably; the mental modes, reverie and persuasion, are unique in their anticipation of future actions, even if other times occur, especially the actual present in reverie, and the general or philosophical present in persuasion. Now if you also consider that the concrete modes usually have a particular or singular reference, and the abstract ones a general or plural reference, you might reduce all eight modes to two-word-formulas this way: description, *it is*; definition, *they* (things) *are*; narration, *he ran*; process, *they* (people) *would run* or *they run*; drama, *you* (singular) *come*; dialogue, *you* (general or plural) *believe*; reverie, *I will*; persuasion, *we should*. If I am right, these are the basic promptings in the modes of rhetoric, but it would be a very foolish writer who would fashion his thoughts to suit them, instead of the other way around.

All persuasion aspires toward philosophy. Universality can always be discovered in local issues, but an exclusively local interest is heading toward concretion. The more rarefied the abstractions the more arguable: my experience warrants different theses from yours. Of the branches of philosophy, the natural has now swelled out of all proportions and thinks it deserves the separate name and rank of science, but persuasion is still chiefly at the service of the other branch of philosophy, moral. Scientific discourse, except at the highest levels, becomes "technical," which means a mere exchange of second-hand information. On moral subjects (including any consideration of human affairs) opinion still competes, has to compete, with fact. When all is said and done, and even before, men still want to know how to lead their lives, and that is the subject permanently worthy of persuasion.

The disgrace of rhetoric, from the most ancient times, has been that persuasion is equally at the service of the honest altruist and of the most cunning and hypocritical sophist. Plato, mainly in the *Gorgias*, altogether dismisses rhetoric in favor of dialectic, which is the only way of uncovering the truth. In the *Protagoras* he shows his distrust of long harangues from a single speaker. Aristotle, better adjusted to his society, gives advice on how to sway the judges as well as prove your case—no matter which, so long as you win. (*Rhetoric*, II, i) Quintilian insists that the perfect orator must be a good man, but is unable to show any necessary connection between the two. (*Institutes*, II, xv, 33) Today, courses in "communications" and "semantics" are not so sure whether they serve God or Mammon, truth or advertising. Handbooks of composition, and especially of speech, recommend slanting the argument differently if you are addressing laborers or capitalists, for instance. It may be that a writer's view of things is necessarily related to his time

and place and perception, and I have argued that a writer
can only achieve originality by a sophisticated awareness of
the climate of opinion around him. But when he has discerned it he has the choice of arguing for the most neglected
opinions, which may or may not get him anywhere, or
for the most widespread opinions, which will probably land
him a job or a vote or a sale. In these of all times, then, I fear
I may be accused of naïveté for urging that a writer, or
speaker, has some obligation to offer you his best version
of the truth, and to say the same things to every audience.
I will be addressed as a laborer only if the speaker is a capi-
talist, and vice versa. In fact, I will not be condescended to at
all. The keen writer will put himself through a mental dialogue at least before he sets out to write a single-voiced
persuasion. He will write in constant awareness of the best
objections to his views. Persuasion may be defined as dialogue in one voice, but the second voice is suggested if
submerged. The best audience, whatever the time or
place or occasion, is Socrates—if he should happen to
differ with you. Though I am not Socrates, I will be
addressed as Socrates or turn elsewhere. The honest writer
will prefer a moral victory to a trivial one. An argument
that satisfies all objectors, real and hypothetical, present and
absent, will from even the most objective, or sophistical,
viewpoint, be stronger than one which has merely swayed
whatever groundlings turned up for the talk.

No one can measure the sincerity of a writer or speaker,
but you can usually decide whether the possible objections
have been answered. You can also decide whether he has
made any effort to tell you what you need to know, or only
what he can be sure you already believe. The strongest
argument is both original and unanswerable. But if a writer
with an unsophisticated thesis is able to answer the most
sophisticated objections to it he satisfies the criterion of
originality as well as the writer with a daring thesis. It is not

to be expected anyway that originality will lead a writer out of this world. "Originality," says Northrop Frye, "returns to the origins of literature, as radicalism returns to its roots." (*Anatomy of Criticism*, pp. 97-8) The mark of an original writer, persuasive and otherwise, will be his discovery of a better common basis for mankind than anyone else. If his society heeds him, it will be doing itself the favor of closing in on elusive truth.

LET US SPEND ONE DAY as deliberately as Nature, and not be thrown off the track by every nutshell and mosquito's wing that falls on the rails. [2]Let us rise early and fast, or break fast, gently and without perturbation; let company come and let company go, let the bells ring and the children cry,— determined to make a day of it. Why should we knock under and go with the stream? Let us not be upset and overwhelmed in that terrible rapid and whirlpool called a dinner, situated in the meridian shallows. Weather this danger and you are safe, for the rest of the way is down hill. With unrelaxed nerves, with morning vigor, sail by it, looking another way, tied to the mast like Ulysses. If the engine whistles, let it whistle till it is hoarse for its pains. If the bell rings, why should we run? We will consider what kind of music they are like. [10]Let us settle ourselves, and work and wedge our feet downward through the mud and slush of opinion, and prejudice, and tradition, and delusion, and appearance, that alluvion which covers the globe, through Paris and London, through New York and Boston and Concord, through Church and State, through poetry and philosophy and religion, till we come to a hard bottom and rocks in place, which we can call *reality*, and say, This is, and no mistake; and then begin, having a *point d'appui*, below freshet and frost and fire, a place where you might found a wall or a state, or set a lamp-post safely, or perhaps a gauge, not a Nilometer, but a Realometer, that future ages might know how deep a freshet of shams and appearances had gathered from time to time. [11]If you stand right fronting and face to face to a fact, you will see the sun glimmer on both its surfaces, as if it were a cimeter, and feel its sweet edge dividing you through the heart and marrow, and so you will happily conclude your mortal career. Be it life or death, we crave only reality. [13]If we are really dying, let us hear the rattle in our throats and feel cold in the extremities; if we are alive, let us go about our business.

[14]Time is but the stream I go a-fishing in. I drink at it; but while I drink I see the sandy bottom and detect how shallow it is. Its thin current slides away, but eternity remains. I would drink deeper; fish in the sky, whose bottom is pebbly with stars. I cannot count one. I know not the first letter of the alphabet. I have always been regretting that I was not as wise as the day I was born. The intellect is a cleaver; it discerns and rifts its way into the secret of things. I do not wish to be any more busy with my hands than is necessary. [23]My head is hands and feet. I feel all my best faculties concentrated in it. [25]My instinct tells me that my head is an organ for burrowing, as some creatures use their snout and fore paws, and with it I would mine and burrow my way through these hills. I think that the richest vein is somewhere hereabouts; so by the diving-rod and thin rising vapors I judge; and here I will begin to mine.

HENRY DAVID THOREAU, *Walden*, 2

[1]IT GOES WITHOUT SAYING that you will not write a good novel unless you possess the sense of reality; but it will be difficult to give you a recipe for calling that sense into being. [2]Humanity is immense, and reality has a myriad forms; the most one can affirm is that some of the flowers of fiction have the odour of it, and others have not; as for telling you in advance how your nosegay should be composed, that is another affair. [3] It is equally excellent and inconclusive to say that one must write from experience; to our suppo-sitious aspirant such a declaration might savour of mockery. [4]What kind of experience is intended, and where does it

begin and end? [5]Experience is never limited, and it is never complete; it is an immense sensibility, a kind of huge spider-web of the finest silken threads suspended in the chamber of consciousness, and catching every air-borne particle in its tissue. [6]It is the very atmosphere of the mind; and when the mind is imaginative—much more when it happens to be that of a man of genius—it takes to itself the faintest hints of life, it converts the very pulses of the air into revelations. [7]The young lady living in a village has only to be a damsel upon whom nothing is lost to make it quite unfair (as it seems to me) to declare to her that she shall have nothing to say about the military. [8]Greater miracles have been seen than that, imagination assisting, she should speak the truth about some of these gentlemen. [9]I remember an English novelist, a woman of genius, telling me that she was much commended for the impression she had managed to give in one of her tales of the nature and way of life of the French Protestant youth. She had been asked where she learned so much about this recondite being, she had been congratulated on her peculiar opportunities. These opportunities consisted in her having once, in Paris, as she ascended a staircase, passed an open door where, in the household of a pasteur, some of the young Protestants were seated at table round a finished meal. The glimpse made a picture; it lasted only a moment, but that moment was experience. She had got her direct personal impression, and she turned out her type. [14]She knew what youth was, and what Protestantism; she also had the advantage of having seen what it was to be French, so that she converted these ideas into a concrete image and produced a reality. [15]Above all, however, she was blessed with the faculty which, when you give it an inch takes an ell, and which for the artist is a much greater source of strength than any accident of residence or of place in the social scale. [16]The power to guess the unseen from the seen, to trace the implication of things, to judge the whole piece by the pattern, the condition of feeling life in general so completely that you are well on your way to knowing any particular corner of it—this cluster of gifts may almost be said to constitute experience, and they occur in country and in town, and in the most differing stages of education. [17]If experience consists of impressions, it may be said that impressions *are* experience, just as (have we not seen it?) they are the very air we breathe. Therefore, if I should certainly say to a novice, "Write from experience and experience only," I should feel that this was rather a tantalising monition if I were not careful immediately to add, "Try to be one of the people on whom nothing is lost!"

HENRY JAMES, "The Art of Fiction"

INJUSTICE IS DONE to the old classical rules of artistic criticism, because we do not treat them as artistic criticism. We first turn them into police regulations, and then complain of them for being so. [3]But I suspect, with the submission proper to ignorance, that the art canons of Aristotle and others were much more generally artistic, in the sense of atmospheric. We allow a romantic critic to be as dogmatic as Ruskin, and still feel that he is not really being so despotic as Boileau. [5]If a modern, like Maeterlinck, says that all drama is in an open door at the end of an empty passage, we do not take it literally, like a notice requiring an extra exit in case of fire. [6]But if an ancient, like Horace, says that all drama demands a closed door, which shall hide Medea while she murders her children, then we do receive it as something rigid and formal, like the order to close the shutters on air-raid nights. Now how far the classical critics took their rules absolutely I do not know. But I am substantially sure that there is a true instinct at the back of them, whatever exceptions be allowed at the edges. [9]The unities of time and place, that is the idea of keeping figures and events within the frame of a few hours or a few yards, is naturally derided

as a specially artificial affront to the intellect. [10]But I am
sure it is an especially true suggestion to the imagination. It
is exactly in the artistic atmosphere, where rules and reasons
are so hard to define, that this unification would be most
easy to defend. This limitation to a few scenes and actors
really has something in it that pleases the imagination and
not the reason. [13]There are instances in which it may be
broken boldly; there are types of art to which it does not
apply at all. [14]But wherever it can be satisfied, something
not superficial but rather subconscious is satisfied. Something
revisits us that is the strange soul of single places; the shadow
of haunting ghosts or of household gods. Like all such things,
it is indescribable when it is successful; it is easier to describe
the disregard of it as unsuccessful. Thus Stevenson's master-
piece, *The Master of Ballantræ*, always seems to me to fall
into two parts, the finer which revolves round Durisdeer and
the inferior which rambles through India and America. The
slender and sinister figure in black, standing on the shore or
vanishing from the shrubbery, does really seem to have come
from the ends of the earth. In the chapters of travel he only
serves to show that, for a boy's adventure tale, a good villain
makes a bad hero. And even about Hamlet I am so heretical
as to be almost classical; I doubt whether the exile in England does not rather dwarf than dignify the prisoner of Den-
mark. I am not sure that he got anything out of the pirates
he could not have got out of the players. And I am very sure
indeed that this figure in black, like the other, produces a
true though intangible effect of tragedy when, and because,
we see him against the great grey background of the house
of his fathers. In a word it is what Mr. J. B. Yeats, the poet's
stimulating parent, calls in his excellent book of essays 'the
drama of the home'. [24]The drama is domestic, and is dramatic because it is domestic.

[25]We might say that superior literature is centripetal,
while inferior literature is centrifugal. [26]But oddly enough,
the same truth may be found by studying inferior as well as

superior literature. What is true of a Shakespearean play is equally true of a shilling shocker. The shocker is at its worst when it wanders, and escapes through new scenes and new characters. The shocker is at its best when it shocks by something familiar; a figure or fact which is already known though not understood. A good detective story also can keep the classic unities; or otherwise play the game. I for one devour detective stories; I am delighted when the dagger of the curate is found to be the final clue to the death of the vicar. But there is a point of honour for the author; he may conceal the curate's crime, but he must not conceal the curate. [33]I feel I am cheated when the last chapter hints for the first time that the vicar had a curate. [34]I am annoyed when a curate, who is a total stranger to me, is produced from a cupboard or a box in a style at once abrupt and belated. [35]I am annoyed most of all when the new curate is only the tool of a terrible secret society ramifying from Moscow or Thibet. These cosmopolitan complications are the dull and not the dramatic element in the ingenious tales of Mr. Oppenheim or Mr. Le Queux. They entirely spoil the fine domesticity of a good murder. It is unsportsmanlike to call spies from the ends of the earth, as it is to call spirits from the vasty deep, in a story that does not imply them from the start. [39]And this because the supply is infinite; and the infinite, as Coventry Patmore well said, is generally alien to art. Everybody knows that the universe contains enough spies or enough spectres to kill the most healthy and vigorous vicar. [41]The drama of detection is in discovering how he can be killed decently and economically, within the classic unities of time and place.

G. K. CHESTERTON, "A Defence of Dramatic Unities"

[1]IN SCHOOLS AND COLLEGES, in these audio-visual days, doubt has been raised as to the future of reading—whether the

printed word is on its last legs. One college president has re-marked that in fifty years "only five per cent of the people will be reading." For this, of course, one must be prepared. But how prepare? [5]To us it would seem that even if only one person out of a hundred and fifty million should con-tinue as a *reader*, he would be the one worth saving, the nucleus around which to found a university. We think this not impossible person, this Last Reader, might very well stand in the same relation to the community as the queen bee to the colony of bees, and the others would quite properly dedicate themselves wholly to his welfare, serving special food and building special accomodations. [7]From his nup-tial, or intellectual, flight would come the new race of men, linked perfectly with the long past by the unbroken chain of the intellect, to carry on the community. But it is more likely that our modern hive of bees, substituting a coaxial cable for spinal fluid, will try to perpetuate the race through audio-visual devices, which ask no discipline of the mind and which are already giving the room the languor of an opium parlor.

[9]Reading is the work of the alert mind, is demanding, and under ideal conditions produces finally a sort of ecstasy. [10]As in the sexual experience, there are never more than two persons present in the act of reading—the writer, who is the impregnator, and the reader, who is the respondent. This gives the experience of reading a sublimity and power unequalled by any other form of communication. It would be just as well, we think, if educators clung to this great phenomenon and did not get sidetracked, for although books and reading may at times have played too large a part in the educational process, that is not what is happening today. Indeed, there is very little true reading, and not nearly as much writing as one would suppose from the towering piles of pulpwood in the dooryards of our paper mills. Readers and writers are scarce, as are publishers and reporters. [15]The reports we get nowadays are those of men who have not gone

to the scene of the accident, which is always farther inside
one's own head than it is convenient to penetrate without
galoshes.

                    E. B. WHITE, "The Future of Reading"

[1]A UNIVERSITY EXISTS to impart truth not only to its students, but to the world. It has achieved only half its purpose
if its graduates fail to influence the world with the right
thinking they have learned. Intercollegiate debating, even
more than most academic courses, aids in educating the
world as well as the individual.

Aristotle held that truth is naturally superior to falsehood,
and that if it does not prevail the fault must lie with its
advocates. If the university's academic program has been
successful, its graduates will have the truth; debating insures
that they will be able to change the world with it. This is
the best justification for debating. [7]Those who advocate it
for the sake of benefits to the individual, such as self-
assurance in personal life or persuasiveness in business, risk
putting it on the level of dancing lessons as a self-improve-
ment project.

Aside from the self-evident value of training in speech,
debating teaches the student to see all sides of an issue, to
avoid hasty conclusions, and to counter false reasoning. He
may at different times argue both sides of the same question, an opportunity that is not usual in either the classroom
or in conversation, without falling into the sin of seeking to
persuade others to do what is wrong. [10]Debating is a
game, in which it is understood by all that the speaker does
not necessarily believe what he says personally or advocate
that his listeners act on it.

Topics are selected so as to admit of valid arguments both
for the affirmative and the negative. In the past few years
debators have argued such issues as whether the nation
should adopt a system of compulsory health insurance,

whether labor organizations should come under anti-trust laws, or whether the free nations of the world should establish a free trade organization. Perhaps there is a right and wrong answer to each of these questions, but the answer changes with each debate. Truth does not change, but the question in effect changes depending on the definitions used by each team. If my opponent means by "labor organizations" every labor union, regardless of size, I may believe that labor organizations should not be subject to certain laws; if he means only large national unions, I may agree with him. Similarly, varying definitions of other terms may change the answer. Besides this change, the means of achieving the desired action changes with each debate. The question then becomes not a choice between two directly opposed alternatives, one right and one wrong, but among several possibilities, depending on the lines of attack and defense chosen by each team. [19]In debating, as in chess, every game is a new game; every question is a new question.

It is clearly immoral to persuade others to do what is wrong. If debating teaches such persuasion it has no place in a university. [22]A distinction must be drawn between convincing and persuading, however. In convincing, one appeals to the intellect to show that his reasoning is correct, but seeks no action. You may convince me by mathematical proofs that in a given problem x equals two, but I will not be tempted to do much about it. Persuading involves the will as well as the intellect. [26]A clever advertising man may persuade me to buy his product without showing me any real proof of its superiority.

The debator wins or loses his case mostly through conviction. [28]At the end of a debate I may be forced to admit that I cannot answer your arguments at the moment. I may feel like a man who has been given a physical beating by a stronger opponent. [30]But I will not have changed my belief, nor will I act on your proposal, for conviction does not always lead to persuasion. A college debate does not persuade others to do wrong, simply because the opposition is not ready to be persuaded, and seldom is there any more audience than the opposition.

[32]Competitive debating is an intellectual exercise designed to strengthen the reasoning faculty. Debators do not seek to persuade in a particular case; they seek to learn how to convince or persuade in any discussion. By knowing this, they will later be able to advance arguments for the truths they have learned through their other studies.

[35]What of the objection that oratorical skill may be used to advocate evil, even to trick others? [36]Surely it might be, but this is not sufficient reason for discouraging such skill. Any ability may be misused by an evil man; one task of the university is to produce graduates who are not evil men, but good men. The debating coach has a strong obligation to warn against the misuse of the skills he teaches, an obligation to insure that these skills will be used for the sake of the good and the true, but the obligation is not his alone. This study which teaches the art of discovering the possible means of conviction and persuasion cannot be expected to teach, all by itself, the proper use of such skill. Moral training is the task of the entire university, all of the disciplines working together. If all have done their job, the product will be a good man, able to use for good ends the skills given him by every particular study.

RICHARD KNOX

[1]WHY WOULD YOU WANT to be a writer? [2]Even though your experiences and observations are crammed with material for good stories, you don't have to tell them. That you are aware of them, that you remember them could be enough to satisfy you. [4]Good writing is honest and it's hard to write honestly. Furthermore, it may hurt to have others read what you have written honestly. Human nature is much more likely to incline you to avoid, rather than seek out,

what is hard and hurtful. [7]Nowhere else do people better display their ingenuity than in the knickknacks and novelties they devise to hide the unsightly or anesthetize the wounds to their sensitive nature. [8]A housewife who is tired of hard work conceals the clutter and dust by pulling venetian blinds. [9]A person who fears the pain of a dentist's drill escapes it by having novocaine. Why should you expose yourself to the hard work and pain good writing involves when you could avoid both by simply refusing to write at all?

[11]Perhaps you have done a little writing and the excitement of it has muffled its frustration. There are, however, easier and quicker ways to find excitement: go climb a mountain or tailgate a car. The mountain has a summit, no matter how distant it may be. [14]And if your tailgating should prove terminal, it's all over quickly. But the effort to write honestly is an endless search to give form to the specks of sorrow and serenity that flicker through your life. [16]They may seem clear and firm inside you, but they become as elusive as shadows when you try to share them with another. Because you cherish them, you want to set them down in all the fullness of what they mean to you. [18]But with every word you write, they become increasingly fragile in the light of the chance that they may not even matter to someone else.

If you insist upon trying to record them, you will find the writing process itself hard and the results painful. [20]You must restrain your impatience as you put together the words you hope will make your reader see what you see, feel what you feel. [21]You must stifle your vanity and cross out the embellishments you've hit upon which say something gracefully at the price of distorting the truth. Often what you see will be as unflattering to your ego as a passport picture. Moreover, you know that you would not recognize the clumsiness and meanness you see in others if they did not already exist in you. The only solace you have for the resentment you arouse in others is the knowledge that you do not wish to judge or condemn them any more than you would yourself. You are already lonely enough and you would not, if you could, sever yourself from the bond between them and you.

But you can never be sure that you will make others see what you see. [27]If you show them something cruel, they may see it as amusing; or they may insist the sordidness is only in you. [28]If you show them a moment of compassion or someone noble and pure, they may yawn or scoff. [29]You long to make them feel the wetness of your tears, but they may remain unmoved. Perhaps it is your fault that they have not understood or cared, but it hurts to find them indifferent to what is poignant to you.

[31]Why would you want to be a writer? Maybe for you there is no other choice. [33]If you feel smothered by closed blinds, if your pain is beyond the reach of novocaine, then all you can do is strain and hurt. You must find words to tell of pain you've felt or caused others to feel. You must find words to show love and kindness so precious that even their memory forever sustains you. Pain, love, aspiration—through them you know what is real in life. And what is real to you you must find a way to make real to another. Writing may be that way.

CAROL MC CORMICK

Commentary

Definition occurs in the Thoreau, 14, 23, 25; in the James, 2, 5-6, 15, 16-17; in the Chesterton, 3, 24, 39, 41; in the White, 9-10, 15; in the Knox, 1, 10, 19, 22-26, 32; in the McCormick, 4. Process is suggested in the Thoreau, 2, 10, 11, 13; in the Chesterton, 33, 34, 35; in the White, 7; in the Knox, 28-30; in the McCormick, 7, 8, 9, 16-18, 20-21, 27, 28, 29. Dialogue is suggested in the James, 1, 3-4, 7-8; in the Chesterton, 5-6, 9-10, 13-14, 25-26; in the White, 1-5; in the Knox, 7, 35-36; in the McCormick, 1-2, 11-14, 31-33.

Of the concrete modes, narration occurs in the James, 9-14. Reverie is remarkably suggested in the Thoreau, by the switch to first person singular from 14 on.

In each of these examples the writer commits himself to a striking and probably unpopular opinion, but shows a sophisticated awareness of the possible objections to his opinion. Like all interesting persuasion, then, these could be considered meta-dialogues. The opinions finally defeated here are: there are too many intrusions and obstacles to a simple and clear view of reality; writers should utilize their own experience; the unities of time and place are artificial and need not be observed; reading will soon be given up; college debating serves no worthwhile academic object; writing is too hard and unrewarding. If you begin reading these selections holding these opinions you will somehow be answered. And you will also come away with a contrary opinion, a thesis or recommendation of action: see reality, train your perception, observe the unities, read, encourage debating, and write. The skill of the writers is shown in manipulating ideas that you will accept in such a way as to persuade you of an unlikely opinion.

Rhetorical Dominance

If Christ had said, "Why hath one been forsaken?" he would have lost the special force of the second and first persons. Or if he had said, "Blessed are the meek: for they inherited the earth," he would have lost the special force of the future tense. Both would be lapses in rhetorical dominance. Now some statements, possibly these, are strong enough to weather any such lapse; most aren't.

By orders of rhetoric, temporal discourse is dominant over static, mimetic over temporal, and mental over mimetic. By modes of rhetoric, in prevailingly concrete discourse, narration is dominant over description, drama over narration, and reverie over drama; in prevailingly abstract discourse, process is dominant over definition, dialogue over process, and persuasion over dialogue. But because division into orders or modes is chiefly determined by the means of procedure from sentence to sentence, you cannot establish the mode unless you have two or more consecutive sentences in the same order or mode. What is to be said of discourse so mixed and compressed (say poetry) that it shifts faster than that? Willynilly the discussion must be limited to the single sentence.

Dominance turns out to be simply a matter of how directly the reader's sympathy can be commanded. For example, in the syntax of a single sentence, the subject dominates the object, and the object the object of the preposition: the nominative case touches you more directly than the accusative or dative. Even if a minor issue or character is placed in the position of subject, it will temporarily dominate. Then, the nearby (*the, this, now, here*) dominates the faraway (*a, that, then, there*). These two appeals may conflict and nearly balance in a sentence like "A (or that) cat caught the (or this) bird."

The harder and more significant area for dominance is the morphology of subjects and predicates, and in order to schematize the distinctions needed for rhetoric I must distort English grammar somewhat. Consider four persons, in both singular and plural: *it—they* (things); *he* or *she—they* (persons); *you* (singular)—*you* (plural); *I—we*. Now consider four tenses in two aspects, single and recurrent or "perfective" and "imperfective": aorist or static (in English, present); past; present, an actual present (in English, often "present progressive"); future. In these four scales, two of persons or subjects, and two of tenses or predicates, each term is dominant over its predecessor. That is (to put them in their customary company), fourth-person aorist statements (*it is* or *they are*) are lowest on the scale of dominance; next, third-person past statements (*he ran* or *they would run*); next, second-person present statements (*you come* or *you believe*); finally, first-person future statements (*I will* or *we should*). In any given passage, the persons and tenses highest on these scales will be dominant.

Take this prevailingly concrete passage:

> How careful was I, when I took my way,
> Each trifle under truest bars to thrust,
> That to my use it might unused stay
> From hands of falsehood, in sure wards of trust!

But thou, to whom my jewels trifles are,
Most worthy comfort, now my greatest grief,
Thou, best of dearest and mine only care,
Art left the prey of every vulgar thief.
Thee have I not lock'd up in any chest,
Save where thou art not, though I feel thou art,
Within the gentle closure of my breast,
From whence at pleasure thou mayst come and part;
  And even thence thou wilt be stolen, I fear,
  For truth proves thievish for a prize so dear.   (48)

The first quatrain is past-tense (though not third-person) narration, the second is present-tense second-person drama, the third, with its mixture of second and first persons, is mixed drama and reverie, and the couplet more purely future-tense first-person reverie. This poem, like most of Shakespeare's sonnets, qualifies as "lyric" though only line 13 is unmistakably lyric, because that line is dominant over all other lines in other modes. Actually the narrative of the first quatrain is not really a story, but a little allegory, of negative significance to the thinker—"This is how I have not treated you." And the drama of the second quatrain is not really spoken, but simply a dramatic reflection of the speaker, so at least you must assume by the ending. The first two quatrains by themselves might qualify as drama, for the second quatrain would be dominant over the first; only the first quatrain by itself could pass as narration. The last line is abstract, but it is no higher than process (the second order), and so it too remains subservient to line 13.

Take this prevailingly abstract passage:

The expense of spirit in a waste of shame
Is lust in action; and till action lust
Is perjur'd, murtherous, bloody, full of blame,
Savage, extreme, rude, cruel, not to trust,
Enjoy'd no sooner but despised straight,
Past reason hunted, and no sooner had

> Past reason hated, as a swallow'd bait
> On purpose laid to make the taker mad;
> Mad in pursuit and in possession so;
> Had, having, and in quest to have, extreme;
> A bliss in proof and, prov'd, a very woe;
> Before, a joy propos'd; behind, a dream.
>> All this the world well knows; yet none knows well
>> To shun the heaven that leads men to this hell. (129)

The first sentence is a static definition. The rest of the poem to the couplet is in the mode of process; temporal progression is variously asserted: "till" (2), "no sooner . . . straight" (5), "no sooner" (6), "in pursuit . . . in possession" (9), "in proof . . . prov'd" (11), "before . . . behind" (12). Line 13, with its dialectic antagonism, is indicative of dialogue. The last line is anticipatory or recommendatory, and so remotely future, or persuasive, and dominant. The couplet makes the rest of the poem subservient to the thesis, If possible, shun lust—though the majority of the poem is in the mode of process. This sonnet is concrete only in the analogy "as a swallow'd bait /On purpose laid to make the taker mad," which is no higher than narration (the second order), and so it too remains subservient to line 14.

In these sonnets dominance is easily determined; both are fairly stable in the scale of abstraction, and the order of dominance is climactic. Other sonnets are harder:

> Were 't aught to me I bore the canopy,
> With my extern the outward honouring,
> Or laid great bases for eternity,
> Which prove more short than waste or ruining?
> Have I not seen dwellers on form and favour
> Lose all, and more, by paying too much rent,
> For compound sweet foregoing simple savour,
> Pitiful thrivers, in their gazing spent?
> No, let me be obsequious in thy heart,
> And take thou my oblation, poor but free,

> Which is not mix'd with seconds, knows no art,
> But mutual render, only me for thee.
>   Hence, thou suborn'd informer! a true soul
>   When most impeach'd stands least in thy control.   (125)

This sonnet is most lyric in its dominant first quatrain, which is hypothetical, "Were 't aught" equivalent to "Would it have meant much" or "Would it have been worth it after all." The third quatrain and the couplet are dramatic, but toward two different second persons (a strange occurrence in such a short poem), the loved one and the informer. The second quatrain is really abstract, third-person plural process, for the "Have I not seen" is equivalent to "Are there not"; because it is only at the second order of rhetoric this quatrain remains subservient to the lyric quatrain. A reading of the poem by rhetorical dominance might prefer this order: quatrain 2, couplet, quatrain 3, quatrain 1, despite the question and answer relationship of quatrains 1 and 3. This order clarifies the overall relationships in the poem. The speaker cries out against the informer who has "impeach'd" him with the charge of being a "dweller on form and favour." Instead, he (a true soul) wishes to be internally obsequious, for external observances (bearing the canopy) prove too short.

Another hard sonnet is this one:

> That thou are blam'd shall not be thy defect,   1
> For slander's mark was ever yet the fair;   2
> The ornament of beauty is suspect,   3
> A crow that flies in heaven's sweetest air.   4
> So thou be good, slander doth but approve   5
> Thy worth the greater, being woo'd of time;   6
> For canker vice the sweetest buds doth love,   7
> And thou present'st a pure unstained prime.   8
> Thou hast pass'd by the ambush of young days,   9
> Either not assail'd or victor being charg'd,   10
> Yet this thy praise cannot be so thy praise   11
> To tie up envy evermore enlarg'd;   12

> If some suspect of ill mask'd not thy show,   13
> Then thou alone kingdoms of hearts shouldst
>   owe.   14 (70)

This sonnet seems to be mainly concrete, in the second person, and so dramatic. But line 1 is future, lines 13 and 14
("If . . . Then") and also 5 and 6 ("So thou be good") and 11
and 12 are hypothetical, and so mental reverie or "lyric."
Line 8 is present, and so is clearly dramatic. Lines 9 and 10
are in "present perfect" and so have a narrative quality as
compared with the rest. Lines 2 and 3 are abstract, static definitions—of "the fair," for "was ever yet" amounts to "is";
and of "suspect" (suspicion), "ornament" ironic or paradoxical. Lines 4 and 7 are concretely synonymous, 4 with 3 and
7 with 2; the four lines 2, 3, 4, 7 form an abstract realm, but
are no higher than the first or second orders of rhetoric, and
so remain subservient to the concrete realm of the poem. A
reading of the poem by rhetorical dominance might prefer
this order of lines, with a slight scrambling of logical connectives; 2 (dropping "For"), 7, 3, 4, 9, 10, 11, 12, 5 (adding
"but" or "however"), 6, 1 (adding "then" or "therefore"),
13, 14. Of course I do not recommend this as a better order
than Shakespeare's, but as one which might be helpful to a
reader having a hard time of it, as some editors have had with
this sonnet.

Consider the following two improbable quatrains, one concrete and one abstract (composed of first lines from different
sonnets), which make rhetorical dominance successively explicit, if you will overlook the logical incoherence between
the lines. (Some readers may even find them coherent.)

> My mistress' eyes are nothing like the sun.   (130)
> Cupid laid by his brand and fell asleep.   (153)
> Take all my loves, my love, yea, take them all!   (40)
> My glass shall not persuade me I am old.   (22)
> Love is too young to know what conscience is,   (151)
> Like as the waves make towards the pebbled shore.   (60)

No, Time, thou shalt not boast that I do change!   (123)
'Tis better to be vile than vile esteemed.   (121)

I have taken the liberty of making the abstract quatrain climactic, though in this hypothetical example, since both the concrete and abstract realms attain the fourth order (reverie and persuasion), lines 4 and 8 are equally dominant. Actually in Shakespeare's sonnets persuasion is rarely found, whereas reverie is common; and so the sonnets as a whole have a lyric rather than argumentative quality. But by an actual count the purely dramatic lines might surpass the lyric. Drop the lines of reverie from the sonnets and the dramatic lines would be dominant over first- and second-order lines. You would have little letters—as a few of the sonnets actually purport to be— and letters are, at least so far as they involve address, mostly dramatic monologues. It takes only a few lines of reverie here and there (often only the couplets are) to make lyrics.

Each order of rhetoric aspires to be dominated by its superior. In the concrete realm, description has been urged to become narration by pedagogues from Horace to Lessing; narration is often urged toward greater representation or dramatization, especially in its climaxes; and drama often becomes, in its highest moments, rhapsodic or persuasive. Compare Hamlet's "How all occasions do inform against me," (IV, iv, 32) with Dr. Stockmann's "I propose to raise a revolution against the lie that the majority has the monopoly of the truth." (*An Enemy of the People,* Act IV). In the abstract realm, definition aspires toward analysis or process, process begins to entertain dialectic reservations, and dialogue reaches a persuasive climax in its favored speaker. Reverie and persuasion are the two strongest modes, ablest to hold their own, for no other mode can dominate them; they can also most easily accommodate other lower modes without losing their force.

Lapses in rhetorical dominance take place when the matter is at odds with the mode. In the first order, description and definition often legitimately attain narration and process, but if the matter remains static while the mode becomes temporal, you get a feeble story, a coy and elegant variation, as in Pope's descriptive line "the bright mountains prop th' incumbent sky."

In the second order, narration and process often legitimately attain drama or dialogue, but sometimes the writer feels a necessity to become mimetic whether the matter warrants it or not. The result is dull expository or narrative dialogue—"You remember what happened yesterday, John . . ." Shifts from the third to the second person (a mimetic mode) should not occur unless the matter becomes clearly mimetic. Similarly, shifts from the third to the first person (a mental mode) should not occur unless the matter becomes clearly mental. Scrupulous James rejected the first person from his longer narratives altogether as "foredoomed to looseness . . . never much my affair," for then the hero has "the double privilege of subject and object"—lyric subject and narrative object. He characterizes first-person narration as "the terrible *fluidity* of self-revelation" toward "our straight and credulous gape" (Preface to *The Ambassadors*)—which is as appropriate to reverie as it is inappropriate to narration. Actually, of course, all narration is third-person, though it may also include a first person. What James calls "autobiography" is narration in which statements of the type "I hit him" surpass those of the types "He hit me" (the "narrator" in a minor observational position) or "He hit him." It is almost that James feels the protagonist wins his dominance too easily if he is the first person: when all persons are third he must win his dominance by legitimate sportsmanship. The "looseness" that James complains of in first-person narration is actually a characteristic of all narration, and so works predominantly narrative may reach great lengths; all the longest literary works are narrative.

In the third order, drama and dialogue often legitimately attain reverie and persuasion, but the author may feel the necessity for a revelation or uplift when he lacks the matter for one, resulting in a lapse, in mental discourse that should have remained static or temporal or mimetic—when, for example, a soliloquy or an aside is used to convey information as easily given through regular drama. In the other direction, toward the lower orders, the Elizabethan stage called for some description, and a dialogue may call for a definition here and there, but if mimetic discourse is used for description or definition for very long you may wonder why the speakers were gathered together. Similarly, all plays call for some expository narration, and all dialogue for some expository process, but if it is overdone or baldly obvious, a lapse occurs. You can't justify staying in the mimetic order very long unless the matter is concretely or abstractly conflicting. Hugh Blair's complaint against modern dialogues—that there is no real conflict in them and the author might better have written in one voice—applies as well to some plays or some passages of plays. This conflict makes the mimetic order tighter than the temporal, and so there is a better reason than the patience of the audience for restricting the length of a play: plays are rarely longer than novelettes.

In the fourth order, reverie and persuasion are called upon to sustain a very high order or rhetoric, and so are most easily subject to lapses. If a writer grows rhapsodic over a mere description or story or conversation, you may wonder why he entered the character's mind in the first place. If a writer grows pugnacious over a mere definition or process which the reader would have granted him to start with, you may wonder why he hasn't chosen a lower mode. Or his loyalties may be too mixed to submit himself to single-voiced persuasion. Kenneth Burke confesses: "Ideally, I suppose, the chapter should have been written not as by one speaker, but as a dialogue in which several speakers conflictingly participated." (*Counter-Statement*, 2nd ed., p. ix) In both mental modes, the indulgence of the first person and the future tense will lend the passage some legitimacy, for no other modes so appropriately accommodate them. Because the mental order seems to call for intensity, passages of reverie and persuasion are rarely as long as plays, and most lyrics are short. Even *Ulysses* and *Walden* are not really sustained reverie or persuasion.

Rhetorical lapses, and probably a greater number, also occur between the abstract and concrete realms: when an abstract mode is chosen, and the matter turns out to be private or eccentric; when a concrete mode is chosen, and the matter turns out to be familiar or routine. Of course there may be self-conscious violations. A very sophisticated writer (Addison, E. B. White) may adopt a mock naïveté in presenting a routine affair as unique—all in the pose of the objective reporter; or may adopt a philosophic pose of abstraction for clearly private experience. But beginning writers rarely stumble on such happy paradoxes by chance.

I have tried to exclude stylistics from this discussion—the study not of all discourse but of arbitrarily restricted bodies of discourse (English poetry, English neoclassical poetry, Pope's poetry), sometimes with recommendations to exploit or avoid certain stylistic traits picked up along the way. If I were asked, after this survey of the modes of rhetoric, to make a stylistic recommendation, it would be to achieve variety of abstraction, to be alternately concrete and abstract. If I were asked to decide which is dominant over which, I would answer, somewhat tentatively, the abstract over the concrete. Burke defines eloquence as "formal excellence" and "form" as "the creation of an appetite in the mind of the auditor, and the adequate satisfying of that appetite." (pp. 37, 31) But I prefer to differentiate two qualities, vividness and eloquence. Vividness is the use of a more concrete term or statement than you might expect, than is needed to satisfy the appetite created in the auditor. As from *Hamlet*: "Thrift, thrift, Horatio! The funeral bak'd meats/ Did coldly furnish forth the marriage tables.'" (I, ii, 180-1) "He took my father grossly, full of bread." (III, iii, 80) "Here is your husband, like a mildewed ear." (III, iv, 64) "There is a willow grows aslant a brook" (IV, vii, 167). Eloquence is the use of a more abstract term or statement than you might expect, than is needed. Again from *Hamlet:* "Frailty, thy name is woman!" (I, ii, 146) "What a piece of work is man!" (II, ii, 315) "To be or not to be—that is the question" (III, i, 55) "Absent thee from felicity a while" (V, ii, 358). Of the two qualities, vividness seems to me to come down, toward the earth, though not with the dud of bathos; eloquence seems to me to go up, *peri hypsous.*